P9-BZC-799

The EATINGWELL

NEW FAVORITES

COOKBOOK

EatingWell BOOKS

A division of Eating Well Magazine
Box 1001, Ferry Road, Charlotte, Vermont 05445-1001

© 1995 by EATING WELL: The Magazine of Food & Health*

All rights reserved, including the right to reproduce this book, or any part thereof,
in any form, except for the inclusion of brief quotations for review.

EATING WELL: The Magazine of Food & Health*, is a registered trademark of Telemedia Communications Inc.
For subscription information, write to EATING WELL, P.O. Box 54263, Boulder, CO 80322-4263 or call 1-800-EAT-WELL.

Library of Congress Cataloging-in-Publication Data

The Eating well new favorites cookbook: more great recipes from the magazine of food & health.
p.   cm.
Includes index.
ISBN 1-884943-07-1 (hardcover) — ISBN 1-884943-08-X (softcover)
1. Cookery, International.   2. Low-fat diet—Recipes.   3. Menus.   I. Eating well.
TX725.A1E314   1996   94-20212
641.5'636—dc20   CIP

Editorial Director: Scott Mowbray   **Editor:** Susan Stuck   **Managing Editor:** Wendy S. Ruopp
Recipe Editor: Susan Herr   **Test Kitchen Director:** Patsy Jamieson   **Nutrition Editor:** Elizabeth Hiser
Special Contributors: Sharon L. Smith (*Indexer*), David Grist (*Permissions*)

Design Director: Joannah Ralston   **Associate Art Director:** Elise Whittemore-Hill
Photography Stylist: Betty Alfenito   **Food Stylist:** Anne Disrude

Front cover photograph: Linguine with Grilled Shrimp & Black Olives (page 46), by Steven Mark Needham

Distributed by
Artisan, a division of Workman Publishing
708 Broadway, New York, NY 10003

Printed and bound in Canada by
Metropole Litho Inc., Montreal, Quebec

The EATINGWELL NEW FAVORITES COOKBOOK

MORE GREAT RECIPES
FROM THE MAGAZINE OF FOOD & HEALTH

A division of EATING WELL Magazine

CONTENTS

**Rhubarb-Peach
Shortcake
(page 231)**

INTRODUCTION

With more than 200 irresistibly delicious recipes, *The Eating Well New Favorites Cookbook* highlights the very best presented by EATING WELL Magazine since the publication of the first *Eating Well Cookbook*. This new collection of sophisticated, inventive and low-fat dishes has been created by contributors to the magazine or by our Test Kitchen staff, all of whom love to cook and love to eat. If you have not yet discovered the magazine, this cookbook gives you the chance to catch up.

EATING WELL readers have always shared an uncommon curiosity about food and a willingness to discover new flavors. The cuisines of more than two dozen countries are represented here, allowing adventurous cooks to experience anything from Korean Lettuce Bundles with Hot-&-Sweet Meat Filling to Aeolian Seafood Couscous to Japanese Glazed Salmon with Soba. There are American favorites too: Caesar salad, barbecued pork sandwiches, pumpkin pie and many others have all been updated to a low-fat profile.

Leafing through the book, you will find recipes for all occasions and seasons—Thanksgiving turkey, Christmas goose, fruit pies for the summer, hearty breads for the winter, and beautiful cakes for birthday parties at any time of the year.

All the recipes are truly favorites. Test Kitchen Director Patsy Jamieson loves the Mediterranean; at home in Vermont she prepares the Stuffed Leg of Lamb Greek-Style or the Aegean Fish Stew to evoke fragrant memories of her travels. Three-Bean Chili is another favorite and shows up often at staff potlucks. Some recipes are favorites of more than just the EATING WELL staff: literally thousands of people requested our recipe for Died-and-Went-to-Heaven Chocolate Cake after Patsy demonstrated it on CNN's "On the Menu" program.

Food is not only an aromatic and flavorful experience, but a visual one as well. This cookbook, with its more than 75 photographs, brings together the work of many of our favorite photographers; their artistry inspires and instructs cooks.

EATING WELL recipes are built around fundamental, widely recognized healthy-eating guidelines: no more than 30 percent of calories in the overall diet should come from fat, and meals should contain modest meat portions in combination with plenty of grains, vegetables and fruits. We are mindful of not only the total amount of fat in a recipe, but also the source of fat. In a healthy diet, saturated fat should make up less than a third of total fat. Every recipe is followed by a nutrition analysis of calories, protein, fat, carbohydrate, sodium and cholesterol per serving.

The book is divided into 16 chapters, each devoted to a particular category ranging from Appetizers to Poultry to Pies, Tarts & Cakes, even Frozen Desserts. The Menus section (pages 8 and 9) suggests recipes that can be used together to make a meal—the combinations serve as a springboard to your own imagination. The recipes were not created specifically for these menus, so in some cases you may need to double the recipes; in others, you may have leftovers. There is a short section at the back of the book called "The Well-Stocked Kitchen." It describes ingredients that may be unfamiliar to some readers, and gives suggestions for where those items can be found.

Since the magazine's charter issue in 1990, the EATING WELL message for healthful eating has never varied. We are as passionate as ever that healthful food does not compromise taste; these new favorites testify to that.

–Susan Stuck, Editor, EATING WELL Books

For a Hungry Crowd

Three-Bean Chili, *page 99*
Potato-Buttermilk Bread, *page 152*
Spinach & Grapefruit Salad, *page 34*
Carrot Cake, *page 185*

Tropical Pleasure

Carambola, Avocado & Wilted Spinach Salad, *page 41*
Shrimp Creole, *page 120*
Coconut Rice *or* Papaya Rice, *page 78*
Mango Tart, *page 181*

Easter Sunday

Artichoke Soup, *page 28*
Stuffed Leg of Lamb Greek-Style, *page 104*
Roasted Asparagus, *page 72*
Romaine Salad, *page 37*
Crusty Rolls, *page 156*
Sunny Citrus Chiffon Cake, *page 197*
(Fresh Strawberries)

Hearty Hors d'Oeuvres Party

Tuscan White Bean Spread (with Crudités), *page 16*
Smoked Trout Tartlets, *page 17*
Artichoke & Leek Pizza, *page 56*
Crispy Scallops with Soy Dipping Sauce, *page 123*
Lettuce Bundles with
Hot-&-Sweet Meat Filling, *page 23*

A Summer Picnic

Antipasto of Seared Tuna & Roasted Peppers, *page 20*
(Italian Bread)
Artichoke & Swiss Chard Pie, *page 138*
Cold Sliced Chicken in Tuna Sauce, *page 85*
Fennel, Orange & Lemon Salad with Olives, *page 40*
Mocha-Almond Biscotti, *page 203*

Casual Supper with Friends

Linguine with Grilled Shrimp & Black Olives, *page 46*
Parmesan Bread, *page 161*
Radicchio & Fennel Salad, *page 39*
Rustic Plum-Walnut Tart, *page 172*

Easy Brunch

Curried Vegetables with Eggs, *page 132*
Latkes, *page 69*
Crackle-Topped Rhubarb Coffee Cake, *page 142*
Layered Mango Fruit Mélange, *page 148*

Holiday Dinner

Creamy Pureed Fennel Soup, *page 29*
Endive & Watercress Salad, *page 40*
Goose with Kumquat Sauce, *page 96*
Brussels Sprouts & Chestnuts, *page 72*
Garlic Mashed Potatoes, *page 68*
Pumpkin Popovers, *page 168*
Cranberry-Vanilla Bombe, *page 246*

CHAPTER 1

Appetizers

Roasted Garlic with Fresh Thyme & Goat Cheese

Spread sweet roasted garlic and some goat cheese on crusty peasant bread for a robust appetizer.

Preheat oven to 400 degrees F. With a sharp knife, cut off and discard the upper third of each garlic head, exposing the cloves. (Leave the skin intact below the cut.)

Set the garlic heads, cut-side up, in a small baking dish or gratin dish just large enough to hold them. Pour chicken broth over the garlic, add thyme sprigs and season lightly with salt and pepper. Cover the dish tightly with aluminum foil and bake for 1 hour, or until each clove is soft to the touch and the skin resembles lightly browned parchment.

Serve the garlic with the cooking juices spooned over and pass goat cheese and bread separately. To eat, break off a piece of bread and spread with a small amount of cheese, then scoop out the garlic puree from one of the cloves with the tip of a knife and spread on top.

Serves 4.

176 CALORIES PER SERVING: 9 G PROTEIN, 10 G FAT, 14 G CARBOHYDRATE;
265 MG SODIUM; 23 MG CHOLESTEROL.

4 large heads garlic

¾ cup defatted reduced-sodium chicken broth

8 sprigs fresh thyme
Salt & freshly ground black pepper to taste

1 4-ounce log creamy goat cheese, cut into 4 portions

1 baguette (French bread) or crusty peasant bread

**Roasted Garlic with
Fresh Thyme & Goat Cheese**

Roasted Red Pepper Dip

The combination of ginger, garlic and jalapeños brings out the sweetness of roasted red peppers;
serve with sesame crackers and crudités.

1   **7-ounce jar roasted red peppers, drained, rinsed and patted dry**

1   **clove garlic, coarsely chopped**

1   **1-inch-long piece fresh ginger, peeled and coarsely chopped**

1   **jalapeño pepper, seeded and coarsely chopped**

1   **scallion, sliced**

2   **teaspoons reduced-sodium soy sauce**

2   **teaspoons rice-wine vinegar or cider vinegar**

1   **teaspoon honey or sugar**

3-5 **tablespoons fresh breadcrumbs (1 slice white bread)**

In a blender or food processor, combine roasted red peppers, garlic, ginger, jalapeño, scallion, soy sauce, vinegar and honey or sugar. Process until smooth. With the motor running, add breadcrumbs, a little at a time, until the dip is thick and creamy. Taste and adjust seasonings. Transfer to a small bowl. (*The dip can be stored, covered, in the refrigerator for up to 2 days.*)

Makes about 1 cup.

5 CALORIES PER TABLESPOON: 0 G PROTEIN, 0 G FAT, 1 G CARBOHYDRATE; 36 MG SODIUM; 0 MG CHOLESTEROL.

Roasted Eggplant Dip

American cooks were hardly the first to roast vegetables; for centuries, Arab cooks roasted eggplant every time they made baba ghanoush. *Here is a low-fat version of the Middle Eastern specialty.*

1   **large head garlic**

1   **eggplant (1-1¼ pounds), cut in half lengthwise**

1   **small onion, cut into ½-inch-thick slices**

1   **ripe tomato, cored, sliced in half and seeded**

3   **tablespoons fresh lemon juice**

Set oven racks at the two lowest levels; preheat to 450 degrees F. Peel as much of the papery skin from the garlic as possible and wrap the head loosely in aluminum foil. Bake for 30 minutes, or until the garlic is soft. Let cool slightly.

Meanwhile, lightly oil a baking sheet or coat it with nonstick cooking spray. Place eggplant halves on the prepared baking sheet, cut-side down. Roast for 10 minutes. Add onion slices and tomato halves to the baking sheet and roast for 10 to 15 minutes longer, or until all the vegetables are soft. Let cool slightly.

Separate the garlic cloves and squeeze the soft pulp into a medium bowl. Mash with the back of a spoon. Slip skins from the eggplant and tomatoes; coarsely chop. Finely chop the onion.

Add the chopped vegetables to the garlic pulp and stir in the lemon juice, mint, oil, salt and pepper. Cover and refrigerate until cool, 1 to 2 hours. (*The dip can be stored, covered, in the refrigerator for up to 2 days.*) Serve with sliced raw vegetables, crackers or pita breads.

Makes about 2½ cups.

9 CALORIES PER TABLESPOON: 0 G PROTEIN, 0 G FAT, 1 G CARBOHYDRATE; 27 MG SODIUM; 0 MG CHOLESTEROL.

- 2 tablespoons chopped fresh mint
- 1 tablespoon olive oil, preferably extra-virgin
- ½ teaspoon salt
- ¼ teaspoon freshly ground black pepper, or to taste

Black Bean Dip

Serve tortilla chips with this lively dip. Freshly baked low-fat chips have a more pronounced corn flavor than store-bought. To make your own, lightly brush corn tortillas on one side with corn oil and sprinkle the oiled side with salt. Cut the tortillas into 8 wedges and arrange them in a single layer on a baking sheet. Bake them at 400 degrees F until crisp, 8 to 10 minutes.

In a food processor, combine black beans, salsa, lime juice, cilantro and cumin. Process until smooth. Season with salt and pepper and transfer to a small bowl. (*The dip can be stored, covered, in the refrigerator for up to 2 days.*)

Makes about 1½ cups.

24 CALORIES PER TABLESPOON: 2 G PROTEIN, 0 G FAT, 4 G CARBOHYDRATE; 19 MG SODIUM; 0 MG CHOLESTEROL.

- 1 16-ounce can black beans, drained and rinsed
- ½ cup prepared tomato salsa, hot or mild
- 2 tablespoons fresh lime juice
- 2 tablespoons chopped fresh cilantro
- ¼ teaspoon ground cumin
  Salt & freshly ground black pepper to taste

Smoked Salmon Spread

Plain vodka can be substituted for the pepper-flavored vodka, but season generously with cracked pepper.

½ pound smoked salmon

1½ cups nonfat cottage cheese

3 tablespoons pepper-flavored vodka, such as Absolut Peppar

2 tablespoons fresh lemon juice

2 teaspoons Dijon mustard

1 teaspoon prepared horseradish
Freshly cracked black pepper
Dill sprigs for garnish

Cut half of the salmon into chunks. Dice the remaining salmon. Place cottage cheese in a fine-mesh sieve and press firmly to remove excess moisture. Transfer the cottage cheese to a food processor. Add the salmon chunks, vodka, lemon juice, mustard and horseradish. Process until smooth. Transfer the mixture to a bowl and fold in the diced salmon. Refrigerate until chilled. (*The spread may be prepared ahead and stored, covered, in the refrigerator for up to 2 days.*)

To serve, spread on crostini (French bread toasts) or pumpernickel cocktail bread and garnish with a generous sprinkling of cracked pepper and dill.

Makes about 2 cups.

17 CALORIES PER TABLESPOON: 3 G PROTEIN, 0 G FAT, 0 G CARBOHYDRATE; 59 MG SODIUM; 2 MG CHOLESTEROL.

Herbed Yogurt Cheese

Remember to start draining the yogurt the day before blending the cheese.

2 cups yogurt cheese made from nonfat yogurt (*see* "The Well-Stocked Kitchen," *page 248*)

2 scallions, trimmed and finely chopped

2 tablespoons chopped fresh parsley

1 tablespoon chopped fresh basil or ½ teaspoon dried

1 clove garlic, very finely chopped

½ teaspoon salt

¼ teaspoon freshly ground black pepper

In a bowl, blend together yogurt cheese, scallions, parsley, basil, garlic, salt and pepper with a wooden spoon. (*The cheese may be prepared ahead and stored, covered, in the refrigerator for up to 2 days.*)

Serve on crostini (French bread toasts), crackers, or use in sandwiches.

Makes 2 cups.

24 CALORIES PER TABLESPOON: 3 G PROTEIN, 0 G FAT, 3 G CARBOHYDRATE; 66 MG SODIUM; 1 MG CHOLESTEROL.

**Smoked Salmon Spread
and Herbed Yogurt Cheese**

Tuscan White Bean Spread

Peppery arugula and garlic enliven a creamy white bean puree; serve with crostini or breadsticks.

1 16-ounce can white beans, such as great northern or cannellini, drained and rinsed

2 tablespoons olive oil, preferably extra-virgin

1 tablespoon chopped fresh thyme or 1 teaspoon dried thyme leaves

2 teaspoons fresh lemon juice

1 clove garlic, finely chopped

¼ cup chopped arugula
   Salt & freshly ground black pepper to taste

In a food processor, combine beans, oil, thyme, lemon juice and garlic. Process until smooth. Transfer the bean puree to a small bowl. Stir in arugula. Season with salt and pepper. (*The spread can be stored, covered, in the refrigerator for up to 8 hours.*)

Makes about 1½ cups.

34 CALORIES PER TABLESPOON: 2 G PROTEIN, 2 G FAT, 4 G CARBOHYDRATE; 1 MG SODIUM; 0 MG CHOLESTEROL.

Black-Eyed Pea Spread

Serve this delectable, garlicky spread with toasted slices of baguette.

1 16-ounce can black-eyed peas, drained and rinsed, or 1½ cups cooked black-eyed peas

¼ cup tightly packed fresh parsley leaves, plus sprigs for garnish

2 tablespoons fresh lemon juice

2 tablespoons olive oil, preferably extra-virgin

1½ teaspoons chopped garlic

½ teaspoon dried tarragon

¼ teaspoon freshly ground black pepper
   Salt to taste

Reserve a few black-eyed peas for garnish and place the remaining peas in a food processor, along with parsley, lemon juice, oil, garlic, tarragon and pepper. Process until smooth. Taste and adjust seasonings, adding salt if desired. Transfer to a serving bowl and garnish with parsley and the reserved peas. (*The spread can be stored, covered, in the refrigerator for up to 2 days.*)

Makes about 1¼ cups.

30 CALORIES PER TABLESPOON: 1 G PROTEIN, 1 G FAT, 3 G CARBOHYDRATE; 1 MG SODIUM; 0 MG CHOLESTEROL.

Smoked Trout Tartlets

The rich, creamy filling contrasts with the pleasant crunch of the tartlet shell.

TO MAKE PHYLLO TARTLET SHELLS:

Preheat oven to 325 degrees F. Lightly coat 2 mini-muffin pans with nonstick cooking spray. In a small bowl, whisk together egg white, oil and salt.

Lay a sheet of phyllo on a work surface and with a pastry brush lightly coat it with egg-white mixture. Lay a second sheet smoothly on top, taking care to line up the edges before setting the sheet down. (Once you set down the sheet, it cannot be moved.) Brush with egg-white mixture and repeat with one more sheet. Lay a fourth sheet on top but do not brush it.

With a knife, cut the stack of phyllo into 4 strips lengthwise and 6 strips crosswise, making 24 squares. Press the squares into the muffin cups and bake for 8 to 12 minutes, or until golden brown and crisp. Transfer the tartlet shells to a rack and let cool. Repeat the procedure with the remaining 4 sheets of phyllo and the rest of the egg-white mixture. (*The baked tartlet shells may be stored in a closed container at room temperature for 1 week or in the freezer for up to 2 months.*)

TO MAKE SMOKED TROUT FILLING:

In a food processor, combine cream cheese and smoked trout; process until fairly smooth. Add scallions and horseradish and pulse until just combined. Alternatively, finely mince the smoked trout with a knife and combine with the cream cheese, scallions and horseradish in a bowl. (*The smoked trout filling may be made ahead and refrigerated for up to 2 days.*) Shortly before serving, spoon or pipe about 1 heaping teaspoon of filling into each tartlet shell and garnish with shredded cucumber.

Makes 4 dozen tartlets.

50 CALORIES PER TARTLET: 3 G PROTEIN, 2 G FAT, 5 G CARBOHYDRATE; 94 MG SODIUM; 5 MG CHOLESTEROL.

PHYLLO TARTLET SHELLS

- 1 large egg white
- 2 tablespoons olive oil
- ¼ teaspoon salt
- 8 sheets phyllo dough (14x18 inches)

SMOKED TROUT FILLING

- 2 8-ounce packages low-fat cream cheese
- ½ pound smoked trout fillets (2 fillets), skin and pin bones removed
- ⅓ cup chopped scallions (2 scallions)
- 4 teaspoons well-drained prepared horseradish
- 1 cup shredded cucumber

Sicilian-Style Stuffed Artichokes

Artichokes, native to Sicily, are prepared by Sicilians in countless ways. Here the simple bread filling is accented with anchovies, and the lovely flavor permeates the whole vegetable during the steaming process.

Grate zest from lemon, measure 1 teaspoon of zest and reserve. Slice the lemon in half; cut one half into thin slices, keeping the other half intact.

Drain anchovies, reserving the oil. In a bowl, mash the anchovies, then stir in breadcrumbs, parsley, Parmesan, oregano, thyme, pepper and the reserved lemon zest.

Trim artichoke stems, leaving about ½ inch, so that they will stand upright. Pull off the short, tough lower leaves of the artichokes. Cut off the top ½ inch of each artichoke, then use scissors to trim off the sharp points of the remaining leaves. Rub the artichokes, especially the cut portions, with the cut side of the lemon half. Turn the artichokes upside down and rap them on a counter to loosen their leaves, then gently spread the leaves open like a flower. Spoon the breadcrumb filling into the openings. Tap each artichoke lightly on the counter to help the filling settle inside the leaves.

Place the artichokes in a Dutch oven so that they fit comfortably standing up, but are not crowded. (Use 2 pans if necessary.) Drizzle the top of each artichoke with about ½ teaspoon of the reserved anchovy oil. Carefully pour water in the pan to a depth of about 1½ inches. Add the lemon slices and squeeze the juice from the lemon half into the water.

Cover the pot and steam the artichokes over low heat until they are tender when pierced to the core with a skewer but are not so soft that they lose their shape, 35 to 45 minutes. Remove them from the pot with a slotted spoon and let drain on a plate. Serve warm or at room temperature. (*Artichokes can be cooked up to 2 hours ahead and kept at room temperature.*)

Serves 8.

207 CALORIES PER SERVING: 12 G PROTEIN, 3 G FAT, 36 G CARBOHYDRATE; 650 MG SODIUM; 9 MG CHOLESTEROL.

1	lemon
1	2-ounce can anchovies
2¼	cups fresh breadcrumbs, made from day-old firm Italian bread (about 7 slices)
¾	cup chopped fresh parsley
½	cup freshly grated Parmesan cheese (1 ounce)
2	teaspoons dried oregano
1½	teaspoons dried thyme leaves
½	teaspoon coarsely ground black pepper
8	medium artichokes (about 6-8 ounces each)

Sicilian-Style Stuffed Artichokes

Antipasto of Seared Tuna & Roasted Peppers

Roasted red peppers in a jar are a wonderful convenience, but you can certainly roast your own.
The tuna can be grilled over hot coals instead of seared in a pan.

1   ¾-pound fresh tuna steak
    (about 1 inch thick)

¾   teaspoon coarsely ground black
    pepper, or to taste

2   7-ounce jars roasted red peppers,
    drained (about 2 cups)

2   teaspoons olive oil, preferably
    extra-virgin

2   teaspoons fresh lemon juice

1   2-ounce piece Parmigiano-
    Reggiano cheese, at room
    temperature

2   tablespoons drained capers

½   loaf of French or Italian bread,
    thinly sliced

    Capers or caper berries, lemon
    wedges and lettuce for garnish

Sprinkle both sides of tuna steak with ½ teaspoon of the pepper. Lightly oil a large nonstick skillet or coat it with nonstick cooking spray. Heat the skillet over high heat until a drop of water sizzles; add the tuna and cook until the underside is lightly browned, 4 to 5 minutes, then turn and cook just until opaque in the center, 4 to 5 minutes longer. Remove from the skillet and cool to room temperature. (*Tuna can be cooked up to 8 hours ahead. Cool to room temperature, wrap and refrigerate. Return to room temperature before continuing.*)

Shortly before serving, cut the tuna on the bias into ¼-inch slices. Cut the red peppers into ¼-inch slices. Arrange tuna and peppers on a serving plate. Sprinkle with the remaining ¼ teaspoon pepper, then drizzle with olive oil and lemon juice. With a vegetable peeler, shave cheese into thin slices. Scatter the cheese and capers over the tuna and peppers. Serve with bread alongside. Garnish with capers or caper berries, lemon wedges and lettuce.

Serves 8.

128 CALORIES PER SERVING: 13 G PROTEIN, 4 G FAT, 15 G CARBOHYDRATE;
827 MG SODIUM; 25 MG CHOLESTEROL.

**Antipasto of Seared Tuna
& Roasted Peppers**

Sesame & Poppy Seed Straws

A nice, crisp nibble to serve with drinks.

2 tablespoons poppy seeds

2 tablespoons sesame seeds

1 large egg white

2 tablespoons olive oil

¼ teaspoon salt

6 sheets phyllo dough (14x18 inches)

Preheat oven to 400 degrees F. Lightly coat 2 baking sheets with nonstick cooking spray or line with parchment paper. Heat a small heavy skillet over medium heat. Add the poppy seeds and sesame seeds and cook, stirring, until they are aromatic and toasted, 2 to 3 minutes. Turn out onto a plate to cool. In a small bowl, whisk together egg white, oil and salt.

Lay a sheet of phyllo on a work surface with a short side toward you. With a pastry brush, lightly coat the lower half of the sheet with egg-white mixture and sprinkle with 1 teaspoon seeds. Fold the upper half over to cover the lower half. Brush the right half of the folded sheet with egg-white mixture, sprinkle with ½ teaspoon seeds and fold the left half over the seeds. Brush the bottom half of the folded sheet with egg-white mixture, sprinkle with ¼ teaspoon seeds and fold the upper half over. Finally, brush the top with egg-white mixture and sprinkle with ¼ teaspoon seeds. Cut into 10 short strips using a knife or serrated pastry cutter. With a wide spatula, transfer the strips to the baking sheet, placing them about ½ inch apart. Repeat the procedure with the remaining 5 sheets of phyllo, egg-white mixture and seeds.

Bake the straws for 8 to 10 minutes, until golden and crisp. Transfer to a rack to cool. (*The straws may be stored in an airtight container at room temperature for 1 week or in the freezer for up to 2 months.*)

Makes about 5 dozen straws.

19 CALORIES PER STRAW: 1 G PROTEIN, 1 G FAT, 3 G CARBOHYDRATE; 23 MG SODIUM; 0 MG CHOLESTEROL.

Lettuce Bundles with Hot-&-Sweet Meat Filling (*Sangchussamjang*)

These bundles are a popular meal-starter in Korea. The custom is to take a lettuce leaf, add a spoonful of hot steamed rice together with a dollop of the meat filling, roll the whole bundle up and pop it in your mouth. Kochujang, a Korean condiment made with soybean paste and hot chiles, can be found at Asian specialty shops.

Heat sesame oil in a small nonstick sauté pan. Add ground beef and cook until all the red color is gone, 2 to 3 minutes; drain off any fat. Add half of the chopped scallions, wine or sherry, *kochujang* or chile paste, garlic, ginger and sugar to the pan. Cook over very low heat for 7 to 10 minutes. Spoon the filling into a small bowl. (*The filling can be made up to 2 days in advance, covered and refrigerated. Warm before serving.*)

Arrange the lettuce leaves on a serving plate. Sprinkle the remaining scallions over the filling and serve with rice, letting diners make up their own bundles.

Serves 6.

142 CALORIES PER SERVING: 6 G PROTEIN, 4 G FAT, 20 G CARBOHYDRATE; 20 MG SODIUM; 14 MG CHOLESTEROL.

1 teaspoon sesame oil

¼ pound lean ground beef

2 scallions, trimmed and finely sliced on the diagonal

¼ cup rice wine or dry sherry

2 tablespoons *kochujang* or Chinese chile paste with garlic

2 cloves garlic, finely chopped

1 tablespoon finely chopped peeled ginger

1 tablespoon sugar

1 head Boston lettuce, leaves separated and washed

2 cups steamed white rice

CHAPTER 2

Soups

Cold Carrot Soup with Sichuan Seasonings

Distinctive seasonings—peanut, sesame, hot red pepper and lime—play against a backdrop of sweet carrots in a beautiful burnished-orange soup.

In a large saucepan, heat oil over medium heat. Add onions, celery and garlic and sauté until softened, 3 to 5 minutes. Add chicken broth, carrots, ginger and red-pepper flakes and bring to a boil. Reduce heat to low and simmer, covered, until the carrots are very tender, 20 to 30 minutes.

Pour the mixture through a strainer set over a large bowl. Transfer the solids to a food processor or blender and add lime juice, soy sauce, peanut butter, sugar and sesame oil; puree, adding some of the cooking liquid as needed for a smooth consistency. Transfer the puree to the bowl of cooking liquid and stir in milk. Season with salt and pepper. Cover and refrigerate until chilled, at least 1 hour. (*The soup can be stored, covered, in the refrigerator for up to 2 days.*) Ladle into bowls, garnish with scallions and serve.

Makes about 5 cups, serves 6 as an appetizer.

125 CALORIES PER SERVING: 6 G PROTEIN, 4 G FAT, 16 G CARBOHYDRATE; 594 MG SODIUM; 1 MG CHOLESTEROL.

Cold Carrot Soup with Sichuan Seasonings

1 teaspoon vegetable oil, preferably canola oil

1 onion, chopped

1 stalk celery, chopped

1 clove garlic, finely chopped

3 cups defatted reduced-sodium chicken broth, preferably homemade (*page 32*)

1 pound carrots (5-6 medium), peeled and chopped

1 ¾-inch piece of ginger, peeled and cut into thin slices

¼-½ teaspoon red-pepper flakes

2 tablespoons fresh lime juice

1½ tablespoons reduced-sodium soy sauce

1½ tablespoons peanut butter

2-3 teaspoons sugar

1 teaspoon sesame oil

1 cup skim milk

Salt & freshly ground black pepper to taste

1 tablespoon chopped scallions

Roasted Onion Soup

*Sweet caramelized onions, bolstered by roasted shallots and garlic, combine in a luscious
but not overpowering soup that is perfect for a wintry day.*

3   Spanish onions, cut in half
    lengthwise and thinly sliced

3   large shallots, cut in half
    lengthwise and thinly sliced

1   large head garlic, cloves
    separated, peeled and cut in half

2   teaspoons olive oil, preferably
    extra-virgin

4   cups defatted reduced-sodium
    chicken broth, preferably
    homemade (*page 32*)

¼   cup brandy

1   tablespoon chopped fresh thyme
    or 1 teaspoon dried thyme leaves
    Salt & freshly ground black
    pepper to taste

¼   cup freshly grated Parmesan
    cheese

Set oven rack at the lowest level; preheat to 450 degrees F.
Combine onions, shallots, garlic and oil in a large shallow roasting pan. Roast for 20 to 25 minutes, stirring every 5 minutes,
or until the onions are golden. Remove from oven and pour in
1 cup of the chicken broth. Stir liquid in the pan, scraping the
bottom to loosen and dissolve any caramelized bits. (The liquid
will become quite dark.)

Transfer the onion mixture to a soup pot and add brandy,
thyme and the remaining 3 cups chicken broth. Bring to a boil;
reduce heat to low and simmer, covered, for 30 minutes. Season
with salt and pepper. Ladle into bowls and serve. Pass Parmesan
at the table.

Makes about 5 cups, serves 4.

137 CALORIES PER SERVING: 4 G PROTEIN, 4 G FAT, 12 G CARBOHYDRATE;
121 MG SODIUM; 5 MG CHOLESTEROL.

Roasted Tomato Soup

Roasting tomatoes not only intensifies their sweetness, it also makes them very easy to peel.

8-10   ripe tomatoes (3 pounds),
       cored, cut in half and seeded

1½   teaspoons olive oil

2   red onions, chopped

1   clove garlic, finely chopped

Preheat broiler. Lightly oil a baking sheet or coat it with nonstick cooking spray. Place tomatoes on the baking sheet, cut-
side down. Broil until skins are blistered, about 10 minutes. Set
aside to cool. Slip off skins and chop tomatoes coarsely.

Meanwhile, in a saucepan, heat oil over medium-low heat.
Add onions and sauté for 5 minutes. Add garlic and sauté until

the onions are very soft, about 5 minutes longer. Stir in tomatoes and cook, stirring, for 1 minute. Transfer the mixture to a food processor or blender and process until smooth; return to the saucepan. Stir in chicken broth and bring to a boil. Reduce heat to low and simmer for 5 minutes. Remove from heat and stir in basil. Season with salt and pepper. Cover and refrigerate until chilled, at least 1 hour. (*The soup can be stored, covered, in the refrigerator for up to 2 days.*) Ladle into bowls and serve.

Makes about 5 cups, serves 6 as an appetizer.

90 CALORIES PER SERVING: 4 G PROTEIN, 2 G FAT, 16 G CARBOHYDRATE; 216 MG SODIUM; 0 MG CHOLESTEROL.

3 cups defatted reduced-sodium chicken broth, preferably homemade (*page 32*)

3 tablespoons chopped fresh basil
   Salt & freshly ground black pepper to taste

Mediterranean Grilled Vegetable Soup

All the flavors and freshness of a Mediterranean garden in a chilled summer soup.

Prepare a grill or preheat the broiler. Grill or broil bell peppers, skin-side toward the flame, until the skin is blackened, 5 to 10 minutes. Place in a paper bag and set aside for 15 minutes.

Meanwhile, brush zucchini and onion slices with oil and grill or broil until well browned and tender, about 5 minutes. Chop coarsely and set aside.

Peel the peppers. Coarsely chop the yellow pepper and set aside with the reserved zucchini and onions. Place the red peppers in a food processor or blender, along with tomatoes, garlic and oregano; puree until smooth. Transfer to a bowl and stir in 1 cup water, basil, vinegar and the reserved chopped vegetables. Season with salt and pepper. Cover and refrigerate until cool, about 30 minutes. (*The soup can be stored, covered, in the refrigerator for up to 2 days.*) Ladle into bowls and serve.

Makes about 5 cups, serves 6 as an appetizer.

56 CALORIES PER SERVING: 2 G PROTEIN, 1 G FAT, 11 G CARBOHYDRATE; 12 MG SODIUM; 0 MG CHOLESTEROL.

2 red bell peppers, cored, seeded and quartered lengthwise

1 yellow bell pepper, cored, seeded and quartered lengthwise

2 small zucchini (½ pound total), trimmed and quartered lengthwise

1 red onion, peeled and cut into ½-inch-thick slices

1 teaspoon olive oil

3 large vine-ripened tomatoes (1¼ pounds), cored and chopped

1 clove garlic, peeled

½ teaspoon dried oregano

¼ cup slivered basil leaves

1 tablespoon red-wine vinegar
   Salt & freshly ground black pepper to taste

Artichoke Soup

"Sublime" aptly describes this soup. If you like, you can puree the soup and rewarm it before enriching with egg yolk and lemon.

2 lemons, cut in half

4 large artichokes

1 tablespoon olive oil

1 leek, trimmed, cut in half lengthwise, thoroughly cleaned and thinly sliced (1½ cups)

1 large all-purpose potato, peeled and diced

1 celery stalk, chopped

1 bay leaf

4 cups defatted reduced-sodium beef broth

2 tablespoons fresh lemon juice

1 egg yolk
Salt & freshly ground black pepper to taste

Squeeze the juice of 3 lemon halves into a big bowl of cold water; keep the remaining half handy. Peel away the outer leaves of the artichokes, snapping them off at the base, until you reach the pale yellow leaves with darker green tops. Slice off the green tops. Rub each artichoke with the lemon half. With a paring knife, trim the base where you snapped off the leaves, removing any fibrous green portions. Rub with the lemon half. Trim the bottom ¼ inch off the stem and pare away the tough outer skin. Rub with the lemon half. With a melon baller or knife, remove the fuzzy choke. Drop the trimmed artichokes into the lemon water as you work.

Cut the trimmed artichokes into thin wedges. Heat oil in a large soup pot over high heat. Add the artichokes, leeks, potatoes, celery and bay leaf; sauté until the leeks start to wilt, 3 to 5 minutes. Add beef broth and bring to a boil. Cover, reduce heat to low and simmer until potatoes and artichokes are tender, about 30 minutes. Remove from the heat and discard the bay leaf. Let the soup cool for 5 minutes.

In a small bowl, whisk together lemon juice and egg yolk. Slowly add the egg mixture to the soup, stirring constantly. Taste and adjust seasonings with salt and pepper. Ladle into bowls and serve.

Makes about 6 cups, serves 6.

161 CALORIES PER SERVING: 7 G PROTEIN, 5 G FAT, 26 G CARBOHYDRATE; 146 MG SODIUM; 53 MG CHOLESTEROL.

Creamy Pureed Fennel Soup

Smooth, subtle, elegant and easily made ahead for a dinner party. If basil and tarragon are available, they lend a pleasant herbal freshness; add them at the end along with the fennel tops. Because the moisture content of fennel varies, add milk gradually so as not to thin the soup too much. Serve hot or chilled.

Reserve feathery fennel tops and set aside. Thinly slice bulb and stalks.

Heat oil in a large pot. Add the sliced fennel and leek. Cook, covered, over medium-low heat for 5 minutes, stirring from time to time. Uncover and cook, stirring often, until softened, about 5 minutes more. Add chicken broth, apples, potatoes and 1 teaspoon salt; bring to a simmer. Cook, covered, over low heat until the vegetables and apples are very soft, about 30 minutes.

In a blender or food processor, puree the soup in batches, then strain back into the pot. In a small bowl, blend cornstarch and ¼ cup milk; add to the soup and bring to a simmer, stirring. Simmer for 1 minute, stirring constantly. Add additional milk as needed for desired consistency. Add liquor to taste. Season with lemon juice, salt and pepper. Ladle into bowls and sprinkle with chopped fennel tops.

Makes about 6 cups, serves 6.

100 CALORIES PER SERVING: 2 G PROTEIN, 3 G FAT, 17 G CARBOHYDRATE; 470 MG SODIUM; 1 MG CHOLESTEROL.

1   very large or 2 medium fennel bulbs with feathery tops (1½ pounds)

1   tablespoon vegetable oil, preferably canola oil

1   leek, well trimmed, thoroughly cleaned and sliced (1 cup)

6   cups defatted reduced-sodium chicken broth, preferably homemade (*page 32*)

1   tart apple, such as Granny Smith, cored, peeled and sliced

1   medium potato, peeled and sliced

1   teaspoon coarse salt, plus more to taste

1   tablespoon cornstarch

¼-1   cup low-fat milk

1-2   tablespoons anise-flavored liquor, such as Ricard or Pernod

1   tablespoon fresh lemon juice, or to taste

Freshly ground white pepper to taste

Chicken Soup with Provençal Herbs

A baguette and a glass of wine are all you need to turn this soup into a meal. Using dried beans instead of canned makes the cooking process much longer, but the result is a thicker soup with a more complex flavor.

Rinse beans and pick over; put the beans in a bowl, cover with water and set aside to soak for 8 hours or overnight.

In a large pot, heat oil over medium-low heat. Add leeks, carrots and garlic; cook until softened, about 5 minutes. Stir in tomatoes and cook for 5 minutes. Add potatoes and cook for 5 minutes. Add chicken broth, wine, thyme, rosemary and bay leaf; bring to a boil. Drain the beans and add to the pot; cook 2 hours, or until the beans are soft. Remove the bay leaf and herb sprigs. Ladle the soup into bowls and serve.

Makes about 7 cups, serves 6.

320 CALORIES PER SERVING: 12 G PROTEIN, 3 G FAT, 58 G CARBOHYDRATE; 1,233 MG SODIUM; 7 MG CHOLESTEROL.

1 cup dried cannellini beans

1 teaspoon olive oil

2 leeks, well trimmed, thoroughly cleaned and chopped

2 carrots, peeled and diced

1 clove garlic, finely chopped

6 plum tomatoes, seeded and chopped, or one 14-ounce can plum tomatoes, drained, seeded and coarsely chopped

6 new potatoes, peeled and diced

8 cups defatted reduced-sodium chicken broth, preferably homemade (*page 32*)

¾ cup dry white wine

1 sprig fresh thyme or 1 teaspoon dried thyme leaves

1 sprig fresh rosemary or 1 teaspoon dried rosemary

1 bay leaf

Chicken Soup with
Provençal Herbs

Homemade Chicken Broth

1   large stewing chicken (5-6 pounds), quartered
4   large carrots, cut into chunks
1   large onion, quartered
6   cloves garlic, unpeeled
10   black peppercorns

Pour 5 quarts water into an 8- to 10-quart pot. Add chicken pieces, heart, neck and gizzard (reserve liver for another use); bring to a boil over high heat. Skim impurities from the surface. Reduce the heat to medium-low and add remaining ingredients. Simmer, covered with the lid slightly ajar, for 1½ hours, skimming as necessary. Strain the broth through a fine sieve set over a bowl. Discard the vegetables and bones. Refrigerate for at least 2 hours. Skim the fat from the surface. (*The broth can be stored, covered, in the refrigerator for up to 2 days or in the freezer for up to 6 months.*)

Makes about 4 quarts.

Red Lentil Soup with a Spicy Sizzle

A drizzle of sizzling spiced olive oil gives this Turkish lentil-and-bulgur soup a final flourish.

6   teaspoons olive oil
2   onions, chopped (1½ cups)
3   cloves garlic, finely chopped
2   teaspoons ground cumin
8   cups defatted reduced-sodium chicken broth, preferably homemade (*recipe above*)
1½   cups red lentils, rinsed
⅓   cup bulgur
2   tablespoons tomato paste
1   bay leaf
3   tablespoons fresh lemon juice
    Salt & freshly ground black pepper
1   teaspoon paprika
1   teaspoon ground red pepper (cayenne)

In a soup pot, heat 2 teaspoons of the oil over medium heat. Add onions and cook, stirring, until softened, 3 to 5 minutes. Add garlic and cumin and cook for 1 minute. Add broth, lentils, bulgur, tomato paste and bay leaf; bring to a simmer, stirring occasionally. Cover and cook over low heat until the lentils and bulgur are very tender, 25 to 30 minutes. Discard the bay leaf.

Ladle about 4 cups of the soup into a food processor and puree. Return the pureed soup to the soup pot and heat through. Stir in lemon juice and season with salt and pepper to taste. Just before serving, ladle the soup into bowls. Heat the remaining 4 teaspoons oil in a small skillet and stir in paprika and red pepper. Drizzle about ½ teaspoon of the sizzling spice mixture over each bowlful and serve immediately.

Makes about 8 cups, serves 8.

135 CALORIES PER SERVING: 6 G PROTEIN, 5 G FAT, 18 G CARBOHYDRATE; 936 MG SODIUM; 5 MG CHOLESTEROL.

Orange & Saffron-Scented Mussel Soup

The beauty of soup as a first course is that it can be cooked in advance and gently reheated just before serving.

Plunge tomatoes into a pan of simmering water. As the skins split, remove the tomatoes with a slotted spoon. When cool enough to handle, peel, seed and dice the tomatoes. Set aside.

In a large soup pot, heat butter and olive oil over medium-high heat. Add garlic and sauté until light golden, about 30 seconds. Add leeks, carrots and onions; sauté until very soft, about 15 minutes. Add wine, bay leaves, 1½ teaspoons of the thyme, pepper and 2 cups water; bring to a simmer. Reduce heat to low and cook for 15 minutes.

Stir in mussels, raise heat to medium-high and return to a simmer. Cover the pan and cook for 5 minutes, shaking the pan several times to distribute the mussels. With a slotted spoon, remove all the opened mussels to a large bowl. Continue to cook any unopened mussels for 2 more minutes. Remove the remaining mussels, discarding any that do not open.

When the mussels are cool enough to handle, remove them from their shells, working over a bowl to collect the juices. Pull off and discard the dark rubbery rims; set the mussels aside. Strain the accumulated juices and the cooking liquid through a cheesecloth-lined sieve set over a bowl, pressing hard on the solids to extract all the liquid. Return the liquid to the pot and add orange juice, parsley, orange zest, saffron and the remaining ½ teaspoon thyme. Season with salt and pepper. (*The soup may be prepared up to 1 day in advance. Store the broth, tomatoes and mussels in separate, covered containers in the refrigerator.*) Add the reserved tomatoes and mussels and heat gently, not allowing the soup to boil. Ladle into bowls and serve.

Makes about 9 cups, serves 8.

390 CALORIES PER SERVING: 30 G PROTEIN, 10 G FAT, 31 G CARBOHYDRATE; 704 MG SODIUM; 69 MG CHOLESTEROL.

6 plum tomatoes

1½ tablespoons butter

1½ tablespoons olive oil

3 cloves garlic, finely chopped

4 leeks, white and light green parts only, thoroughly cleaned and thinly sliced

3 carrots, finely chopped

2 onions, finely chopped

1 bottle dry white wine, such as Sauvignon Blanc (3 cups)

2 bay leaves

2 teaspoons dried thyme leaves

½ teaspoon freshly ground black pepper

4 pounds fresh mussels, scrubbed and debearded

1 cup fresh orange juice

3 tablespoons parsley, preferably Italian flat-leaf, cut in slivers

1 tablespoon grated orange zest

1 teaspoon saffron threads, crumbled, or ¼ teaspoon powdered saffron

Salt to taste

CHAPTER 3

Salads

Spinach & Grapefruit Salad

The combination of pink grapefruit sections, dark green spinach and white jícama is both visually and texturally appealing. Toasted poppy seeds give an extra lift.

2 teaspoons poppy seeds

½ red onion, thinly sliced

3 grapefruit, preferably pink or red

6 cloves garlic, peeled

2 tablespoons white-wine vinegar

2 tablespoons olive oil, preferably extra-virgin

1 tablespoon whole-grain mustard

½ teaspoon honey

Salt & freshly ground black pepper to taste

¾ pound fresh spinach, trimmed, washed and torn (16 cups)

½ small jícama, peeled and cut into matchsticks

Heat a small skillet over medium heat. Add poppy seeds; toast, stirring constantly, until aromatic, 1 to 2 minutes. Transfer to a bowl and set aside.

Place onions in a small bowl, add cold water to cover and soak for 10 minutes. Drain.

Meanwhile, with a sharp knife, remove skin and white pith from grapefruit and discard. Working over a small bowl to catch the juice, cut the grapefruit segments from their surrounding membrane; reserve the segments in a small bowl. Measure ⅓ cup of the juice and set aside.

Place garlic cloves in a small saucepan and add water to cover. Bring to a simmer over medium heat and cook until tender, about 3 minutes. Drain.

In a blender, combine vinegar, oil, mustard, honey, the cooked garlic and the reserved grapefruit juice. Blend until creamy. Season with salt and pepper.

In a salad bowl, combine spinach, jícama and the reserved onions and grapefruit. Drizzle with the dressing and toss. Arrange on salad plates and garnish with the toasted poppy seeds.

Serves 8.

89 CALORIES PER SERVING: 2 G PROTEIN, 4 G FAT, 13 G CARBOHYDRATE; 60 MG SODIUM; 0 MG CHOLESTEROL.

Spinach & Grapefruit Salad

Salad of Celeriac, Carrots & Beets

A lightened variation on the traditional French céleri-rave en rémoulade.
For a different dimension, substitute apples and watercress for beets.

1 tablespoon whole-grain mustard

1 tablespoon fresh lemon juice

½ teaspoon salt, preferably kosher

2 tablespoons olive oil

¼ cup low-fat plain yogurt

1 celeriac (¾ pound)

1 tablespoon finely chopped shallots

3 carrots (½ pound)

¼ teaspoon dried dillweed

1 tablespoon chopped capers

2 tablespoons chopped fresh parsley

4 cooked beets, peeled and sliced

Blend mustard, lemon juice and salt in a small bowl. Gradually whisk in oil, then yogurt; set aside.

Peel and quarter celeriac. Cut out the spongy core. Shred coarsely in a food processor or with a grater. Transfer to a bowl and mix with shallots and three-quarters of the dressing, separating and tossing strands until well coated. Peel and shred carrots. Mix with the remaining dressing and dill in another bowl. Cover both bowls and refrigerate for 1 hour or up to 8 hours, to allow the flavors to blend.

To serve, toss the celeriac with capers and parsley. Arrange beets on a serving dish, top with the celeriac, followed by the carrots.

Serves 4.

157 CALORIES PER SERVING: 4 G PROTEIN, 8 G FAT, 22 G CARBOHYDRATE; 460 MG SODIUM; 1 MG CHOLESTEROL.

Salad of Mâche & Beets

While the term "mimosa" may bring to mind a champagne cocktail, it is also used to describe a garnish
of sieved hard-cooked egg because it resembles tiny yellow mimosa flowers. Such a garnish is the
final touch for this lovely salad of ruby beets and deep green, delicate leaves of mâche (lamb's lettuce).

2 tablespoons red-wine vinegar

2 tablespoons cranberry juice

2 tablespoons very finely chopped shallots

1 tablespoon whole-grain mustard

2 tablespoons olive oil, preferably extra-virgin

In a small bowl, whisk together vinegar, cranberry juice, shallots and mustard. Slowly whisk in olive oil. Season to taste with salt and pepper. Pour half of the dressing into a separate bowl and set aside. Marinate beets in the remaining dressing for at least 1 hour and up to 6 hours.

Just before serving, use a rubber spatula to press egg through a coarse strainer into a small bowl. Toss the reserved dressing with the mâche or Boston lettuce. Arrange on 6 salad plates. Divide the marinated beets over the lettuce and garnish with some of the sieved egg and a grinding of black pepper.

Serves 6.

83 CALORIES PER SERVING: 3 G PROTEIN, 6 G FAT, 6 G CARBOHYDRATE; 72 MG SODIUM; 36 MG CHOLESTEROL.

Salt & freshly ground black pepper to taste

6 small cooked beets, peeled and cut into thin sticks

1 hard-cooked egg, peeled

9 cups mâche or Boston lettuce

Romaine Salad

Serve this Greek salad with the stuffed leg of lamb found on page 104.

In a small bowl or jar, mix together vinegar or lemon juice, oil, salt, pepper and ouzo, if using. (*The dressing can be mixed ahead and refrigerated for up to 8 hours.*)

Rub a large salad bowl with the scored sides of garlic. Place romaine, scallions, parsley, dill and mint in the bowl. Drizzle the dressing over the salad, toss and serve.

Serves 10.

48 CALORIES PER SERVING: 1 G PROTEIN, 3 G FAT, 4 G CARBOHYDRATE; 10 MG SODIUM; 0 MG CHOLESTEROL.

3 tablespoons balsamic vinegar or fresh lemon juice

2 tablespoons olive oil, preferably extra-virgin

Salt & freshly ground black pepper to taste

2 teaspoons ouzo (anise-flavored liqueur), optional

1 clove garlic, cut in half, cut sides scored with a knife

12 cups torn romaine lettuce (2 heads)

1 small bunch scallions, trimmed and sliced

⅔ cup finely chopped fresh parsley

⅓ cup finely chopped fresh dill

1 tablespoon finely chopped fresh mint

Caesar Salad

During Prohibition, Caesar Cardini's restaurant in Tijuana, Mexico, attracted carloads of wealthy Los Angelenos and Hollywood starlets. On the busy Fourth of July weekend in 1924, Cardini concocted his famous salad with what he had on hand—and seven decades later we revised this American classic.

ROASTED GARLIC DRESSING

- 2 heads garlic
- ¼ cup defatted reduced-sodium chicken broth or water
- 3 tablespoons red-wine vinegar or cider vinegar
- 2 tablespoons olive oil, preferably extra-virgin
- 2 teaspoons Dijon mustard
- 3 anchovy fillets, rinsed and coarsely chopped
- 2 teaspoons Worcestershire sauce
  Salt & freshly ground black pepper to taste

SALAD

- 2 cups cubed French bread (1-inch pieces)
- 1 clove garlic, peeled
- ½ teaspoon salt
- 2 teaspoons olive oil, preferably extra-virgin
- 10 cups torn romaine lettuce (2 small heads)
- ½ ounce Parmesan cheese, shaved with a vegetable peeler
- 3 anchovy fillets, rinsed and halved lengthwise (optional)
  Freshly ground black pepper to taste

TO MAKE ROASTED GARLIC DRESSING:

Preheat oven to 400 degrees F. Pull off loose papery outside skin from garlic, without separating the cloves. Slice about ½ inch off the tip of each head. Wrap the garlic in aluminum foil. Roast for about 40 minutes, or until very soft. Unwrap the garlic and cool slightly. Squeeze the garlic pulp into a blender or food processor. Add chicken broth or water, vinegar, oil, mustard, anchovies and Worcestershire sauce; blend until smooth. Season with salt and pepper. (*The dressing can be stored, covered, in the refrigerator for up to 2 days.*)

TO MAKE SALAD:

Spread the bread cubes on a baking sheet and toast in a 400-degree oven for 10 to 15 minutes, or until golden and crisp. Chop garlic coarsely, sprinkle with salt and mash with the side of the knife blade. Heat oil in a nonstick skillet. Add the mashed garlic and cook, stirring, until golden brown, about 30 seconds. Remove from the heat, add the bread cubes and toss until the garlic is well distributed.

In a large salad bowl, combine lettuce with the dressing and toss well. Add the croutons, Parmesan and anchovy fillets, if using. Grind pepper over the top, toss once and serve.

Serves 6.

135 CALORIES PER SERVING: 5 G PROTEIN, 8 G FAT, 12 G CARBOHYDRATE; 349 MG SODIUM; 2 MG CHOLESTEROL.

Radicchio & Fennel Salad

Radicchio & Fennel Salad

The distinctive and contrasting flavors of fennel and radicchio need only the lightest of dressings.

In a small bowl, whisk together vinegar, chicken broth, oil, mustard, salt and pepper.

Trim stalk and tough outer layer from fennel. Cut in half lengthwise, cut out core and slice the fennel thinly. Place in a bowl and cover with cold water. Let soak for about 10 minutes. Drain and place in a salad bowl. Wash radicchio and cut into thin julienne strips. Add to the fennel. Drizzle the dressing over the salad and toss.

Serves 6.

17 CALORIES PER SERVING: 0 G PROTEIN, 2 G FAT, 2 G CARBOHYDRATE; 21 MG SODIUM; 0 MG CHOLESTEROL.

1 tablespoon balsamic vinegar

1 tablespoon defatted reduced-sodium chicken broth

2 teaspoons olive oil, preferably extra-virgin

1 teaspoon Dijon mustard
  Salt & freshly ground black pepper to taste

1 fennel bulb

1 head radicchio

Endive & Watercress Salad

Pomegranate juice is a flavorful stand-in for some of the oil in the dressing. To squeeze pomegranate juice, press the seeds through a sieve placed over a bowl. Bottled pomegranate juice can be found in health-food stores.

¼ cup pomegranate juice, fresh or bottled

2 tablespoons walnut oil

2 tablespoons white-wine vinegar

½ teaspoon sugar

Salt & freshly ground black pepper to taste

¼ cup walnut or pecan halves

4 heads Belgian endive, trimmed, leaves separated and broken into 1½-inch lengths

1 bunch watercress, large stems removed, leaves washed and dried

1 small red onion, thinly sliced

½ cup pomegranate seeds or raspberries

In a small bowl or a jar, whisk or shake pomegranate juice, walnut oil, vinegar, sugar, salt and pepper together.

Preheat oven to 350 degrees F. Spread walnuts or pecans on a pie plate and toast for about 10 minutes, or until lightly browned and fragrant. Let cool and chop coarsely.

In a salad bowl, combine endives, watercress and red onions. Drizzle the dressing over and toss. Taste and adjust seasonings. Sprinkle pomegranate seeds or raspberries and the toasted nuts over the top and serve.

Serves 8.

70 CALORIES PER SERVING: 1 G PROTEIN, 6 G FAT, 5 G CARBOHYDRATE; 8 MG SODIUM; 0 MG CHOLESTEROL.

Fennel, Orange & Lemon Salad with Olives

Fresh, crunchy, tangy with a bright salt-sweet balance, this salad is a natural for grilled fish or poultry or grain entrées. For a light lunch, add canned tuna or salmon.

3 tablespoons fresh lemon juice

1 tablespoon anise-flavored liquor, such as Ricard or Pernod, or orange juice

¼ teaspoon finely ground white pepper

Blend lemon juice, liquor or orange juice, pepper and salt in a jar. Add oil and shake to emulsify. Combine onions and olives in a small bowl; stir in the dressing.

Finely chop feathery fennel tops. (Reserve stalks for another use.) Quarter fennel bulbs lengthwise and remove any heavy outer layer and part of the core. Cut crosswise into very thin slices. Toss with the tops. Arrange on 4 plates.

Cut peel and pith from oranges. Slice each one into very thin slices, then quarter to form wedges. Arrange these around the fennel. Divide the dressing, onions and olives evenly over all. Serve within 1 hour.

Serves 6.

132 CALORIES PER SERVING: 2 G PROTEIN, 6 G FAT, 21 G CARBOHYDRATE; 296 MG SODIUM; 0 MG CHOLESTEROL.

¼ teaspoon salt

2 tablespoons olive oil, preferably extra-virgin

⅓ cup finely diced red onion

16 green or black olives, pitted and thinly sliced

2 medium fennel bulbs with feathery tops (1½ pounds)

2 large navel oranges

Carambola, Avocado & Wilted Spinach Salad

A pretty, unusual and easy salad. Very tender frisée lettuce also works nicely here.

In a small heavy skillet, heat oil over medium heat, stir in cumin and cook for 30 seconds. Add onions and cook, stirring, until soft, about 2 minutes. Add vinegar, brown sugar, soy sauce and red-pepper flakes, stirring to mix well. Remove from heat.

In a large bowl, toss spinach with 3 tablespoons of the warm dressing. Divide the salad among four plates, arrange carambola and avocado slices over the top and drizzle with the remaining dressing.

Serves 4.

178 CALORIES PER SERVING: 5 G PROTEIN, 12 G FAT, 19 G CARBOHYDRATE; 186 MG SODIUM; 0 MG CHOLESTEROL.

1 tablespoon peanut or corn oil

1 teaspoon ground cumin

2 tablespoons chopped red onion

⅓ cup Japanese rice-wine vinegar

1½ tablespoons brown sugar

1 teaspoon soy sauce

¼ teaspoon red-pepper flakes

1 pound fresh spinach, stemmed, washed and dried

2 carambolas (star fruit), thinly sliced

1 avocado, peeled and sliced

CHAPTER 4

Pasta

Penne with Artichoke Hearts (*Penne ai carciofi*)

Lemon juice and zest brighten the taste of this quick pasta dish.

1   9-ounce package frozen artichoke hearts

10   ounces penne or rigatoni

2   teaspoons olive oil

1   small onion, thinly sliced

1   clove garlic, finely chopped

1½   teaspoons chopped fresh oregano or ½ teaspoon dried oregano

    Salt & freshly ground black pepper to taste

¼   cup dry white wine

2   tablespoons fresh lemon juice

½   cup skim-milk ricotta cheese

1   tablespoon grated lemon zest

Blanch artichokes in lightly salted water for 1 minute; drain well. When cool enough to handle, slice about two-thirds of the artichokes into small wedges and set aside; finely chop the remaining artichokes into a paste and set aside.

In a large pot of boiling salted water, cook penne or rigatoni until al dente, 10 to 15 minutes.

While the pasta is cooking, heat oil in a large nonstick skillet over medium heat. Add onions and garlic; cook, stirring, for 1 minute. Add oregano, salt and a generous grinding of pepper. Stir in ¼ cup water and cook until the water has evaporated and the onions are limp, about 2 minutes. Reduce heat to low, stir in wine, lemon juice and the reserved artichoke wedges and chopped artichokes. Simmer, stirring, until heated through, about 1 minute. (If the mixture becomes dry, add 1 or 2 tablespoons of water.) Add ricotta and stir until creamy.

When the pasta is ready, drain it and add to the skillet with the simmering sauce; toss well. Remove from heat and stir in lemon zest. Taste and adjust seasonings with salt and pepper. Serve immediately.

Serves 4.

378 CALORIES PER SERVING: 15 G PROTEIN, 6 G FAT, 65 G CARBOHYDRATE; 106 MG SODIUM; 10 MG CHOLESTEROL.

Penne with Artichoke Hearts (*Penne ai carciofi*)

Vermicelli with Tomatoes, Olives & Capers (*Vermicelli alla puttanesca*)

For this dish, the sauce is uncooked, so it is ready by the time the vermicelli is cooked. Cooking the pasta until it is al dente is essential because texture is as important as taste.

1   pound vermicelli or spaghettini

4   large, vine-ripened tomatoes, cored and coarsely chopped, or one 28-ounce can plum tomatoes, drained and roughly chopped (3½ cups)

¼   cup chopped fresh parsley, preferably Italian flat-leaf

16 large black olives (packed in brine), pitted and chopped

3   tablespoons drained capers, chopped

4   anchovy fillets, rinsed and finely chopped

2   tablespoons olive oil, preferably extra-virgin

3   large cloves garlic, finely chopped

½   teaspoon freshly ground black pepper, or to taste

¼   cup freshly grated pecorino romano or Parmesan cheese

In a large pot of boiling salted water, cook vermicelli or spaghettini until al dente, about 5 to 7 minutes.

Meanwhile, in a serving bowl, combine tomatoes, parsley, olives, capers, anchovies, oil, garlic and pepper.

When the pasta is cooked, drain it and add to the bowl with the sauce. Toss well to combine. Taste and adjust seasonings. Sprinkle with cheese and serve immediately.

Serves 4.

580 CALORIES PER SERVING: 20 G PROTEIN, 14 G FAT, 95 G CARBOHYDRATE; 437 MG SODIUM; 5 MG CHOLESTEROL.

Linguine with Fennel & Butter Beans

A dusting of grated Parmesan is a perfect balance for the full fennel flavor.

1   tablespoon olive oil

2   fennel bulbs, trimmed, quartered, cored and thinly sliced

3   large carrots, chopped

In a large nonstick skillet, heat oil over medium-low heat. Add fennel, carrots, onions, garlic, fennel seed and red-pepper flakes and cook until the vegetables are tender, about 10 minutes.

Add chicken broth and butter beans and bring to a boil. Reduce the heat to low and simmer, uncovered, until the beans are tender, 10 to 12 minutes. Season with salt and pepper.

Meanwhile, in a large pot of boiling salted water, cook linguine until al dente, 6 to 8 minutes. Drain and transfer to a large shallow bowl. Add the vegetables and toss well. Taste and adjust seasonings. Sprinkle with Parmesan and serve.

Serves 6.

405 CALORIES PER SERVING: 16 G PROTEIN, 5 G FAT, 73 G CARBOHYDRATE; 561 MG SODIUM; 5 MG CHOLESTEROL.

1 large onion, chopped

3 cloves garlic, finely chopped

½ teaspoon fennel seed

½ teaspoon red-pepper flakes

3 cups defatted reduced-sodium chicken broth

1 10-ounce package frozen butter beans (baby lima beans)
Salt & freshly ground black pepper to taste

1 pound linguine

3 tablespoons freshly grated Parmesan cheese

Penne in Spicy Tomato Sauce (*Penne all'arrabbiata*)

Arrabbiata means "in a rage." It could refer either to the cooking technique (it's all prepared so quickly that the cook appears to be in a rage) or to the spicy (enraged) taste of the dish. Both interpretations apply: the dish is quick and easy to prepare and it should be as spicy as you like it (or can stand it).

In a large pot of boiling salted water, cook penne or mostaccioli until al dente, about 10 minutes.

Meanwhile, heat oil in a large nonstick skillet over low heat. Add garlic and red-pepper flakes; cook, stirring, until the garlic is golden, about 1 minute. Add tomatoes, crushing them roughly with a fork. Bring to a simmer over low heat and cook until slightly reduced, about 5 minutes.

When the pasta is ready, drain it and return it to the pot. Stir in the sauce and put the pot over high heat. Stir until the mixture sizzles. Remove from the heat. Add cheese and parsley; toss well. Taste and adjust seasonings; serve immediately.

Serves 4.

553 CALORIES PER SERVING: 22 G PROTEIN, 10 G FAT, 95 G CARBOHYDRATE; 262 MG SODIUM; 10 MG CHOLESTEROL.

1 pound penne or mostaccioli

1 tablespoon olive oil

3 cloves garlic, finely chopped

¼ teaspoon red-pepper flakes, or more to taste

1 28-ounce can plum tomatoes, drained

½ cup freshly grated pecorino romano cheese

¼ cup finely chopped fresh parsley, preferably Italian flat-leaf
Salt & freshly ground black pepper to taste

Linguine with Grilled Shrimp & Black Olives

In Italy, black olives are added to some pasta sauces, such as puttanesca, *or to boldly flavored fish dishes.*

1 pound medium shrimp, peeled and deveined

Salt & coarsely ground black pepper to taste

¾ pound linguine

1 tablespoon extra-virgin olive oil

6 large cloves garlic, peeled and thinly sliced lengthwise

4 vine-ripened tomatoes, coarsely chopped

½ cup brine-cured black olives, pitted and coarsely chopped

½ cup chopped fresh basil

Freshly ground black pepper to taste

½ cup freshly grated Parmesan cheese (optional)

If using bamboo skewers, soak them in water for 30 minutes. Prepare the grill.

Thread shrimp onto skewers and sprinkle with salt and pepper. Grill over a medium-hot fire until just opaque throughout, 3 to 4 minutes per side. Remove the shrimp from the skewers and cut each into 3 or 4 pieces. Set aside.

While the shrimp is grilling, cook linguine in a large pot of boiling salted water until al dente, about 8 minutes. Drain but do not rinse.

Meanwhile, in a large skillet, heat oil over medium heat until hot but not smoking. Add garlic and cook, stirring frequently, until it just starts to brown, about 2 minutes. Add tomatoes, olives, the grilled shrimp and cooked linguine; cook, tossing, until heated through, 2 to 3 minutes. Transfer to a large bowl, mix in basil and season with pepper to taste. Top with cheese, if using, and serve.

Serves 4.

612 CALORIES PER SERVING: 38 G PROTEIN, 19 G FAT, 79 G CARBOHYDRATE; 532 MG SODIUM; 175 MG CHOLESTEROL.

Linguine with Grilled Shrimp & Black Olives

Shellfish Lasagne

The lasagne is baked very briefly to ensure that the flavors remain fresh and bright. Italian anise-flavored liqueurs include Galliano, Sambuca and Anisette. Pernod, a French product, is also excellent.

½ cup dried tomatoes (not packed in oil)

1 tablespoon olive oil

2 onions, coarsely chopped (about 2 cups)

1 medium fennel bulb, trimmed, cored and coarsely chopped

2 cloves garlic, finely chopped

2 pounds plum tomatoes, seeded and coarsely chopped, or two 28-ounce cans tomatoes, drained and coarsely chopped

½ cup chopped fresh parsley

½ teaspoon red-pepper flakes

1 cup bottled clam juice

1 cup dry white wine

¾ pound medium shrimp, in shells

24 small clams, such as littleneck, scrubbed

24 mussels, scrubbed and debearded

½ pound cleaned squid, thinly sliced

½ cup plus 2 tablespoons chopped fresh basil

2 tablespoons anise-flavored liqueur
  Salt & freshly ground black pepper to taste

1 pound fresh pasta sheets or 12 ounces dried lasagne noodles

2 tablespoons freshly grated Parmesan cheese

In a small bowl, cover dried tomatoes with boiling water and let stand for 10 minutes, or until softened. Drain and cut into slivers.

In a very large skillet or Dutch oven, heat oil over medium-low heat. Add onions and fennel and cook until softened, about 5 minutes. Add garlic and cook for 1 minute. Increase heat to medium and stir in tomatoes, parsley, red-pepper flakes and the reserved dried tomatoes. Simmer, stirring often, until the juices are nearly evaporated, 15 to 20 minutes.

Meanwhile, in a large pot, bring clam juice and wine to a boil over high heat. Add shrimp, lower heat and simmer, covered, until the shrimp are pink and just cooked through, about 2 minutes. Transfer to a bowl with a slotted spoon and set aside.

Add clams to the pot, cover and steam about 5 minutes, removing the clams with a slotted spoon as they open, and transferring them to the bowl with the shrimp. Then add mussels to the pot. Cover and steam about 3 minutes, removing the mussels with a slotted spoon as they open. Transfer to the bowl with the clams and shrimp. (Discard any clams or mussels that do not open.)

Strain the shellfish-steaming liquid through a sieve lined with cheesecloth and measure out 1½ cups. (Reserve any extra for another use.) Peel and devein the shrimp. Set aside 8 shrimp, along with 8 clams and 8 mussels in their shells, for garnish; cover and refrigerate. Cut the remaining shrimp in half lengthwise. Remove the remaining clams and mussels from their shells. Pull off the dark rubbery rim from the mussels.

Add squid and the reserved 1½ cups shellfish-steaming liquid to the tomato sauce. Simmer until the squid is cooked through, about 4 minutes. Remove from the heat and stir in the shelled clams and mussels, shrimp, ½ cup chopped basil and anise-flavored liqueur. Taste and season with salt and pepper. (*The sauce can be prepared 1 day ahead and stored, covered, in the refrigerator.*)

Bring a large pot of salted water to a boil. Place a large bowl of cold water near the stove and lay some kitchen towels on the work surface. Cook pasta in boiling water, a few sheets at a time, until barely tender, 1 to 2 minutes for fresh pasta or 8 to 10 minutes for dried. Remove the pasta with a slotted spoon and drop it into the cold water, then spread it on the kitchen towels.

Lightly oil one 9-by-13-inch lasagne pan or 8 individual gratin dishes. Moisten the bottom of the pan (or dishes) with a spoonful of the tomato-shellfish sauce. Add a layer of pasta, using about ⅓ of the sheets, cutting to fit if necessary. Then spoon on half of the tomato-shellfish sauce. Make another layer with half of the remaining pasta, then add the rest of the tomato-shellfish sauce. Top with remaining pasta sheets. (*The lasagne can be prepared ahead and stored, covered, in the refrigerator for up to 8 hours.*)

Preheat the oven to 450 degrees F. Sprinkle the lasagne with cheese. Bake for 10 to 20 minutes, or until the tip of a sharp knife or skewer inserted in the center is hot to the touch. Place the shrimp and shellfish that have been reserved for garnish decoratively on top and heat for another 2 to 3 minutes, until they are warm. Remove from the oven and sprinkle with 2 tablespoons chopped basil. If baking the lasagne in a large pan, let it stand for 5 minutes before cutting into squares, spooning any juices left in the baking dish over each serving. (*The lasagne will be juicy.*)

Serves 8.

520 CALORIES PER SERVING: 46 G PROTEIN, 7 G FAT, 64 G CARBOHYDRATE; 635 MG SODIUM; 203 MG CHOLESTEROL.

Fresh Fettuccine with Shiitake & Celery

Fresh pasta, a generous helping of silky shiitake mushrooms and crisp celery are accented with lemon for a surprising and subtle effect. If you like, add fresh sage for another dimension to the dish.

¾   **pound fresh shiitake**

2   **tablespoons olive oil**

2   **teaspoons sesame oil**

2   **cups thinly sliced inner celery stalks**

3   **cloves garlic, finely chopped (1 tablespoon)**

½   **cup defatted reduced-sodium chicken broth or vegetable broth**

1   **teaspoon grated lemon zest Salt & freshly ground black pepper**

½   **cup finely chopped fresh parsley**

¾   **pound fresh (not dried) fettuccine or linguine**

2   **tablespoons fresh lemon juice, plus more to taste**

Reserve shiitake stems for another use. Clean caps with a soft brush. Slice the caps in half and toss thoroughly with 2 teaspoons of the olive oil. Let stand for at least 15 minutes. Meanwhile, put a large pot of water on to boil for the pasta.

Heat 1 tablespoon of the remaining olive oil and 1 teaspoon of the sesame oil in a very large skillet over high heat. Add celery and the mushroom caps and toss for 1 minute. Add garlic and toss for 1 minute. Pour in broth, cover and cook for 1 minute, or until the caps are tender but the celery is still quite crisp. If necessary, uncover and boil a moment longer to evaporate the liquid. Stir in lemon zest, salt, pepper and parsley; toss to blend.

Cook fettuccine or linguine in boiling salted water until al dente, 2 to 4 minutes. Drain well, then combine in a heated dish with the shiitake mixture. Season with lemon juice, salt, pepper and the remaining 1 teaspoon each of olive oil and sesame oil; toss and serve.

Serves 4.

297 CALORIES PER SERVING: 8 G PROTEIN, 11 G FAT, 45 G CARBOHYDRATE; 178 MG SODIUM; 39 MG CHOLESTEROL.

Cold Buckwheat Noodles Korean-Style

Chilled buckwheat noodles swim in a sharp, vinegary broth, garnished with boiled beef and crunchy slices of Asian pear. Buy either Korean naengmyon *or Japanese* soba *noodles.*

1   **pound beef for boiling (arm pot roast or round steak)**

1½   **tablespoons sesame seeds Pinch of salt**

Bring about 2 quarts water to a boil and add beef. Skim the surface several times, then reduce the heat, cover and simmer the beef until tender, about 1 to 1½ hours.

Allow the meat to cool in the broth, then remove it, trim off any fat and gristle; thinly slice.

In a small heavy skillet, toast sesame seeds over medium heat until they begin to brown and have a toasted aroma. Transfer to a mortar, add salt and crush with a pestle.

In a small bowl, combine the sliced beef with soy sauce, sesame oil, garlic, a generous grinding of black pepper and the ground sesame seeds. Cover and refrigerate until just before serving time. Chill the broth for at least 1 hour and skim off any fat from the surface. (*The meat and broth can be made 24 hours in advance and stored, covered, in the refrigerator.*) Mix the broth with vinegar, sugar and salt. Return the broth mixture to the refrigerator until serving time.

TO MAKE MARINATED CUCUMBERS:

Sprinkle salt over cucumbers, cover with cold water and set aside for 20 minutes. Drain, rinse well and squeeze out excess moisture. In a small bowl, combine the cucumbers with vinegar, sugar and ground red pepper. Refrigerate until serving time.

TO MAKE VINEGAR-MUSTARD SAUCE:

Stir together soy sauce, vinegar and dry mustard in a small bowl. Set aside.

TO FINISH DISH:

Cook the buckwheat noodles in a large pot of boiling water until al dente, 3 to 5 minutes. Drain and rinse well in cold water. (*The noodles can be cooked up to 2 hours ahead and chilled.*)

To serve, put some noodles in each soup bowl. Pour in the chilled broth mixture about halfway up each bowl. Top with a few slices of beef, some Marinated Cucumbers, a few slices of hard-cooked egg and a slice of Asian pear, if using. Add 1 or 2 ice cubes to each bowl to keep the soup and noodles very cold. Serve with the Vinegar-Mustard Sauce, to be mixed with the noodles to taste.

Serves 6.

172 CALORIES PER SERVING: 26 G PROTEIN, 6 G FAT, 6 G CARBOHYDRATE; 234 MG SODIUM; 70 MG CHOLESTEROL.

3 tablespoons reduced-sodium soy sauce

1 tablespoon sesame oil

1 clove garlic, finely chopped
Freshly ground black pepper to taste

6 tablespoons rice vinegar or cider vinegar

1 tablespoon sugar
Salt to taste

MARINATED CUCUMBERS

1 tablespoon salt

1 cucumber, thinly sliced

1 tablespoon rice vinegar or cider vinegar

1½ teaspoons sugar

½ teaspoon ground red pepper (cayenne)

VINEGAR-MUSTARD SAUCE

3 tablespoons reduced-sodium soy sauce

4½ teaspoons rice vinegar or cider vinegar

1½ teaspoons English dry mustard

NOODLES & GARNISH

1 pound buckwheat noodles

2 hard-cooked eggs, sliced

1 Asian pear, peeled, cored and sliced (optional)

CHAPTER 5

Pizza & Sandwiches

Pizza *alla siciliana*

Look for Sicilian olives for this pizza.

¾ pound Pizza Dough (*page 54*)
Semolina or cornmeal for
dusting

1 tablespoon olive oil, preferably
extra-virgin

½ cup tomato sauce (*page 54*)

6 black olives, pitted and sliced

6 green olives, pitted and sliced

3 anchovy fillets, rinsed, patted dry
and chopped

1 tablespoon drained capers

1 tablespoon freshly grated
Parmesan cheese

Place a pizza stone, baking tiles or an inverted baking sheet on the bottom or on the lowest rack of a cold oven; preheat for 30 minutes to 500 degrees F or the highest setting.

Place dough on a lightly floured surface and pat into a disk. Use a rolling pin or your hands to roll or stretch the dough into a circle that is ¼ inch thick and 10 to 12 inches in diameter. Transfer to a semolina- or cornmeal-dusted pizza peel or inverted baking sheet.

Brush the dough with a little of the olive oil. Spread tomato sauce over the dough almost to the edge. Distribute olives, anchovies and capers over the sauce. Sprinkle with Parmesan. Drizzle with the remaining olive oil.

Carefully slide the pizza onto the heated pizza stone, tiles or baking sheet and bake for 6 to 8 minutes, or until the bottom is crisp and browned and the top is bubbling.

Makes one 12-inch pizza.

158 CALORIES FOR EACH OF 6 SLICES: 4 G PROTEIN, 5 G FAT, 25 G CARBOHYDRATE; 469 MG SODIUM; 3 MG CHOLESTEROL.

Pizza *alla siciliana*

Tomato Sauce for Pizza, Neapolitan-Style

In Naples, pizza can be topped with fresh tomatoes, but a cooked sauce is more common. This one freezes well.

1	tablespoon olive oil
2-3	cloves garlic, peeled and sliced
3½	pounds vine-ripened tomatoes, cut in chunks, or two 28-ounce cans plum tomatoes, drained and coarsely chopped
1	teaspoon salt
½	teaspoon sugar

In a large heavy saucepan, heat olive oil over medium-low heat. Add garlic and cook, stirring, until it starts to soften, 30 to 60 seconds. Add tomatoes, salt and sugar and bring to a boil. Cook briskly over medium heat, stirring frequently, until the tomatoes cook down to a thick mass, 15 to 25 minutes, depending on the juiciness of the tomatoes.

Puree the tomatoes by working them through the medium disk of a food mill or through a coarse sieve. If the sauce seems too thin, return it to medium-low heat and cook, stirring constantly, until it is the desired consistency. Cool completely before spreading over the pizza.

Makes about 2 cups.

Pizza Dough

This recipe makes dough for two pizzas; if you plan to make only one, refrigerate or freeze half after the dough has risen. Note the cake flour in the ingredients—this produces a wonderfully tender crust.

1	teaspoon active dry yeast
1⅔-2	cups unbleached or all-purpose white flour
1	cup cake flour
1	teaspoon salt

In a small bowl, sprinkle yeast over ¼ cup warm water; stir until dissolved. In a mixing bowl, combine 1⅔ cups of the unbleached or all-purpose flour, cake flour and salt. Make a well in the center of the dry ingredients and pour in the dissolved yeast. With a wooden spoon, gradually stir in the flour, adding ½ cup warm water as you mix.

Turn the dough out onto a lightly floured surface and knead until very smooth, soft and no longer sticky, about 10 minutes, adding additional flour as needed to keep the dough from sticking. (The dough should still be quite wet, however.) Transfer to an oiled bowl and turn to coat lightly. Cover with plastic wrap and let rise until doubled, 2 to 2½ hours.

About 10 minutes before baking the pizza, turn the dough onto the floured board, punch it down and knead briefly. Use a pastry cutter or a sharp knife to divide the dough in half. Pat each half into a ball and flatten into a disk. Proceed as directed in pizza recipes. (*The dough can be made ahead, enclosed in a plastic bag and stored in the refrigerator for up to 2 days or in the freezer for up to 2 months. Bring to room temperature before using.*)

Makes about 1½ pounds of dough, enough for two 12-inch pizzas.

Pizza Margherita

Fresh mozzarella is the cheese of choice for an authentic Pizza Margherita.

Place a pizza stone, baking tiles or an inverted baking sheet on the bottom or on the lowest rack of a cold oven; preheat for 30 minutes to 500 degrees F or the highest setting.

Place dough on a lightly floured surface and pat into a disk. Use a rolling pin or your hands to roll or stretch the dough into a circle that is ¼ inch thick and 10 to 12 inches in diameter. Transfer to a semolina- or cornmeal-dusted pizza peel or inverted baking sheet.

Brush the dough with a little of the olive oil. Spread tomato sauce over the dough almost to the edge. Distribute mozzarella slices on top and season with salt and pepper. Arrange basil leaves over the mozzarella. Sprinkle with Parmesan. Drizzle with the remaining olive oil.

Carefully slide the pizza onto the heated pizza stone, tiles or baking sheet and bake for 6 to 8 minutes, or until the bottom is crisp and browned and the top is bubbling.

Makes one 12-inch pizza.

181 CALORIES FOR EACH OF 6 SLICES: 7 G PROTEIN, 6 G FAT, 24 G CARBOHYDRATE; 397 MG SODIUM; 9 MG CHOLESTEROL.

¾ pound Pizza Dough (*recipe above*)
Semolina or cornmeal for dusting

1 tablespoon olive oil, preferably extra-virgin

½ cup tomato sauce (*page 54*)

2 ounces mozzarella cheese, sliced ⅛ inch thick
Salt & freshly ground black pepper to taste

½ cup loosely packed fresh basil leaves (1 small bunch), rinsed

¼ cup freshly grated Parmesan cheese

Artichoke & Leek Pizza

Pancetta is available at Italian markets, specialty stores and some supermarkets.

2 medium or 4 small artichokes

½ lemon

1 ounce pancetta, diced

1 tablespoon olive oil, preferably extra-virgin

1 onion, finely chopped
   Freshly ground black pepper to taste

1 large leek, well trimmed, thoroughly cleaned and thinly sliced
   Salt to taste

¾ pound Pizza Dough (*page 54*)
   Semolina or cornmeal for dusting

2 ounces mozzarella cheese, coarsely grated (⅔ cup)

3 tablespoons freshly grated Parmesan cheese

Place a pizza stone, baking tiles or an inverted baking sheet on the bottom or on the lowest rack of a cold oven; preheat for 30 minutes to 500 degrees F or the highest setting.

Peel away and discard the tough outer leaves of the artichokes, snapping them off at the base, until you reach the pale yellow leaves with the darker green tops. Slice off the darker green tops and rub the artichokes with the cut side of the lemon half. With a paring knife, trim each artichoke where you snapped off the leaves, removing any green portions. Rub with the lemon. Trim the bottom ¼ inch off the stem and pare away the tough outer skin. With a melon baller or paring knife, remove the fuzzy choke from the center of each artichoke. Cut the hearts into quarters, then cut each quarter into 4 pieces. Squeeze the lemon into a bowl of water and place the artichoke pieces into the acidulated water to keep them from turning brown.

Heat a skillet over medium heat, add pancetta and cook, stirring, until golden, about 4 minutes. Drain the pancetta on paper towels; set aside. Pour off the fat from the skillet. Add 1½ teaspoons of the olive oil and onions to the skillet. Cook, stirring occasionally, until the onions are soft but not brown, about 3 minutes. Add the drained artichoke pieces and stir to mix well. Add pepper and ⅔ cup water. Cover and cook over low heat until the artichoke pieces are tender and most of the liquid has cooked away, about 15 minutes. Add leeks and stir to mix well. Taste and adjust seasonings, adding salt if desired. Let cool completely.

Place dough on a lightly floured surface and pat into a disk. Use a rolling pin or your hands to roll or stretch the dough into a circle that is ¼ inch thick and 10 to 12 inches in diameter. Transfer to a semolina- or cornmeal-dusted pizza peel or inverted baking sheet.

Brush the dough with a little of the remaining olive oil. Distribute the artichoke mixture and the reserved pancetta over the dough. Sprinkle the cheeses over the artichoke mixture. Drizzle with the remaining olive oil.

Carefully slide the pizza onto the heated pizza stone, tiles or baking sheet and bake for 6 to 8 minutes, or until the bottom is crisp and browned and the top is bubbling.

Makes one 12-inch pizza.

207 CALORIES FOR EACH OF 6 SLICES: 9 G PROTEIN, 5 G FAT, 31 G CARBOHY-DRATE; 386 MG SODIUM, 10 MG CHOLESTEROL.

The Eating Well PBT (Portobello, Basil & Tomato Sandwich)

A new take on the BLT. Smoky grilled portobello mushrooms (a.k.a. vegetarians' prime rib)
add a toothsome richness to this meatless sandwich.

2 tablespoons reduced-fat mayonnaise

2 tablespoons nonfat sour cream or nonfat plain yogurt

1 teaspoon fresh lemon juice

1 tablespoon olive oil

2 4-ounce portobello mushrooms, stems removed, caps wiped clean and sliced ⅜ inch thick

Salt & freshly ground black pepper to taste

8 slices sourdough bread

1 clove garlic, halved

1 cup loosely packed basil leaves, washed, dried and torn into shreds (if large)

2 vine-ripened tomatoes, cored and sliced

In a small bowl, stir together mayonnaise, sour cream or yogurt, and lemon juice.

Prepare a grill or preheat the broiler. Brush olive oil over the cut sides of the mushrooms. Grill or broil the mushroom slices until tender and golden, 2 to 3 minutes per side. Season with salt and pepper. Meanwhile, toast bread on the grill or under the broiler. Rub both sides of the bread with garlic clove.

Spread half of the mayonnaise mixture over 4 toasted bread slices and arrange basil on top. Top with the grilled mushroom slices, followed by tomato slices and salt and pepper to taste. Finish with a dollop of the remaining mayonnaise mixture and cover with the remaining pieces of toast. Cut sandwiches in half and serve immediately.

Serves 4.

261 CALORIES PER SERVING: 9 G PROTEIN, 6 G FAT, 43 G CARBOHYDRATE; 328 MG SODIUM; 3 MG CHOLESTEROL.

Roasted Vegetable & Feta Sandwich

Inspired by a New Orleans sandwich, the muffaletta, this jazzy vegetarian version is far more healthful.

1 medium eggplant (about 1 pound)

1 tablespoon olive oil, preferably extra-virgin

1 7-ounce jar roasted red peppers, drained, rinsed and chopped

Prepare a grill or preheat the broiler. Cut eggplant crosswise into ½-inch-thick slices. Brush ½ tablespoon of the oil over both sides of the eggplant slices. Grill or broil the eggplant until lightly browned and tender, 3 to 4 minutes per side. Let cool slightly. Chop the eggplant coarsely and mix with red peppers. Season with salt and pepper.

In a small bowl, mash feta with a fork. Add lemon juice, oregano, red-pepper flakes and the remaining ½ tablespoon oil; blend until smooth and spreadable. Season with pepper.

Slice loaf in half horizontally and scoop out about 1 inch of the soft interior from each half. (Reserve for another use, such as breadcrumbs.) Spread the seasoned feta in the bottom half of the loaf. Spoon the chopped eggplant and peppers over the cheese and place the bread top firmly on the bottom half. Cut into wedges. Serve immediately or wrap and store in a cool place for up to 8 hours.

Serves 6.

315 CALORIES PER SERVING: 11 G PROTEIN, 7 G FAT, 51 G CARBOHYDRATE; 597 MG SODIUM; 17 MG CHOLESTEROL.

Salt & freshly ground black pepper to taste

4 ounces feta cheese, preferably imported

2 teaspoons fresh lemon juice

1 teaspoon dried oregano
   Pinch of red-pepper flakes

1 round loaf country bread (about 9 inches across)

Roasted Vegetable & Feta Sandwich

Barbecued Pork & Coleslaw Sandwiches

Two Southern favorites are combined here: pork in sweet barbecue sauce and crunchy coleslaw.

COLESLAW

- 3 tablespoons cider vinegar
- 4 teaspoons sugar
- 2 teaspoons vegetable oil, preferably canola oil
- 1 teaspoon Dijon mustard
- ¼ teaspoon celery seeds
- ¼ teaspoon mustard seeds
- 1 cup shredded green cabbage
- 1 cup shredded red cabbage
- 1 carrot, grated
  Salt & freshly ground black pepper to taste

BARBECUE SAUCE

- 1 teaspoon vegetable oil, preferably canola oil
- 1 onion, chopped
- 1 clove garlic, finely chopped
- 1 cup catsup
- ¼ cup cider vinegar
- 1 tablespoon brown sugar
- 1 teaspoon dry mustard
- 1 teaspoon Worcestershire sauce
- ¼ teaspoon Tabasco sauce
  Salt to taste

PORK & ROLLS

- 2 ¾-pound pork tenderloins, trimmed of fat and membrane
- 6 Kaiser or other large rolls, cut in half crosswise

TO MAKE COLESLAW:

In a mixing bowl, whisk together vinegar, sugar, oil, Dijon mustard, celery seeds and mustard seeds. Add green and red cabbage and carrots; toss well. Season with salt and pepper.

TO MAKE BARBECUE SAUCE:

In a saucepan, heat oil over medium heat. Add onions and garlic and sauté for 4 to 5 minutes, or until golden brown. Add catsup, vinegar, sugar, mustard, Worcestershire, Tabasco and salt. Cook, stirring, for 1 to 2 minutes, or until the mixture boils. Remove from the heat and set aside.

TO COOK PORK AND ASSEMBLE SANDWICHES:

Preheat the broiler. Place tenderloins on a broiler pan and season with salt and pepper. Broil 4 inches from the heat for 6 minutes, or until lightly browned. Turn the tenderloins over and broil for 6 to 7 minutes longer, or until the internal temperature registers 160 degrees F. (The center should be juicy with just a trace of pink.) Let the meat stand for 5 minutes before cutting into thin strips. Add the meat to the barbecue sauce and toss well.

To assemble the sandwiches, layer the coleslaw and the pork mixture inside rolls.

Serves 6.

400 CALORIES PER SERVING: 30 G PROTEIN, 9 G FAT, 52 G CARBOHYDRATE; 661 MG SODIUM; 79 MG CHOLESTEROL.

Barbecued Pork & Coleslaw Sandwiches

Spicy Black Bean Sandwiches with Chipotle Mayonnaise

Chipotles are smoked jalapeño peppers. They are often sold in cans, packed in adobo sauce. They can be found in the Mexican section of a large supermarket or at a specialty food store.

1 tablespoon reduced-fat mayonnaise

3 tablespoons nonfat sour cream or nonfat plain yogurt

2 teaspoons chopped chipotle peppers in adobo sauce

1 16-ounce can black beans, drained and rinsed

¾ cup chopped red onion

3 tablespoons chopped fresh cilantro

1 clove garlic, finely chopped

1 tablespoon mild chili powder

1 teaspoon ground cumin

2 tablespoons fresh lime juice

Salt to taste

4 pita breads

½ small head of iceberg lettuce, shredded

1 ripe avocado, pitted, peeled and sliced

1 vine-ripened tomato, cored and sliced

In a small bowl, stir together mayonnaise, sour cream or yogurt and chipotle peppers; set aside.

In a large bowl, combine black beans, red onion, cilantro, garlic, chili powder, cumin, lime juice and salt. Lightly mash the beans while stirring, until all ingredients are incorporated and the mixture just holds together.

Slice off the top third of each pita and spoon some bean mixture into each one. Top with the chipotle mayonnaise, shredded lettuce, avocado slices and tomato slices. Serve within 30 minutes.

Serves 4.

266 CALORIES PER SERVING: 8 G PROTEIN, 11 G FAT, 36 G CARBOHYDRATE; 283 MG SODIUM; 1 MG CHOLESTEROL.

Grilled Chicken Sandwiches with Sherried Peaches

A peachy, peppery relish makes a lively contrast to the grilled chicken.

Heat 1 teaspoon of the oil in a large nonstick skillet over medium-low heat. Add onions and cook, stirring, until softened and starting to color, 5 to 7 minutes. Add sugar, stirring until it dissolves and starts to bubble, about 2 minutes. Add peaches and cook another 4 minutes, or until the mixture turns golden brown. Add vinegar and sherry, bring to a simmer and cook, stirring, until thickened and jamlike, 5 to 10 minutes. Stir in crushed peppercorns and season with salt. Transfer to a bowl and set aside.

Prepare a grill or preheat the broiler. Place each chicken breast between two layers of plastic wrap and flatten gently with a rolling pin or heavy skillet until approximately ¼ inch thick. Brush the chicken breasts lightly with the remaining 1 teaspoon oil and season with salt and pepper. Grill or broil the chicken until no longer pink inside, 3 to 4 minutes per side. While the chicken is cooking, toast the rolls on the grill or under the broiler.

Place lettuce leaves on the bottom halves of the toasted rolls, followed by the grilled chicken. Top with the sherried peaches and the roll tops.

Serves 4.

439 CALORIES PER SERVING: 33 G PROTEIN, 7 G FAT, 56 G CARBOHYDRATE; 378 MG SODIUM; 72 MG CHOLESTEROL.

2 teaspoons vegetable oil, preferably canola oil

2 onions, quartered and sliced (about 2 cups)

¼ cup sugar

2 peaches, peeled, pitted and chopped

⅓ cup sherry vinegar or cider vinegar

⅓ cup dry sherry

1 teaspoon black peppercorns, crushed

Salt to taste

4 4-ounce boneless, skinless chicken breasts, trimmed of fat

Freshly ground black pepper to taste

4 Kaiser or other large rolls, split

4 large lettuce leaves

CHAPTER 6

Vegetables & Grains

Potato, Sweet Potato & Leek Terrine

Here vegetables are layered in a clay-pot cooker or two loaf pans and baked in the oven. When unmolded, the terrine is a beautiful golden brown on the outside and tender within. Serve with roast chicken or pork tenderloin.

Soak the bottom and lid of a clay cooker of at least 3-quart capacity in cool water for 15 minutes. Heat butter and oil in a large nonstick skillet over medium-high heat. Add the leeks, thyme, salt and pepper and sauté until tender, about 5 minutes.

Line the bottom of the soaked clay cooker with aluminum foil or baking parchment. Lightly brush the foil or paper and the sides of the clay cooker with oil or coat it with nonstick cooking spray. (*Alternatively, line the bottom and sides of two 4½-by-8½-inch loaf pans with foil. Brush with oil or coat with nonstick cooking spray.*)

Arrange half of the all-purpose potatoes in overlapping layers in the bottom of the clay cooker (or loaf pans). Spoon in one-third of the leeks. Arrange one-half of the sweet potato slices over the leeks, then top with another third of the leeks. Layer the remaining potatoes, leeks and sweet potatoes.

Cover, place the clay cooker on the lowest rack of a cold oven and set the oven temperature at 425 degrees F. Bake for 1½ hours, or until the vegetables are tender. (*If using loaf pans, cover them with foil and bake for 1 hour.*) Remove from the oven and let sit, covered, for 10 minutes. Loosen the edges with a knife and unmold onto a platter.

Serves 8.

304 CALORIES PER SERVING: 6 G PROTEIN, 4 G FAT, 64 G CARBOHYDRATE; 304 MG SODIUM; 1 MG CHOLESTEROL.

Potato, Sweet Potato & Leek Terrine

1	tablespoon butter
1	tablespoon olive oil
2	large leeks, well trimmed, thoroughly cleaned and thinly sliced
1	tablespoon chopped fresh thyme or 1 teaspoon dried thyme leaves
1	teaspoon salt
½	teaspoon freshly ground black pepper
1½	pounds all-purpose potatoes, preferably Yukon Gold (about 4 medium), peeled and cut into ⅛-inch-thick slices
1½	pounds sweet potatoes (about 3 medium), peeled and cut into ⅛-inch-thick slices

Southern-Style Curried Sweet Potatoes

*Curry was in no way an unusual flavor in an old-style Southern meal, and recipes
for the spice blend appear in some of the earliest Southern cookbooks.*

4½ pounds sweet potatoes (8 or 9
    medium), peeled and cut into
    1-inch pieces

1   teaspoon salt, plus more to taste

1   cup loosely packed dried apricots
    (¼ pound), cut into ¼-inch
    slivers

½   cup raisins

1   tablespoon vegetable oil,
    preferably canola oil

1   onion, finely chopped

2   teaspoons mild curry powder,
    preferably Madras

    Freshly ground black pepper to
    taste

Place sweet potatoes in a large pot and add enough cold water
to cover by 1 inch. Add 1 teaspoon salt and bring to a boil over
high heat. Reduce heat to medium and cook, uncovered, until
tender but not mushy, 8 to 12 minutes. Drain well.

Meanwhile, in a small bowl, combine apricots, raisins and
1 cup boiling water; let sit until plumped, about 10 minutes.

In a large wide pot, heat oil over medium-high heat. Add
onions and cook, stirring often, until softened, about 2 minutes. Add curry powder and cook, stirring, until fragrant, about
2 minutes. Add the cooked sweet potatoes, apricots, raisins and
the fruit-soaking liquid. Season with salt and pepper. Stir gently
over medium-low heat until warmed through. (*The recipe can be
prepared ahead and stored, covered, in the refrigerator for up to 2 days. Reheat
on the stovetop or in the microwave before serving.*)

Serves 10.

340 CALORIES PER SERVING: 5 G PROTEIN, 2 G FAT, 77 G CARBOHYDRATE;
250 MG SODIUM; 0 MG CHOLESTEROL.

Butternut Squash, Carrot & Parsnip Ragoût

*Root vegetables take on a sweet intensity when gently braised in a good broth.
Serve this ragoût with roast chicken, grilled salmon fillets or pan-seared pork tenderloin.*

1   teaspoon olive oil

3   cups peeled and cubed
    butternut squash (about 1
    pound)

    Salt & freshly ground black
    pepper to taste

Preheat oven to 350 degrees F. In a shallow roasting pan on the
stovetop, heat olive oil over medium heat. Add squash, season
with salt and pepper and toss gently. Add ½ cup of the chicken
broth and transfer the pan to the oven. Bake for 15 minutes, or
until squash is just tender; do not overcook.

Meanwhile, in a large nonstick skillet, heat butter over

medium heat. Add carrots, parsnips, sugar, and salt and pepper to taste; cook until the vegetables are lightly browned, about 3 minutes. Add another ½ cup of the broth, cover the pan and simmer until tender, about 10 minutes. Transfer to a dish and set aside.

Add leeks and the remaining ¼ cup broth to the skillet, season with salt and pepper, cover the pan and simmer until tender, about 10 minutes. Add the reserved squash, carrots and parsnips and toss gently. Taste and adjust seasonings, adding a grating of nutmeg. (*The ragoût can be prepared ahead and stored, covered, in the refrigerator for up to 8 hours. Reheat gently on the stovetop or in the microwave before serving.*)

Serves 6.

139 CALORIES PER SERVING: 2 G PROTEIN, 3 G FAT, 28 G CARBOHYDRATE; 48 MG SODIUM; 5 MG CHOLESTEROL.

1¼ cups defatted reduced-sodium chicken broth
1 tablespoon butter
2 cups diced carrots
2 cups diced parsnips
1 teaspoon sugar
2 large leeks, well trimmed, thoroughly cleaned and chopped
   Freshly grated nutmeg to taste

Sauté of Root Vegetables

To simplify cutting the carrots and rutabaga into julienne strips, use a food processor fitted with an ⅛-inch or ¼-inch slicing disk, then cut the slices into thin strips by stacking them and reslicing in the opposite direction.

In a large nonstick skillet, melt butter over medium heat. Add carrots, leeks, rutabagas and celeriac or parsnips; sauté until softened, 3 to 5 minutes. Add chicken broth and thyme and bring to a simmer. Reduce heat to low, cover and cook, stirring occasionally, until the vegetables are tender and the broth has evaporated, 10 to 15 minutes. Season with salt and pepper. (*The recipe can be prepared up to 8 hours ahead and stored, covered, in the refrigerator. Reheat gently on the stovetop, adding a little water if necessary, before serving.*)

Serves 8.

77 CALORIES PER SERVING: 1 G PROTEIN, 1 G FAT, 16 G CARBOHYDRATE; 29 MG SODIUM; 3 MG CHOLESTEROL.

2 teaspoons butter
2 cups julienned carrots (4 small)
2 cups julienned leeks (3 leeks, white and light green parts only)
2 cups julienned rutabaga (⅓ large)
2 cups julienned celeriac or parsnips
1 cup defatted reduced-sodium chicken broth
1 tablespoon chopped fresh thyme or 1 teaspoon dried thyme leaves
   Salt & freshly ground black pepper to taste

Crushed Red Potatoes with Winter Greens

Flecks of red potato skin and deep green from the winter greens add festive color to the dish.

1   pound greens, such as collards, mustard greens, broccoli rabe and/or escarole (8 cups)

2   pounds small red potatoes, scrubbed

1   tablespoon olive oil, preferably extra-virgin

2   cloves garlic, finely chopped

½   cup buttermilk
    Salt & freshly ground black pepper to taste

Remove tough fibrous stems and any wilted or yellow leaves from greens. Wash the leaves well and cut into 1-inch pieces. Set aside. In a large saucepan, cook potatoes in boiling salted water until tender, about 15 minutes. Remove with a slotted spoon and transfer to a medium bowl. Crush with a potato masher or the back of a large spoon and set aside. Add the greens to the boiling potato water and cook until tender, 2 to 3 minutes. Drain and set aside.

Dry the pot, and return to medium heat. Heat oil, add garlic and sauté until fragrant, about 1 minute. Add the cooked greens and toss with the garlic. Stir in the potatoes and buttermilk. Season with salt and pepper. (*The recipe can be prepared up to 1 hour ahead and kept warm over a larger pan of barely simmering water.*)
Serves 8.

128 CALORIES PER SERVING: 3 G PROTEIN, 2 G FAT, 26 G CARBOHYDRATE; 19 MG SODIUM; 0 MG CHOLESTEROL.

Garlic Mashed Potatoes

What could be more satisfying than mashed potatoes? The challenge lies in making them rich and creamy without an excess of butter and cream. In this version, the potatoes are flavored with poached garlic, thinned with chicken broth and enriched with a small amount of reduced-fat sour cream. The recipe can easily be doubled or tripled.

2   pounds all-purpose potatoes, preferably Yukon Gold (4-6 potatoes), peeled and cut into chunks

6   cloves garlic, peeled

1   teaspoon salt, plus more to taste

Place potatoes and garlic in a large saucepan and cover with cold water. Add 1 teaspoon salt and bring to a boil. Cook, covered, over medium heat until the potatoes are tender, about 10 minutes. Drain the potatoes and return them to the pan. Shake the pan over low heat to dry the potatoes slightly. Remove the pan from the heat.

Mash the potatoes with a potato masher or a hand-held electric mixer (do not use a food processor). Add enough hot chicken broth to make a smooth puree. Stir in sour cream and season with salt, pepper and nutmeg. (*The potatoes can be prepared up to 1 hour ahead and kept warm over a larger pan of barely simmering water.*)

Serves 4.

191 CALORIES PER SERVING: 4 G PROTEIN, 1 G FAT, 42 G CARBOHYDRATE; 551 MG SODIUM; 2 MG CHOLESTEROL.

½-¾　cup defatted reduced-sodium chicken broth, heated

2　tablespoons reduced-fat sour cream

　Freshly ground black pepper

　Grated nutmeg to taste

Latkes

EATING WELL *frequent contributor Nina Simonds developed this low-fat version of the traditional potato pancake served at Hanukkah. She says that even though her mother swore by red potatoes, she prefers a starchier potato like an Idaho in this recipe. Serve the pancakes plain or with applesauce.*

Set oven racks at middle and lower positions; preheat oven to 450 degrees F. Prepare 2 baking sheets by brushing each one with 2 teaspoons of the oil.

Using a hand grater or the shredding blade of a food processor, grate potatoes. Place in a large bowl and add onions, flour, salt and pepper; toss with 2 forks to mix well. Add egg, egg white and the remaining 1 teaspoon oil; toss to mix.

Drop rounded tablespoonfuls of the potato mixture onto the prepared baking sheets and press lightly to form cakes. Bake for 10 minutes, or until golden brown on the bottom. Turn the latkes over, switch the position of the baking sheets, and bake for about 5 minutes longer, or until golden brown.

Transfer to a platter, arranging the latkes browned-side up, and serve. (*Latkes may be prepared ahead and stored, covered, in the refrigerator overnight. Reheat at 350 degrees for 10 minutes.*)

Makes about 24 latkes.

56 CALORIES PER LATKE: 1 G PROTEIN, 1 G FAT, 10 G CARBOHYDRATE; 96 MG SODIUM; 9 MG CHOLESTEROL.

5　teaspoons vegetable oil, preferably canola oil

2　pounds russet (Idaho) potatoes (4-5 potatoes), peeled

¾　cup finely chopped red onion (1 medium)

¼　cup all-purpose white flour

1　teaspoon salt

¼　teaspoon freshly ground black pepper

1　large egg, lightly beaten

1　large egg white, lightly beaten

Savoy Cabbage with Peppers

Serve this wintry dish with ham or roast pork tenderloin.

2 teaspoons vegetable oil, preferably canola oil

½ teaspoon caraway seeds

½ teaspoon mustard seeds

4 cups thinly sliced Savoy cabbage

1 jalapeño pepper, seeded and finely chopped

¼ cup defatted reduced-sodium chicken broth

¼ cup chopped bottled roasted red peppers

Salt & freshly ground black pepper to taste

In a large nonstick skillet, heat oil over medium heat. Add caraway and mustard seeds and cook, stirring, for 1 minute. Stir in cabbage and jalapeños and cook, stirring, for 1 minute. Stir in chicken broth and cover the pan tightly. Reduce heat to low and simmer until the cabbage is tender, 5 to 6 minutes. Stir in red peppers and season with salt and pepper. (*The cabbage can be made up to 8 hours ahead and stored, covered, in the refrigerator. Reheat gently on the stovetop or in the microwave before serving.*)

Makes 3½ cups, serves 4.

51 CALORIES PER SERVING: 2 G PROTEIN, 3 G FAT, 6 G CARBOHYDRATE; 48 MG SODIUM; 0 MG CHOLESTEROL.

Stew of Fennel with Carrots & Pearl Onions

This stew makes a satisfying vegetarian main dish. It is also a hearty side dish to roast chicken or lamb; a few spoonfuls of the roasting pan juices (defatted, of course) stirred in just before serving will enhance the flavor.

4 fennel bulbs

1 tablespoon butter

1 teaspoon olive oil

2 cups frozen pearl onions, thawed

1 teaspoon sugar

4 large carrots, cut into thick matchsticks

1-1½ cups defatted reduced-sodium chicken broth or vegetable broth

Cut off fennel stalks and remove strings from the bulbs with a vegetable peeler. Cut each bulb into 8 wedges, but do not remove the core. Bring salted water to a boil in a large saucepan, add the fennel and blanch for 5 minutes. Drain and set aside.

In a large cast-iron or nonstick skillet, heat ½ tablespoon of the butter and ½ teaspoon of the oil together over medium-high heat. Add half of the fennel and sauté until nicely browned on all sides, about 8 minutes. Transfer to a dish and reserve. Repeat with the remaining butter, oil and fennel. Add onions to the skillet, sprinkle with sugar and sauté, shaking the skillet back and forth, until nicely browned, 5 to 6 minutes.

Return the fennel to the skillet; add carrots and 1 cup broth. Season with salt and pepper and simmer, covered, until the vegetables are tender, 15 to 20 minutes, adding more broth as needed to keep the stew moist. (*The vegetables can be prepared up to 2 days ahead and stored, covered, in the refrigerator. Warm on the stovetop or in the microwave.*) Garnish with fennel fronds or parsley before serving.

Serves 6.

87 CALORIES PER SERVING: 2 G PROTEIN, 3 G FAT, 13 G CARBOHYDRATE; 132 MG SODIUM; 7 MG CHOLESTEROL.

Salt & freshly ground black pepper to taste

2 **tablespoons finely chopped fennel fronds or fresh parsley for garnish**

Stew of Fennel with Carrots & Pearl Onions

Roasted Asparagus

Roasting vegetables brings out their sweetness.

2 pounds asparagus

2 teaspoons olive oil

Salt & freshly ground black pepper to taste

1 teaspoon balsamic vinegar

Preheat oven to 450 degrees F. Snap off the tough ends of asparagus and, if desired, peel the stalks. In a shallow roasting pan or baking sheet with sides, toss the asparagus with oil and season with salt and pepper. Spread the asparagus in a single layer. (If the pan is not large enough, use two pans.)

Roast for 10 to 15 minutes, until tender and browned, shaking once during roasting. Sprinkle with balsamic vinegar and toss. Taste and adjust seasonings. Let cool to room temperature; serve within 2 hours.

Serves 6.

51 CALORIES PER SERVING: 4 G PROTEIN, 2 G FAT, 7 G CARBOHYDRATE; 6 MG SODIUM; 0 MG CHOLESTEROL.

Brussels Sprouts & Chestnuts

Fresh chestnuts are available in the fall.

24 fresh chestnuts (¾ pound)

1 stalk celery

1 lemon

1½ pounds Brussels sprouts, trimmed

¼ cup defatted reduced-sodium chicken broth

1 tablespoon butter

Salt & freshly ground black pepper to taste

Using a sharp knife, score a cross on the flat side of each chestnut. Using a slotted spoon, dip the chestnuts, 4 or 5 at a time, into a saucepan of boiling water. Remove the chestnuts and peel away the shells and inner brown skins. Place the peeled chestnuts in a large saucepan and add enough boiling water to cover. Add celery stalk and simmer, covered, for 30 to 45 minutes, or until tender. Drain, discarding the celery, and refresh with cold water. Set aside.

With a vegetable peeler, remove the zest from half the lemon. (Save the lemon for another use.) Cut the zest into julienne strips and place in a small saucepan; cover with cold water and bring to a boil. Drain and set aside.

With a paring knife, cut a small cross, ⅛ inch deep, in the

stem end of each Brussels sprout. Bring a large saucepan of salted water to a boil. Add the Brussels sprouts and cook, uncovered, until tender, 6 to 8 minutes. Drain and refresh with cold water.

In a large skillet, heat chicken broth and butter. Add the chestnuts and Brussels sprouts and toss over medium heat until heated through. Season with salt and pepper and garnish with the julienned lemon zest.

Serves 8.

144 CALORIES PER SERVING: 4 G PROTEIN, 2 G FAT, 29 G CARBOHYDRATE; 50 MG SODIUM; 4 MG CHOLESTEROL.

Wilted Winter Greens & Black-Eyed Peas

The soft, sweet nature of black-eyed peas is a fine contrast for the somewhat bitter "mess of greens" like the ones called for here. Rather than using the traditional high-fat salt pork to cook with the greens, use flavorful, lean Southern country ham or Italian prosciutto.

Soak peas overnight in cold water. (*Alternatively, place peas in a large saucepan, cover with water and bring to a simmer. Cook for 2 minutes. Remove from the heat and let stand for 1 hour.*)

Drain the peas, rinse well and place in a large saucepan. Add water to cover and bring to a boil. Reduce heat to medium; cook, stirring occasionally, until tender, about 45 minutes. Add salt to taste. Let sit, covered, for ½ hour, then drain and rinse.

Slice greens into ¼-inch-wide strips. Heat oil in a very large skillet over high heat. Add country ham or prosciutto and sauté until lightly browned, about 2 minutes. Add the greens and cook, stirring constantly, until wilted, 5 to 10 minutes, adding a little water if necessary. Add the reserved black-eyed peas and heat through. Season with vinegar, salt and pepper.

Serves 10.

79 CALORIES PER SERVING: 4 G PROTEIN, 2 G FAT, 13 G CARBOHYDRATE; 107 MG SODIUM; 3 MG CHOLESTEROL.

½ pound dried black-eyed peas (1⅓ cups)
  Salt to taste

2 pounds greens, such as collards, kale and/or escarole, trimmed and washed

1 tablespoon vegetable oil, preferably canola oil

2 ounces country ham or prosciutto, diced (½ cup)

2 tablespoons red-wine vinegar, or to taste
  Freshly ground black pepper to taste

Sesame Green Beans

The beans are good hot or at room temperature.

1 pound green beans, trimmed
1 teaspoon olive oil
2 teaspoons sesame seeds
  Salt & freshly ground black
  pepper to taste

Preheat oven to 450 degrees F. On a baking sheet with sides, toss beans with oil, then spread the beans out in a single layer. Roast the beans for about 12 minutes, stirring once, or until wrinkled, browned and tender.

In a small dry skillet over medium heat, stir sesame seeds until fragrant and toasted, about 1 minute. Crush the seeds lightly and toss with the beans. Season with salt and pepper.

Serves 4.

58 CALORIES PER SERVING: 2 G PROTEIN, 2 G FAT, 9 G CARBOHYDRATE; 4 MG SODIUM; 0 MG CHOLESTEROL.

Bulgur with Asian Accents

Peppery radish sprouts give pizzazz to this light and simple salad.

1¼ cups bulgur
2 cups lightly packed radish sprouts
1 bunch scallions, trimmed and chopped
¼ cup rice-wine vinegar
1½ tablespoons reduced-sodium soy sauce
1 tablespoon sesame oil
1 tablespoon finely chopped fresh ginger
1½ teaspoons Chinese chile paste with garlic
1 teaspoon honey
¼ cup toasted cashews

Bring 1⅔ cups water to a boil in a saucepan; stir in bulgur, remove from the heat, cover and set aside for about 30 minutes, or until the water has been absorbed. Spread the bulgur out on a baking sheet to cool to room temperature, about 15 minutes.

In a serving bowl, combine the cooled bulgur, sprouts and scallions.

In a small bowl, whisk together vinegar, soy sauce, sesame oil, ginger, chile paste and honey. Pour over the salad and toss well. Garnish with cashews and serve. (*The recipe can be made without the sprouts up to 2 hours ahead and stored, covered, in the refrigerator; add the sprouts just before serving.*)

Makes 5 cups, serves 4.

260 CALORIES PER SERVING: 9 G PROTEIN, 8 G FAT, 43 G CARBOHYDRATE; 211 MG SODIUM; 0 MG CHOLESTEROL.

Bulgur with Asian Accents

Quinoa with Sun-Dried Tomatoes

*This ancient Peruvian grain has a nutty, almost sweet flavor that really needs no accent but is excellent
with sun-dried tomatoes and shallots. It can be found in health-food stores and some supermarkets.*

1   cup quinoa
1   teaspoon butter
8   sun-dried tomatoes (not oil-
    packed), chopped
2   shallots, finely chopped
1   clove garlic, finely chopped
2   cups defatted reduced-sodium
    chicken broth or water
    Pinch of ground red pepper
    (cayenne)
2   tablespoons chopped fresh parsley
    Salt & freshly ground black
    pepper to taste

Place quinoa in a fine-meshed sieve and rinse under warm running water for 1 minute. Set aside.

Heat butter in a heavy medium saucepan over medium heat. Add tomatoes, shallots and garlic and sauté for 3 to 5 minutes, or until the shallots are softened. Add chicken broth or water and bring to a boil. Stir in the quinoa and ground red pepper, return to a boil, then reduce heat to low and simmer, covered, for about 30 minutes, or until the liquid has been absorbed. Let sit for 5 minutes and fluff grains with a fork to separate. Stir in parsley and season with salt and pepper.

Serves 4.

226 CALORIES PER SERVING: 9 G PROTEIN, 4 G FAT, 42 G CARBOHYDRATE; 351 MG SODIUM; 3 MG CHOLESTEROL.

The Sultan's Lentils

*The tartness of lemon juice plays against the sweet flavors of dried fruits,
mint and cinnamon; serve alongside grilled lamb or chicken.*

½   teaspoon ground cinnamon
1½ teaspoons salt
1   cup bulgur
½   cup red lentils
½   cup chopped dates
½   cup chopped dried apricots
½   cup chopped fresh parsley
⅓   cup chopped fresh mint

Bring 1½ cups water, cinnamon and 1 teaspoon of the salt to a boil in a small saucepan; stir in bulgur, remove from the heat, cover and set aside for about 30 minutes, or until the water has been absorbed. Spread the bulgur out on a baking sheet to cool to room temperature, about 15 minutes.

Meanwhile, combine lentils and the remaining ½ teaspoon salt in a saucepan; add enough water to cover by 1 inch. Bring to a simmer and cook until the lentils are just tender, about 5 minutes. Drain and rinse under cold water, pressing firmly to remove excess water.

Combine the cooled bulgur and lentils in a serving bowl with dates, apricots, parsley, mint, oil, lemon juice and zest, and half of the pine nuts. Toss well. Sprinkle with the remaining pine nuts. (*The salad can be made up to 1 day ahead and stored, covered, in the refrigerator.*)

Makes 6 cups, serves 6.

255 CALORIES PER SERVING: 8 G PROTEIN, 8 G FAT, 44 G CARBOHYDRATE; 543 MG SODIUM; 0 MG CHOLESTEROL.

- 2 tablespoons olive oil, preferably extra-virgin
- ¼ cup fresh lemon juice
- 2 teaspoons grated lemon zest
- 3 tablespoons pine nuts, toasted and chopped

Citrusy Couscous with Olives

A refreshing accompaniment to grilled chicken or fish.

In a large bowl, stir together couscous, orange-juice concentrate, oil, mustard, thyme, orange zest and ½ teaspoon salt. Stir in 2 cups boiling water, cover and set aside until the liquid has been absorbed, about 5 minutes.

Fluff the couscous with a fork. Add parsley, scallions, olives, oranges and lemon juice; toss to blend. Season with salt and pepper. (*The couscous can be prepared up to 2 hours ahead and stored, covered, in the refrigerator.*)

Makes about 6 cups, serves 6.

250 CALORIES PER SERVING: 7 G PROTEIN, 6 G FAT, 43 G CARBOHYDRATE; 269 MG SODIUM; 0 MG CHOLESTEROL.

- 1½ cups couscous, preferably whole-wheat (10 ounces)
- ¼ cup orange-juice concentrate, thawed
- 2 tablespoons olive oil, preferably extra-virgin
- 1 tablespoon Dijon mustard
- 1 tablespoon chopped fresh thyme or 1 teaspoon dried thyme leaves
- 1 teaspoon grated orange zest
- ½ teaspoon salt, plus more to taste
- 1 cup chopped fresh parsley
- ½ cup chopped scallions (4 scallions)
- ¼ cup sliced black olives, preferably Kalamata (12 olives)
- 1 navel orange, peeled, sectioned and diced
- 1 tablespoon fresh lemon juice
  Freshly ground black pepper to taste

Coconut Rice

Canned coconut milk gives this Caribbean rice dish a subtle creaminess. If you cannot find the "lite" variety, substitute ¼ cup regular unsweetened coconut milk mixed with ½ cup water.

½ tablespoon vegetable oil, preferably canola oil

2 large cloves garlic, finely chopped

2 teaspoons finely chopped fresh ginger

2 cups long-grain white rice

¾ cup "lite" coconut milk

1 teaspoon salt

Heat oil in a heavy saucepan over medium heat. Add garlic and ginger and cook, stirring, until fragrant but not brown, about 45 seconds. Add rice and cook, stirring, until the individual grains are shiny, about 1 minute.

Add coconut milk, 2½ cups water and salt. Bring to a boil. Reduce the heat to low, cover, and simmer until all of the liquid has been absorbed and the grains are tender, 18 to 20 minutes.

Remove the pan from the heat and let stand, covered, for 5 minutes. Fluff with a fork before serving.

Serves 6.

250 CALORIES PER SERVING: 5 G PROTEIN, 3 G FAT, 51 G CARBOHYDRATE; 359 MG SODIUM; 0 MG CHOLESTEROL.

Papaya Rice

Papaya holds its shape and color beautifully when cooked, so don't worry about mushy rice. Include a few teaspoons of the seeds, if desired, for a bitter, peppery, dark and crunchy accent.

2 teaspoons vegetable oil, preferably canola oil

1 tablespoon finely chopped fresh ginger

1 small clove garlic, finely chopped

½ teaspoon ground cardamom

1 cup papaya nectar or mango juice

1¼ cups long-grain white rice, preferably basmati or jasmine

½ teaspoon salt

1¾ cups diced papaya

In a heavy 2-quart saucepan, heat oil over medium heat. Add ginger and garlic; cook, stirring, for 1 minute. Stir in cardamom. Combine papaya nectar or mango juice with 1½ cups water and add to the pot along with rice and salt; bring to a rolling boil, stirring occasionally. Add diced papaya, bring to a simmer, then reduce the heat to the lowest point.

Cover the pan and cook for 20 minutes. Remove from the heat and let stand, covered, for 15 minutes. Fluff the rice and serve.

Serves 4.

252 CALORIES PER SERVING: 4 G PROTEIN, 3 G FAT, 53 G CARBOHYDRATE; 273 MG SODIUM; 0 MG CHOLESTEROL.

Pilaf with Lime Zest, Almonds & Raisins

Turkish in inspiration, this pilaf is a delightful accompaniment to many Mediterranean dishes.

Preheat oven to 400 degrees F. Spread almonds on a pie plate and bake for 5 minutes, or until golden. Set aside.

Heat oil in a heavy saucepan over medium heat. Add onions and pine nuts and sauté until the onions are soft and the pine nuts slightly browned, 5 to 7 minutes. Stir in rice and cook an additional 4 to 5 minutes, stirring frequently. Add chicken broth, raisins, lime zest, saffron, cinnamon, salt, red-pepper flakes and cardamom; stir well. Reduce heat to low, cover, and simmer until all the liquid has been absorbed, 15 to 18 minutes. Remove from the heat and fluff with a fork. Stir in the almonds and serve.

Serves 4.

286 CALORIES PER SERVING: 6 G PROTEIN, 6 G FAT, 53 G CARBOHYDRATE; 274 MG SODIUM; 0 MG CHOLESTEROL.

2	tablespoons blanched slivered almonds
1½	teaspoons vegetable oil, preferably canola oil
1	onion, finely chopped
2	tablespoons pine nuts
1	cup white rice, preferably arborio
2¼	cups defatted reduced-sodium chicken broth
⅓	cup golden raisins
2	teaspoons grated lime zest
1	teaspoon saffron threads, crumbled, or ¼ teaspoon powdered saffron
½	teaspoon ground cinnamon
½	teaspoon salt
¼	teaspoon red-pepper flakes
⅛	teaspoon ground cardamom

Roasted Chicken Breasts with *Gremolata*

Gremolata, a mixture of herbs, garlic and lemon zest, is stuffed under the skin, contributing its extraordinary fragrance to the chicken. To ensure moist and succulent meat, the skin is left on for roasting, but removed before carving. This is an excellent treatment for all kinds of poultry; for a turkey, make a double or triple batch of gremolata. Serve with mashed potatoes.

Preheat oven to 425 degrees F. Place a rack in a roasting pan or large ovenproof skillet; lightly oil the rack or spray it with non-stick cooking spray.

With the side of a chef's knife, mash garlic to a paste with ¼ teaspoon salt. In a small bowl, combine the mashed garlic with parsley, rosemary or thyme, lemon zest and pepper.

Press the breast bone of each whole chicken breast with the heel of your hand to flatten slightly. Discard any visible fat. Carefully separate the chicken skin from the flesh with your fingers. Stuff the herb mixture between the flesh and the skin. Place the chicken breasts on the prepared rack and roast for about 35 minutes, or until the chicken is no longer pink in the center.

Transfer the chicken to a carving board, and cover to keep warm. Pour the drippings from the pan into a small bowl and chill in the freezer. Add wine to the roasting pan and bring to a boil, stirring to scrape up any brown bits. Boil until reduced by half, 3 to 5 minutes. Pour in chicken broth, return to a boil and cook for about 5 minutes to intensify the flavors.

Skim the fat from the chilled pan drippings and add the drippings to the sauce. Whisk arrowroot or cornstarch mixture into the sauce. Cook, whisking, until slightly thickened, about 1 minute. Stir in mustard. Taste and adjust seasonings.

Remove the skin and carve the chicken into thin slices. Serve with the sauce alongside.

Serves 4.

190 CALORIES PER SERVING: 27 G PROTEIN, 4 G FAT, 3 G CARBOHYDRATE; 527 MG SODIUM; 75 MG CHOLESTEROL.

- **2** cloves garlic, peeled and crushed
- **¼** teaspoon kosher salt, plus more to taste
- **3** tablespoons chopped fresh parsley
- **1** tablespoon chopped fresh rosemary or thyme
- **2** teaspoons grated lemon zest Freshly ground black pepper to taste
- **2** whole bone-in chicken breasts with skin (1½-2 pounds)
- **¾** cup dry white wine
- **1** 14-ounce can defatted reduced-sodium chicken broth
- **2** teaspoons arrowroot or cornstarch mixed with 1 tablespoon cold water
- **1** teaspoon Dijon mustard

Jamaican Chicken with Rice & Beans

Pickapeppa sauce is a sweet-and-sour, mild hot pepper sauce, imported from Jamaica.
You can find it in the condiment section of many supermarkets.

1   cup long-grain white rice

⅓   cup fresh lime juice

2   tablespoons plus 1 teaspoon olive oil

2   teaspoons unsulfured molasses

2   cloves garlic, finely chopped

1   jalapeño pepper, seeded and finely chopped
    Salt & freshly ground black pepper to taste

1   15-ounce can adzuki beans or black beans, drained and rinsed

½   cup chopped scallions (3 scallions)

1   7-ounce jar roasted red peppers, drained, rinsed and diced

6   tablespoons chopped fresh cilantro

1   pound boneless, skinless chicken breasts, trimmed of fat

¼   cup Pickapeppa sauce
    Lime wedges for garnish

Bring a pot of salted water to a boil. Add rice and cook over medium heat until the rice is tender but still firm, 12 to 15 minutes. Drain in a sieve and rinse under cold water to separate the grains. Drain well and set aside.

In a large bowl, whisk together lime juice, 2 tablespoons oil, molasses, garlic and jalapeño. Season with salt and pepper. Add beans, scallions, red peppers, 4 tablespoons of the cilantro and the cooked rice. Set aside.

Meanwhile, prepare a grill or preheat the broiler and broiler pan. Brush chicken with the remaining 1 teaspoon oil and grill or broil, basting with Pickapeppa sauce, until the meat is no longer pink in the center, about 4 minutes per side. Let cool slightly.

Cut the chicken pieces in half lengthwise and cut into thin slices against the grain. Add to the rice mixture. Taste and adjust seasonings with salt and pepper. (*The salad may be prepared up to 1 day ahead and stored, covered, in the refrigerator.*)

Garnish with lime wedges and the remaining 2 tablespoons cilantro.

Makes about 8 cups, serves 6.

356 CALORIES PER SERVING: 26 G PROTEIN, 7 G FAT, 47 G CARBOHYDRATE; 127 MG SODIUM; 44 MG CHOLESTEROL.

Cold Sliced Chicken in Tuna Sauce

This is based on the classic Italian dish vitello tonnato; *the secret to the rich taste and velvety quality of the sauce is the addition of mellow roasted garlic and a small quantity of flavorful olive oil.*

Preheat oven to 400 degrees F. Rub off excess papery skin from the garlic head without separating the cloves. Slice about ½ inch off the top of the garlic head. Place the garlic on a square of aluminum foil or in a ceramic garlic roaster. Sprinkle with 2 teaspoons water and pinch the edges of the foil together to make a package. Roast for 40 to 45 minutes, or until the cloves are very soft. Unwrap and let cool slightly.

Meanwhile, place chicken breasts in a large skillet or saucepan. Pour chicken broth over the chicken; bring to a simmer over medium heat. Immediately turn the chicken breasts over with tongs or a fork, cover the pan and remove from the heat. Let steep for 20 minutes, or until the chicken is no longer pink inside. Cover and refrigerate, letting the chicken cool in the broth.

Place tuna and anchovies in a food processor and process until very smooth. Squeeze the roasted garlic cloves out of the skins into the processor. Add mayonnaise, yogurt, lemon juice, capers, oil and mustard. Blend until very smooth. Taste and adjust seasonings with salt and pepper.

Slice the chicken breasts on the diagonal into ¼-inch-thick slices. Spread one-third of the tuna sauce on a serving platter. Arrange the chicken on the sauce, then cover with the remaining sauce. Cover tightly with plastic wrap and refrigerate at least 2 hours or overnight.

Remove the chicken from the refrigerator a few minutes before serving. Garnish with lemon slices, capers and parsley.

Serves 8.

190 CALORIES PER SERVING: 24 G PROTEIN, 8 G FAT, 6 G CARBOHYDRATE; 286 MG SODIUM; 57 MG CHOLESTEROL.

1 plump head garlic

6 boneless, skinless chicken breasts, trimmed of fat (1½ pounds)

1 14-ounce can defatted reduced-sodium chicken broth

1 6-ounce can solid white tuna packed in water, drained

4 anchovy fillets, rinsed and patted dry

½ cup reduced-fat mayonnaise

½ cup nonfat plain yogurt

3-4 tablespoons fresh lemon juice

3 tablespoons capers, rinsed, plus additional for garnish

2 tablespoons extra-virgin olive oil

½ teaspoon Dijon mustard

Salt & freshly ground black pepper to taste

Thin lemon slices for garnish

Fresh parsley, preferably Italian flat-leaf, for garnish

Capon Braised in a Sealed Pot

The capon cooks in record time because the roasting pan is tightly sealed with a flour, or luting, paste. As it is impossible to monitor the progress of the cooking bird without breaking the seal, check the weight of the capon before you begin and calculate the cooking time based on 5 minutes per pound.

LUTING PASTE

  3 cups all-purpose white flour

10 large egg whites

CAPON & SAUCE

  1 7-to-9-pound capon

⅓ cup all-purpose white flour

  1 teaspoon paprika

½ teaspoon salt

½ teaspoon freshly ground black pepper

  1 tablespoon olive oil

  2 ounces pancetta, finely chopped

  3 onions, chopped

  2 stalks celery, chopped

  1 carrot, chopped

  8 cloves garlic, chopped

12 whole black peppercorns

  2 tablespoons chopped fresh parsley

  1 tablespoon chopped fresh sage or 1 teaspoon dried rubbed sage

  1 tablespoon chopped fresh rosemary or 1 teaspoon dried

  1 tablespoon chopped fresh thyme or 1 teaspoon dried thyme leaves

  1 bottle full-flavored white wine, preferably Gewürztraminer (3 cups)

  4 teaspoons cornstarch mixed with 2 tablespoons cold water

TO PREPARE LUTING PASTE:

In a large mixing bowl, combine flour and egg whites. Beat with an electric mixer until the dough is soft and pliable. (The paddle attachment of a stand-up mixer works best.) If the dough is too dry, add a little water until it has a thick, pastelike consistency. Cover with plastic wrap and set aside.

TO PREPARE CAPON:

Preheat oven to 425 degrees F. Coarsely chop giblets, cut neck into several pieces and reserve. (Set liver aside for another use.) Remove skin and fat from the capon. Rinse the bird in cold water and pat dry. Fold the wings under the bird and tie the legs together.

In a small bowl, combine flour, paprika, salt and pepper. Sprinkle the capon evenly with the flour mixture. In a very large, heavy skillet, heat oil over medium-high heat. Brown the capon, turning with a meat fork, until well browned on all sides, 2 to 3 minutes per side. Remove the capon from the skillet and set it in a large roasting pan that has a tight-fitting lid.

Add the giblets and neck to the skillet, along with pancetta, and cook over medium heat until browned, 1 to 2 minutes. Add onions, celery and carrots; cook until well browned, 15 to 20 minutes. Add garlic, peppercorns, parsley, sage, rosemary and thyme; sauté for 2 minutes longer. Pour in wine and bring to a boil, scraping up any bits from the bottom of the pan. Remove from the heat and pour the mixture around the capon.

Cover the pan and seal with the reserved luting paste by spreading it with a rubber spatula along the seam around the edge of the pan. Place the pan in the oven and roast for 35 to 45 minutes (see recipe note above).

Remove the pan from the oven. Wait 10 minutes, then break

the seal by prying off the lid with a stiff metal spatula. Check for doneness with an instant-read thermometer; the breast meat should register 170 degrees F. (If not done, cover and return to the oven for 15 minutes.) Transfer the capon to a platter, cover loosely with foil and keep warm.

Strain the cooking liquid through a fine sieve into a medium saucepan. Bring to a simmer, skimming off any fat and foam. Whisk the cornstarch mixture into the sauce and cook, whisking, until slightly thickened. Taste and adjust seasonings. Carve the capon and serve with the sauce.

Serves 8.

304 CALORIES PER 4-OUNCE SERVING: 34 G PROTEIN, 13 G FAT, 14 G CARBO-
HYDRATE; 355 MG SODIUM; 107 MG CHOLESTEROL.

Grilled Lemon & Cinnamon Chicken

The following recipe features the classic Greek combination of garlic, lemon, cinnamon and oregano, with a fresh chile pepper added for some heat.

In a large shallow dish, combine lemon juice, garlic, oregano, cinnamon, tomato paste and jalapeño. Season with salt and pepper. Add chicken and turn to coat well. Cover with plastic wrap and marinate in the refrigerator for at least 2 hours or up to 8 hours, turning occasionally.

Prepare a grill or preheat the broiler. Drain the chicken and discard the marinade. Grill or broil the chicken on a lightly oiled rack until no longer pink inside, 5 to 6 minutes per side. Garnish with lemon quarters and oregano, if desired, and serve.

Serves 4.

167 CALORIES PER SERVING: 27 G PROTEIN, 4 G FAT, 6 G CARBOHYDRATE;
67 MG SODIUM; 72 MG CHOLESTEROL.

½ cup fresh lemon juice

3 cloves garlic, finely chopped

1 tablespoon chopped fresh oregano or 1 teaspoon dried

½ tablespoon ground cinnamon

½ teaspoon tomato paste

1 jalapeño pepper, seeded and finely chopped
   Salt & freshly ground black pepper to taste

4 boneless, skinless chicken breasts (1 pound), trimmed of fat

1 lemon, quartered

4 sprigs fresh oregano for garnish (optional)

Skillet-Braised Chicken Thighs with Chickpeas

The spicing in this Spanish dish is lively but not overpowering.

12 bone-in chicken thighs (3½-4 pounds), skinned and trimmed of fat

½ cup all-purpose white flour for dredging
   Salt & freshly ground black pepper to taste

1½ tablespoons olive oil

2 small dried red chile peppers, crumbled

2 onions, quartered and thinly sliced

2 cloves garlic, finely chopped

1 teaspoon paprika

1 teaspoon dried marjoram

2 large vine-ripened tomatoes, seeded and chopped

2 large green bell peppers, cored, seeded and thinly sliced

1 cup defatted reduced-sodium chicken broth

1 19-ounce can chickpeas, drained and rinsed

2 tablespoons chopped fresh parsley for garnish

In a shallow dish, dredge chicken thighs in flour, shaking off the excess. Season both sides with salt and pepper. In a large cast-iron or nonstick skillet, heat 1 tablespoon of the oil over high heat. Add the chicken, partially cover the pan and cook until the chicken is nicely browned, about 2 minutes per side (it will not be fully cooked). Remove from the skillet and set aside.

Reduce the heat to medium and add the remaining ½ tablespoon oil to the skillet. Add dried chile peppers and cook until they turn dark, about 2 minutes. Remove with a slotted spoon and discard. Add onions and garlic to the skillet; cook until soft and lightly browned, 5 to 7 minutes. Add paprika and marjoram and cook, stirring, for 1 minute. Add tomatoes, green peppers and salt and pepper to taste; cook for 5 minutes longer.

Return the chicken to the skillet, along with ½ cup of the chicken broth. Cover and simmer until the chicken is tender and no longer pink inside, 20 to 25 minutes. Add chickpeas and the remaining ½ cup broth; simmer for 5 to 8 minutes. Blot off any fat that rises to the surface with paper towels. Taste and adjust seasonings. (*The dish can be made up to 2 days in advance and stored, covered, in the refrigerator. Reheat gently on the stovetop or in the microwave oven before serving.*) Garnish with parsley.

Serves 6.

291 CALORIES PER SERVING: 21 G PROTEIN, 11 G FAT, 28 G CARBOHYDRATE; 411 MG SODIUM; 51 MG CHOLESTEROL.

Clay-Pot Chicken with a Spice Rub

*Marinating the chicken beforehand and cooking it slowly ensure that the
vibrant Southwestern flavors permeate the meat.*

In a small skillet over medium heat, toast chili powder, cumin
seeds and salt, stirring constantly, until aromatic, 1 to 2 minutes. Transfer to a plate and set aside.

Sprinkle chicken with lime juice. Season the surface and
cavity with the toasted spice mix. Tie the legs together and tuck
the wing tips under the back. Set in a shallow dish, cover with
plastic wrap and refrigerate for 2 to 3 hours to allow the flavors
to develop.

Soak the bottom and lid of a clay cooker of at least 3-quart
capacity in cool water for 15 minutes.

Place the chicken in the soaked cooker, cover and place in a
cold oven. (*The chicken can also be cooked in a covered Dutch oven.*) Set
the temperature at 350 degrees F and bake for 1 hour, or until
the juices run clear when the thigh is pierced with a fork and a
meat thermometer in the thigh registers 180 degrees F. Transfer
the chicken to a warm platter. Strain the cooking juices into a
small bowl or pitcher. Skim off any fat that rises to the top before serving the juices alongside the chicken.

Serves 4.

173 CALORIES PER 3-OUNCE SERVING: 28 G PROTEIN, 4 G FAT, 7 G CARBO-
HYDRATE; 118 MG SODIUM; 72 MG CHOLESTEROL.

2   teaspoons chili powder

1   teaspoon cumin seeds

½   teaspoon salt

1   3½-pound chicken, skinned and
    trimmed of fat

2   tablespoons fresh lime juice

Bourbon-&-Mustard Glazed Turkey with Corn Bread Stuffing

Serve the turkey with Southern-Style Curried Sweet Potatoes (page 66) and
Wilted Winter Greens & Black-Eyed Peas (page 73).

Preheat oven to 325 degrees F. Place an oiled rack on the bottom of a large roasting pan. Lightly oil a 2-quart baking dish.

Remove giblets and neck from turkey cavity and reserve for the stock. (Discard liver.) Remove any visible fat from the turkey. Rinse it inside and out with cold water and pat dry. Season the cavity with salt and pepper.

Spoon about half of the Corn Bread Stuffing into the turkey and neck cavities, securing the neck cavity with a skewer. Transfer the remaining stuffing to the prepared baking dish, cover with aluminum foil and refrigerate.

For the bourbon-and-mustard glaze, stir together ¼ cup of the bourbon, ¼ cup of the mustard and ¼ cup of the brown sugar. With your fingers, separate the turkey skin from the breast meat, taking care not to tear the skin. Rub about half of the glaze under the skin onto the breast meat; set aside the remaining glaze. Season the bird with salt and pepper.

Tie the drumsticks together and tuck wing tips under the back. Place breast-side up in the prepared roasting pan. Cover with oiled aluminum foil and roast for 2½ hours. Remove the foil, brush the turkey all over with some of the reserved glaze and baste with pan juices. Continue roasting, uncovered, 1½ to 2 hours longer, brushing with glaze and basting from time to time. The turkey is done when a meat thermometer inserted into the thickest part of the thigh registers 180 degrees F and registers 165 degrees F when inserted into the stuffing.

TO MAKE GIBLET STOCK:

While the turkey is roasting, heat oil over medium-high heat in a saucepan. Add the giblets, neck, onions and carrots; cook, stirring often, for 10 to 15 minutes, until well browned. Add chicken broth, garlic, parsley, thyme, peppercorns and 1 cup

1	**12-to-14-pound turkey with giblets** **Salt & freshly ground black pepper to taste** **Corn Bread Stuffing** (*page 92*)
¾	**cup bourbon**
¼	**cup plus 2 tablespoons Dijon or spicy brown mustard**
¼	**cup plus 1 teaspoon packed brown sugar**
3	**tablespoons cornstarch mixed with ¼ cup cold water**

GIBLET STOCK

1	**teaspoon vegetable oil, preferably canola oil**
1	**onion, chopped**
1	**carrot, chopped**
3½	**cups defatted reduced-sodium chicken broth**
2	**cloves garlic, unpeeled** **A few sprigs fresh parsley** **A few sprigs fresh thyme or ½ teaspoon dried thyme leaves**
6-8	**whole black peppercorns**

Bourbon-&-Mustard Glazed Turkey
with Corn Bread Stuffing

91

water; bring to a boil. Reduce the heat to low and simmer for 30 minutes. Strain and chill; skim off the fat.

TO MAKE GRAVY:

Transfer the turkey to a carving board. Scoop the stuffing into a serving bowl, cover and keep warm. Place the dish of extra stuffing in the oven to heat. Cover the turkey loosely with aluminum foil and let rest for 15 to 30 minutes before carving.

Meanwhile, pour the drippings from the roasting pan through a strainer into a small bowl, then chill in the freezer so that the fat can be skimmed off. Add the remaining ½ cup bourbon to the roasting pan and cook, stirring and scraping up any brown bits, for about 1 minute. Strain into a medium saucepan. Add the giblet stock and bring to a simmer. Skim off the fat from the chilled pan juices before adding to the pan. Slowly add cornstarch mixture to the simmering sauce, whisking until slightly thickened. Stir in the remaining 2 tablespoons mustard and 1 teaspoon brown sugar. Taste and adjust seasonings. Remove the string from the turkey and carve, discarding the skin. Serve with gravy and stuffing.

Serves 10, with leftovers.

453 CALORIES FOR 3-OUNCE TURKEY SERVING PLUS STUFFING: 33 G PROTEIN, 9 G FAT, 49 G CARBOHYDRATE; 659 MG SODIUM; 87 MG CHOLESTEROL.

Corn Bread Stuffing

If you like, bake the corn bread a week or two in advance and freeze it.

2 cups yellow cornmeal, preferably stone-ground

2 cups all-purpose white flour

1 tablespoon baking powder

2 teaspoons salt, plus more to taste

1 large egg, lightly beaten

2 cups skim or low-fat milk

Preheat oven to 375 degrees F. Lightly oil an 8-inch square baking dish or coat it with nonstick cooking spray.

Combine cornmeal, flour, baking powder and 2 teaspoons salt in a large bowl and mix well. In a separate bowl, whisk together egg, milk and 1½ tablespoons of the oil; add to the dry ingredients and stir just until evenly moistened.

Turn the batter into the prepared baking dish and bake for 25 to 30 minutes, or until a toothpick inserted in the center comes out clean. Let cool in the pan on a rack. Cut into 1-inch cubes.

In a large nonstick skillet, heat the remaining ½ tablespoon oil over medium-high heat. Add onions and celery and cook, stirring often, until softened, about 5 minutes. Transfer to a large bowl and add the cubed corn bread and parsley; toss to mix. Slowly add chicken broth, tossing until the corn bread is well moistened. Season with salt and pepper.

Makes about 12 cups, serves 10.

244 CALORIES PER SERVING: 7 G PROTEIN, 5 G FAT, 44 G CARBOHYDRATE; 58 MG SODIUM; 22 MG CHOLESTEROL.

2 tablespoons olive oil
2 cups chopped onions
2 cups chopped celery
¼ cup chopped fresh parsley
2½ cups defatted reduced-sodium chicken broth
Freshly ground black pepper to taste

Hoisin-Orange Turkey Roll-Ups

Look for Mandarin pancakes in Chinese markets or purchase them directly from a local Chinese restaurant.

Line a steamer basket with a heavy kitchen towel. Separate pancakes or tortillas and lay them on the towel. Cover with the overhanging edges of the towel. Set into a pot filled with ½ inch water; cover tightly. Bring to a boil and boil for 1 minute. Remove from the heat and let stand, covered, for 15 minutes.

Meanwhile, heat a large nonstick skillet or wok over high heat. Add turkey and cook, stirring, until no longer pink, about 5 minutes. Transfer to a colander and drain off fat; set aside.

Add oil to the skillet or wok. Add ginger and garlic; stir-fry until fragrant, about 30 seconds. Add shiitakes and scallions; stir-fry until the mushrooms are tender, about 2 minutes. Stir in hoisin sauce, orange-juice concentrate, soy sauce, 1 tablespoon water and the reserved turkey; stir until heated through.

To serve, line a warm Mandarin pancake or tortilla with a lettuce leaf, spoon on some of the turkey mixture, garnish with carrots and cucumber, if desired, wrap up and serve.

Serves 4.

362 CALORIES PER SERVING: 22 G PROTEIN, 10 G FAT, 44 G CARBOHYDRATE; 929 MG SODIUM; 56 MG CHOLESTEROL.

8 Mandarin pancakes or flour tortillas
¾ pound ground turkey
1 teaspoon peanut oil
2 tablespoons finely chopped fresh ginger
2 cloves garlic, finely chopped
½ pound shiitake mushrooms, stems removed, caps finely chopped
8 scallions, trimmed and chopped
¼ cup hoisin sauce
1 tablespoon frozen orange-juice concentrate
1 teaspoon reduced-sodium soy sauce
8 lettuce leaves, washed
½ cup grated carrots (optional)
½ cup grated cucumber (optional)

Roasted Quail in a Pinot Noir Sauce with Wilted Spinach

Among friends, it is permitted to pick up the tiny quail bones with your fingers to get at every chewy morsel.

4 teaspoons olive oil

1 onion, quartered and thinly sliced

2 teaspoons sugar

1 cup dry red wine, preferably Pinot Noir

1 cup defatted reduced-sodium chicken broth

3 tablespoons currants

2 tablespoons drained capers

2 tablespoons chopped fresh rosemary or 2 teaspoons dried, crushed

4 quail, about 6 ounces each
   Salt & freshly ground black pepper to taste

1 teaspoon cornstarch mixed with 2 teaspoons cold water

WILTED SPINACH

1 tablespoon olive oil

1½ tablespoons pine nuts, coarsely chopped

1 pound spinach, stemmed, washed, torn and drained
   Salt & freshly ground black pepper to taste

Heat 2 teaspoons oil in a large heavy ovenproof skillet over medium heat. Add onions and sugar and cook for 5 minutes. Reduce the heat to low and continue cooking, stirring often, until the onions are deeply colored and caramelized, 7 to 10 minutes. Add wine, chicken broth, currants, capers and rosemary. Simmer until reduced to 1½ cups, about 15 minutes. Transfer the sauce to a small bowl and set aside. Rinse and dry the skillet. (*The sauce can be prepared ahead to this point and refrigerated for up to 2 days.*)

Preheat oven to 400 degrees F. With a sharp knife, split each quail down one side of the backbone. Turn over and press to flatten. Remove any excess fat. Lightly season both sides of the birds with salt and pepper.

Heat the remaining 2 teaspoons oil in the skillet over high heat. Brown the quail, breast-side down, for 4 minutes. Turn and brown the other side for 4 minutes more. Transfer to a plate. Return the sauce to the skillet and bring to a simmer. Add the quail, breast-side up, and baste with sauce. Transfer the skillet to the oven and roast for about 15 minutes, or until the thigh juices run clear when pierced with a knife.

TO MAKE WILTED SPINACH:

Heat oil in a large skillet over medium-high heat. Add pine nuts and stir until golden, about 1 minute. Add spinach, in batches if necessary, and toss until just wilted, about 2 minutes. Season with salt and pepper.

Transfer the quail to a warm platter. Return the skillet to the stovetop and whisk cornstarch mixture into the sauce. Bring to a simmer, stirring constantly, until slightly thickened, about 1 minute. Season with salt and pepper. To serve, pour the sauce over the quail and surround with Wilted Spinach.

Serves 4.

253 CALORIES PER SERVING: 20 G PROTEIN, 9 G FAT, 14 G CARBOHYDRATE; 74 MG SODIUM; 1 MG CHOLESTEROL.

Roasted Quail in a Pinot Noir Sauce with Wilted Spinach

Goose with Kumquat Sauce

A very festive treatment of a festive bird. If kumquats are not available,
substitute the zest of two oranges, cut in julienne strips.

1   10-pound goose
    Salt & freshly ground black
    pepper to taste
2   oranges, quartered
2   onions, quartered

KUMQUAT SAUCE

1   teaspoon vegetable oil
1   onion, chopped
1   carrot, chopped
4   cups defatted reduced-sodium
    chicken broth, preferably
    homemade (*page 32*)
2   cloves garlic, unpeeled
    A few sprigs fresh parsley
    A few sprigs fresh thyme or
    ½ teaspoon dried thyme leaves
6-8 whole black peppercorns
¼   cup sugar
2   cups kumquats, scrubbed and
    sliced, large seeds removed
¼   cup red-wine vinegar
1   tablespoon arrowroot or
    cornstarch
1   tablespoon brandy

TO PREPARE GOOSE:

Preheat oven to 325 degrees F. Remove giblets and neck from goose and reserve for the kumquat sauce. (Set liver aside for another use.) Remove any excess fat from the goose. Rinse the goose with cold water and pat dry.

Season the cavity of the goose with salt and pepper and stuff it with oranges and onions (they flavor the goose; they are not served). Tie the legs together with butcher's twine and tuck the wing tips under the back. Set the goose on a rack in a roasting pan. With a skewer or a fork, prick holes in the skin, being careful not to pierce the flesh. Roast the goose for 2½ to 3 hours, or until the juices run clear when the thigh is pierced with a skewer and a meat thermometer registers 180 to 185 degrees F. Spoon off the fat that accumulates in the pan every 30 minutes. Transfer the goose to a cutting board, cover loosely and let rest for 15 minutes before carving.

TO MAKE KUMQUAT SAUCE:

While the goose is roasting, in a heavy saucepan heat oil over medium-high heat. Add the reserved goose giblets and neck, onions and carrots; cook, stirring occasionally, for 15 to 20 minutes, or until well browned. Add chicken broth, garlic, parsley, thyme and peppercorns and bring to a boil. Reduce the heat to low and simmer, uncovered, for 30 minutes. Strain through a fine sieve and skim the fat from the surface; set broth aside.

In a heavy saucepan, combine sugar with 1 cup water. Bring to a boil over high heat and boil for 5 minutes. Reduce heat to medium and add kumquats. Poach the kumquats until they are translucent, about 10 minutes; remove from the syrup with a slotted spoon and reserve. Increase the heat to high and cook, without stirring, until the syrup turns amber, about 5 minutes. Remove from the heat and carefully add vinegar. Return to medium-high heat and cook for 5 to 7 minutes, or until reduced again to ¼ cup. Stir in the reserved broth and bring to a boil. Reduce the heat to low. In a small bowl, stir arrowroot or cornstarch into brandy. Whisk the mixture into the sauce and cook, stirring, until the sauce is thickened and glossy. Stir in the poached kumquats. Taste and adjust seasonings with salt and pepper.

TO SERVE:

Carve the goose, discarding the skin. Spoon a little sauce over the meat and pass the rest in a sauce boat.

Serves 8.

399 CALORIES PER 4-OUNCE SERVING: 35 G PROTEIN, 15 G FAT, 29 G CARBO-HYDRATE; 289 MG SODIUM; 109 MG CHOLESTEROL.

Duck & Vegetable Stir-Fry

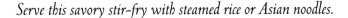

Serve this savory stir-fry with steamed rice or Asian noodles.

In a small bowl, stir together chile paste, 2 tablespoons water, vinegar, soy sauce and cornstarch; set aside.

Heat oil in a wok or large skillet over high heat. Add garlic and ginger and stir-fry until fragrant, about 30 seconds. Add broccoli and bok choy and stir-fry until the broccoli is bright green, about 2 minutes. Add shiitakes and stir-fry until softened, about 1 minute. Add poultry meat and stir until heated through. Add the reserved chile-paste mixture and stir until slightly thickened, about 1 minute. Serve immediately.

Serves 4.

173 CALORIES PER SERVING: 15 G PROTEIN, 8 G FAT, 11 G CARBOHYDRATE; 238 MG SODIUM; 44 MG CHOLESTEROL.

2 tablespoons Chinese chile paste with garlic

1 tablespoon rice-wine vinegar or distilled white vinegar

2 teaspoons reduced-sodium soy sauce

1 teaspoon cornstarch

2 teaspoons vegetable oil, preferably peanut oil

4 cloves garlic, finely chopped

2 tablespoons finely chopped fresh ginger

3 cups broccoli florets (1 large head)

3 cups sliced bok choy (3 stalks)

1 cup sliced fresh shiitake

2 cups cooked dark poultry meat (duck, goose or turkey thighs)

CHAPTER 8

Beef, Pork & Lamb

Three-Bean Chili

In this chili, a little beef goes a long way, slowly simmered with the magic combination of toasted spices, ancho chiles, sun-dried tomatoes and a touch of chocolate. Black, kidney and great northern beans round out the dish.

In a small dry skillet, toast cumin seeds over medium heat, stirring, until aromatic, 1 to 2 minutes. Transfer to a mortar and pestle or spice grinder; grind to a fine powder. Transfer to a small bowl; add chili powder, paprika, oregano and ground red pepper. Stir to combine; set aside.

Heat ½ tablespoon of the oil in a large heavy pot over high heat. Add beef, in batches if necessary, and sauté until browned on all sides, about 3 minutes. Transfer to a plate lined with paper towels and set aside.

Lower heat to medium, add the remaining ½ tablespoon oil. Add onions and green peppers. Cook, stirring, until the onions have softened and are golden brown, 7 to 10 minutes. Add garlic, jalapeños, dried tomatoes, anchos, if using, and the reserved spice mixture. Stir until aromatic, about 2 minutes. Pour in beer, bring to a simmer and cook for 10 minutes, scraping up any brown bits clinging to the bottom of the pan. Add canned tomatoes and their juices, chocolate, sugar, bay leaves and the reserved beef. Pour in 2 cups of water and bring to a simmer. Cover the pot and simmer, stirring occasionally, for 1½ to 2 hours, or until the beef is very tender.

Drain and rinse kidney beans, great northern beans and black

Three-Bean Chili

2	tablespoons cumin seeds
2	tablespoons chili powder
1	tablespoon paprika
2	teaspoons dried oregano
½	teaspoon ground red pepper (cayenne)
1	tablespoon olive oil
1	pound beef round, trimmed, cut into ½-inch chunks
3	onions, chopped
1	green bell pepper, chopped
6	cloves garlic, finely chopped
2	jalapeño peppers, seeded and finely chopped
8	dried tomatoes (not packed in oil), snipped into small pieces
2	dried ancho chiles, seeded and snipped into strips (optional)
12	ounces dark beer
1	28-ounce can plum tomatoes, with juices
1	tablespoon grated unsweetened chocolate

1   teaspoon sugar, or to taste
2   bay leaves
1   19-ounce can kidney beans
1   19-ounce can great northern
    beans
1   19-ounce can black beans
¼   cup chopped fresh cilantro
2   tablespoons fresh lime juice
    Salt & freshly ground black
    pepper

beans, add to the pot and cook until the chili is thick, 30 to 45 minutes more. Remove the bay leaves. Stir in cilantro and lime juice; season with salt and pepper. (*The chili can be prepared ahead and stored in the refrigerator for up to 2 days or in the freezer for up to 6 weeks.*)

Makes about 10 cups, serves 8.

428 CALORIES PER SERVING: 31 G PROTEIN, 8 G FAT, 59 G CARBOHYDRATE; 409 MG SODIUM; 41 MG CHOLESTEROL.

Korean Grilled Beef (*Bulgogi*)

In Korean restaurants, bulgogi *is often cooked with great theatrics at the tables, on a hot brass or iron shield.*

1   tablespoon sesame seeds
    Pinch of salt
1½ pounds boneless sirloin steak,
    trimmed of fat
6   scallions, trimmed and thinly
    sliced
4   cloves garlic, finely chopped
3   tablespoons finely chopped fresh
    ginger
3   tablespoons reduced-sodium soy
    sauce
1   tablespoon rice vinegar or cider
    vinegar
1½ teaspoons vegetable oil
1½ teaspoons sugar
    Generous grinding of black
    pepper

In a small heavy skillet, toast sesame seeds over medium heat until they begin to brown and have a toasted aroma. Transfer to a mortar, add salt and crush with a pestle. Set aside.

Score steak deeply (nearly through to the other side) in a 1-inch crisscross diamond pattern. Turn over and score the second side (do not worry if the meat breaks up into 2 or 3 pieces). Cover with plastic wrap and pound lightly with a mallet or heavy pan to tenderize.

In a shallow dish large enough to hold the steak, combine scallions, garlic, ginger, soy sauce, vinegar, oil, sugar, pepper and the ground sesame seeds. Add the steak and turn to coat with the marinade. Cover and marinate in the refrigerator for at least 2 hours or up to 8 hours, turning from time to time.

Prepare a hot charcoal fire. Once the coals are white-hot, remove the meat from the marinade and grill until medium-rare, about 4 minutes per side. Slice into thin strips and serve at once.

Serves 6.

206 CALORIES PER SERVING: 26 G PROTEIN, 10 G FAT, 4 G CARBOHYDRATE; 336 MG SODIUM; 76 MG CHOLESTEROL.

Beef, Watercress & Roquefort Burgers

Roquefort cheese, peppery watercress and beef is quite simply a fabulous combination of flavors.

In a bowl, mix bulgur with ½ cup warm water; let stand for 30 minutes.

Prepare a grill or preheat the broiler. Add beef, watercress, salt and pepper to the plumped bulgur and mix thoroughly but lightly. Shape the mixture into eight ⅓-inch-thick patties. Sandwich cheese between the patties to form 4 cheese-filled burgers.

Grill or broil the patties on a lightly oiled rack until browned and cooked through, about 5 minutes per side. Serve on buns.

Serves 4.

386 CALORIES PER SERVING: 24 G PROTEIN, 15 G FAT, 39 G CARBOHYDRATE; 755 MG SODIUM; 61 MG CHOLESTEROL.

- ⅓ cup bulgur
- ¾ pound lean ground beef
- ½ cup chopped watercress leaves
- ½ teaspoon salt
- ¼ teaspoon freshly ground black pepper
- 3 tablespoons crumbled Roquefort cheese (1 ounce)
- 4 onion buns, split and toasted

Braised Veal Shanks with Green Chiles & Sage

Chiles and sage impart a Southwestern flavor to the rich meat. This is even better the second day.

Preheat oven to 325 degrees F. On a plate, mix flour, salt and pepper. In a deep skillet or Dutch oven, heat 2 teaspoons of the oil over medium-high heat. Lightly dredge veal in the flour mixture. Brown the veal on all sides; drain on paper towels.

Add the remaining 1 teaspoon oil to the pan, then add onions and sauté until softened, 5 to 7 minutes. Stir in mild green chiles, jalapeños and garlic; sauté for 1 minute. Return the meat to the pan, stir in sage, oregano, bay leaves and ½ cup water. Bring to a simmer. Cover the pan and place it in the oven.

Bake for 1½ to 2 hours, or until the veal is very tender, turning the meat every 30 minutes. Remove the bay leaves and serve.

Serves 4.

326 CALORIES PER SERVING: 42 G PROTEIN, 9 G FAT, 18 G CARBOHYDRATE; 1,337 MG SODIUM; 144 MG CHOLESTEROL.

- ¼ cup all-purpose white flour
- ½ teaspoon salt
- ½ teaspoon ground black pepper
- 3 teaspoons olive oil
- 2 pounds veal shanks, sawed into 1-inch-thick pieces, trimmed of fat
- 2 onions, thinly sliced
- 4 4-ounce cans diced mild green chiles, with juices
- 1 jalapeño pepper, chopped
- 2 large cloves garlic, finely chopped
- 2 tablespoons chopped fresh sage
- ½ teaspoon dried oregano
- 2 bay leaves

Pork Tenderloin with Fennel

A garlicky fennel-seed crust and a delicate sauce enriched with pureed fresh fennel are two of the best things that could happen to pork. The tenderloin is by far the leanest cut of pork, with only 4 grams of fat in a cooked 3-ounce portion.

4   cloves garlic, crushed

1   tablespoon fennel seeds

½   teaspoon salt, plus more to taste

½   teaspoon freshly ground black pepper, plus more to taste

1   tablespoon olive oil

2   ¾-pound pork tenderloins, trimmed of fat and membrane

1½ cups chopped fennel bulb, plus fronds for garnish

1   small onion, chopped

1¼ cups defatted reduced-sodium chicken broth

½   cup dry white wine

1   tablespoon reduced-fat sour cream (optional)

Preheat oven to 425 degrees F. Mash garlic, fennel seeds and ½ teaspoon salt together on a cutting board with the flat side of a large knife. Transfer to a small bowl; stir in pepper and ½ table-spoon of the oil.

Rub the fennel-seed mixture evenly over tenderloins, pressing it into the crevices. Fold the thin tails underneath and secure with butcher's string or a toothpick.

Heat a large ovenproof skillet (cast iron is perfect) over medium-high heat. Add the tenderloins and cook until lightly browned on one side, about 1½ minutes. Turn the tenderloins over, transfer the skillet to the oven and roast for about 20 minutes, or until the pork's internal temperature registers 150 degrees F.

Meanwhile, heat the remaining ½ tablespoon oil in a heavy saucepan over medium-low heat. Add fennel and onions and cook, stirring often, until softened, 3 to 5 minutes. Add chicken broth and bring to a simmer. Cover and cook over low heat until the vegetables are tender, 10 to 15 minutes. Transfer to a blender or food processor and puree. Return to the sauce-pan and keep warm.

When the pork is ready, transfer it to a carving board, cover loosely and keep warm. Place the skillet (do not wipe it) over medium-high heat. Pour in wine and bring to a boil, stirring. Boil until reduced by half, about 2 minutes. Add to the fennel sauce, along with sour cream, if using. Taste and adjust seasonings. Remove the string or toothpick from the tenderloins and carve into ½-inch-thick slices. Spoon the sauce onto plates and fan the pork slices over the top. Garnish with a few fennel fronds.

Serves 6.

192 CALORIES PER SERVING: 26 G PROTEIN, 7 G FAT, 5 G CARBOHYDRATE; 476 MG SODIUM; 80 MG CHOLESTEROL.

Pork Tenderloin with Fennel

Stuffed Leg of Lamb Greek-Style (*Gemisto Arni me Pilafi*)

Lamb is the centerpiece of a Greek Easter dinner table. Ask the butcher to partially bone the leg of lamb, removing the aitchbone, hip bone and leg center bone, but to leave the hindshank in place. Make certain the butcher wraps the bones along with the meat; you will need them to make a broth for the pilaf. If you purchase a boned, butterflied leg, you can use canned chicken or beef broth in the pilaf.

LAMB

2 tablespoons nonfat plain yogurt

1 teaspoon olive oil

1 clove garlic, finely chopped

1 teaspoon chopped fresh thyme or ¼ teaspoon dried thyme leaves

  Salt & freshly ground black pepper to taste

1 5-pound leg of lamb, partially boned (*see recipe note above*), trimmed of fat

PILAF

3 tablespoons poppy seeds

1 tablespoon olive oil

3 large onions, finely chopped

3 cups bulgur

⅔ cup currants

1½ teaspoons chopped fresh thyme or ½ teaspoon dried thyme leaves

1 teaspoon salt

½ teaspoon freshly ground black pepper

5 cups lamb broth (*page 106*; add water if necessary to make 5 cups), heated

TO MARINATE LAMB:

In a large shallow dish, stir together yogurt, oil, garlic, thyme, salt and pepper. Add lamb and turn to coat. Cover with plastic wrap and refrigerate for at least 2 hours or up to 4 hours.

TO MAKE PILAF:

Meanwhile, toast poppy seeds in a small dry skillet over low heat until fragrant, about 2 minutes. Transfer to a small dish and set aside.

Heat oil in a Dutch oven (about 4-quart capacity) over medium heat. Add onions and cook, stirring, until softened, about 2 minutes. Stir in bulgur, currants, thyme, salt, pepper and the reserved poppy seeds. Slowly pour in 1 cup of the hot broth and cook, stirring, until all the liquid has been absorbed. Repeat with enough of the remaining broth, adding it 1 cup at a time, until the bulgur is tender and fluffy. (You may not need all the broth.) Taste and adjust seasonings. Let cool completely. (*The pilaf can be prepared ahead and stored, covered, in the refrigerator for up to 2 days.*)

TO STUFF AND ROAST LAMB:

Preheat oven to 450 degrees F. Place the lamb, skin-side down, on a cutting board. Place about 2 cups of the pilaf down the center of the meat, where the bones were removed. Bring the edges together and secure with butcher's string. Set on a rack in a roasting pan. Transfer the remaining pilaf to a lightly oiled 2-quart casserole and set aside.

Roast the lamb for 15 minutes. Reduce the oven temperature to 350 degrees F and roast for about 1 hour longer, or until a meat thermometer registers 145 to 150 degrees F for medium.

During the last 15 minutes of roasting, put the casserole of pilaf in the oven to heat through. Place the lamb on a carving board to rest for 15 to 30 minutes. Remove the string and carve.

Serves 10, with lamb leftovers.

366 CALORIES PER SERVING (3 OUNCES OF LAMB): 30 G PROTEIN, 10 G FAT, 40 G CARBOHYDRATE; 282 MG SODIUM; 76 MG CHOLESTEROL.

Lamb Broth

1½ pounds lamb bones
1 onion, peeled and studded with 1 whole clove
1 carrot, peeled
½ cup celery leaves
½ cup parsley stems
1 clove garlic, peeled
1 teaspoon salt
8 whole black peppercorns

Place lamb bones in a stockpot. Pour in 12 cups cold water or enough to cover. Bring to a boil and skim off froth. Add remaining ingredients and simmer, partially covered, over low heat for 2 hours.

Strain the broth through a fine sieve, discarding the bones and vegetables. Let cool. Chill and skim off the fat. (*The broth can be stored, covered, in the refrigerator for up to 2 days or in the freezer for up to 6 months.*)

Makes 4 to 6 cups.

Lamb Curry with Apples

With a little planning, Sunday's roast becomes Monday's easy dinner. Serve this curry over rice.

1 teaspoon cumin seeds
1 teaspoon coriander seeds
1 tablespoon yellow mustard seeds
3 Golden Delicious apples
2 teaspoons olive oil
2 large onions, finely chopped
6 cloves garlic, finely chopped
1 jalapeño pepper, seeded and finely chopped
2 tablespoons curry powder, preferably Madras
1 teaspoon paprika
½ teaspoon ground cinnamon
1 14-ounce can defatted beef broth
1 pound cooked lamb meat from the leg, cut into ½-inch cubes

In a small dry skillet over medium heat, toast cumin and coriander seeds, stirring, until they are aromatic, about 1 minute. Transfer to a spice mill or mortar and pestle, and grind to a powder; set aside.

In the same skillet, toast mustard seeds until they start to pop, about 1 minute; set aside.

Peel, core and chop 1 of the apples. Heat oil in a Dutch oven over medium heat. Add onions and chopped apple; sauté until softened and golden, 5 to 7 minutes. Add garlic, jalapeño peppers, curry powder, paprika, cinnamon, the reserved mustard seeds and 1 teaspoon of the ground cumin-coriander mixture; sauté until aromatic, about 2 minutes.

Add beef broth, lamb, raisins and crystallized ginger; bring to a simmer. Cover and cook over low heat for 15 minutes. Peel, core and cut the remaining 2 apples into ½-inch chunks; add them to the lamb mixture and simmer until the lamb is tender and the apples are soft, about 10 minutes longer. Stir in the remaining ground cumin-coriander mixture. Season with salt and pepper.

Serves 6.

252 CALORIES PER SERVING: 19 G PROTEIN, 7 G FAT, 30 G CARBOHYDRATE; 275 MG SODIUM; 50 MG CHOLESTEROL.

½ cup golden raisins

2 tablespoons slivered crystallized ginger

Salt & freshly ground black pepper to taste

Lamb Osso Buco

A variation on the northern Italian classic, this recipe substitutes lamb shanks for the usual veal. Ask the butcher to saw the shanks into 1½-inch-thick pieces for you.

Preheat oven to 350 degrees F. In a shallow dish, combine flour, salt and pepper. Roll lamb pieces in the flour; shake off excess.

Heat ½ tablespoon of the oil in a Dutch oven or heavy oven-proof skillet over medium-high heat. In two batches, brown the lamb on all sides, about 8 to 10 minutes per batch, using the remaining ½ tablespoon oil for the second batch. Remove the lamb to a bowl and set aside. Reduce the heat to medium, add onions, carrots and celery to the pan and cook, stirring, until softened, 3 to 5 minutes. Add garlic and cook until aromatic, about 30 seconds.

Stir in tomato sauce, wine or vermouth, basil, thyme and bay leaf. Add the reserved lamb and return to a simmer. Cover and bake for about 1½ hours, or until the lamb is tender, turning the meat once after 45 minutes. Discard the bay leaf; taste and adjust seasonings. (*The recipe can be prepared ahead. Cover and refrigerate for up to 2 days or freeze for up to 6 months. Thaw, if necessary, and heat on the stovetop or in a 350-degree-F oven for about 30 minutes before serving.*) Sprinkle with parsley and serve.

Serves 6.

291 CALORIES PER SERVING: 28 G PROTEIN, 8 G FAT, 13 G CARBOHYDRATE; 807 MG SODIUM; 89 MG CHOLESTEROL.

2 tablespoons all-purpose white flour

1 teaspoon salt

½ teaspoon freshly ground black pepper

3 pounds lamb shanks, trimmed of fat and sawed into 1½-inch-thick pieces

1 tablespoon olive oil

1 onion, chopped

2 carrots, chopped

1 stalk celery, chopped

2 cloves garlic, finely chopped

1½ cups tomato sauce

1½ cups dry white wine or vermouth

1 tablespoon chopped fresh basil or 1 teaspoon dried

1½ teaspoons chopped fresh thyme or ½ teaspoon dried thyme leaves

1 bay leaf

1 tablespoon chopped fresh parsley

CHAPTER 9

Fish & Shellfish

Cioppino

This recipe, like many classic cioppino recipes, calls for red wine in the broth, but feel free to substitute white. The assortment of seafood can vary as well: little clams instead of mussels, scallops in place of shrimp.

Heat oil in a stockpot or Dutch oven over medium heat. Add onions and green peppers; cook, stirring, until softened, about 5 minutes. Add garlic and cook until aromatic, about 1 minute. Stir in wine and bring to a boil; cook for 3 minutes, then add tomatoes and their juices, clam juice, parsley, bay leaf, oregano and red-pepper flakes. Cover, leaving the lid slightly ajar; simmer, stirring occasionally, until the broth is rich and thick, 20 to 30 minutes.

Add mussels, cover and cook for 2 minutes. Remove the mussels with tongs as they open, reserving them in a large bowl. Discard any mussels that do not open. Add crab legs, return to a simmer and cook, uncovered, until the crab is heated through, about 5 minutes. Remove with tongs and reserve along with the mussels. Add shrimp, fish and basil; cover and simmer until the shrimp turns pink and the fish is opaque, 2 to 3 minutes. Discard the bay leaf. Taste and adjust seasonings with salt and pepper. Return the reserved mussels and crab legs to the pot. Reheat briefly and serve.

Makes about 12 cups, serves 6.

330 CALORIES PER SERVING: 43 G PROTEIN, 6 G FAT, 17 G CARBOHYDRATE; 652 MG SODIUM; 209 MG CHOLESTEROL.

———
Cioppino

- 1 tablespoon olive oil
- 1 onion, chopped
- 1 green bell pepper, chopped
- 4 cloves garlic, finely chopped
- 1 cup dry red wine
- 1 14-ounce can plum tomatoes, chopped, with juices
- 1 8-ounce bottle clam juice
- ½ cup chopped fresh parsley
- 1 bay leaf
- ½ teaspoon dried oregano
- ¼ teaspoon red-pepper flakes
- 1 pound mussels, scrubbed and debearded
- 1 pound crab legs, cut into 4-inch pieces
- 1 pound medium shrimp, peeled and deveined
- 1 pound firm whitefish fillet, such as cod, haddock or halibut
- ¼ cup chopped fresh basil
   Salt & freshly ground black pepper to taste

Halibut with Herb-Almond Crust

If fresh oregano and mint are not available, substitute 1 teaspoon of dried oregano,
1 teaspoon of dried mint and 2 tablespoons of chopped fresh parsley.

⅓ cup nonfat plain yogurt

1 large egg white

1 tablespoon Dijon mustard

⅔ cup fine, dry, unseasoned breadcrumbs

¼ cup chopped toasted almonds

1 tablespoon chopped fresh oregano

1 tablespoon chopped fresh mint

¼ teaspoon salt

¼ teaspoon freshly ground black pepper

1¼ pounds halibut or mahi-mahi fillet, cut into 4 pieces

4 lemon wedges

Preheat oven to 400 degrees F. Lightly oil a wire rack large enough to hold fillets in a single layer. Put the rack on a baking sheet and set aside.

In a bowl, whisk together yogurt, egg white and mustard until creamy. In a shallow dish, combine breadcrumbs, almonds, oregano, mint, salt and pepper.

Dip each piece of fish in the crumb mixture, then in the yogurt mixture, and once again in the crumb mixture. Set on the prepared rack; they should not touch. Bake for 12 to 15 minutes, until the fish is lightly browned on the outside and opaque in the center. Serve hot with lemon wedges.

Serves 4.

288 CALORIES PER SERVING: 35 G PROTEIN, 8 G FAT, 17 G CARBOHYDRATE; 372 MG SODIUM; 45 MG CHOLESTEROL.

Honey-Macadamia Mahi-Mahi with Pineapple Relish

The colorful dolphinfish, also known by its Hawaiian name mahi-mahi, is a mild-tasting fish
caught in semitropical waters. For best results, select fillets that are at least ½ inch thick.

PINEAPPLE RELISH

1 cup diced fresh pineapple

½ cup unsweetened pineapple juice

¼ cup fresh lime juice

2 tablespoons finely chopped scallion greens

1 teaspoon finely chopped jalapeño or other hot pepper (optional)

TO PREPARE RELISH:

In a small bowl, combine all the relish ingredients. Mix well. (*The relish will keep, covered and refrigerated, for up to 8 hours.*)

TO PREPARE MAHI-MAHI:

Preheat oven to 350 degrees F. Prepare a grill. Toast macadamia nuts in the oven for 8 to 10 minutes, stirring occasionally, until lightly browned. Let cool. Finely chop and set aside.

Rub fillets with oil, then season with salt and pepper. When the fire is medium-hot, put the fillets on the grill. Cook for 3 to 4 minutes on the first side. Turn the fish over and cook for 3 to 4 minutes longer. As the second side is cooking, brush the exposed side lightly with honey and sprinkle with half of the nuts. Turn the fillets over again and cook for 1 minute, meanwhile coating the second side with the remaining honey and nuts. Turn once again and cook 1 minute, or until the crust is golden brown. Remove the fillets from the grill. Cut each fillet into 2 portions and serve, accompanied by Pineapple Relish.

Serves 4.

302 CALORIES PER SERVING: 25 G PROTEIN, 12 G FAT, 24 G CARBOHYDRATE; 91 MG SODIUM; 57 MG CHOLESTEROL.

HONEY-MACADAMIA MAHI-MAHI

¼ cup macadamia nuts

2 8-ounce mahi-mahi fillets, skinned

½ teaspoon vegetable oil
Salt & freshly ground black pepper to taste

3 tablespoons honey

Grilled Bluefish with Chipotle Vinaigrette

The strong flavor of bluefish is mellowed by a vinaigrette spiced with chipotles. Serve this dish hot or cold.

TO MAKE VINAIGRETTE:

In a small bowl, whisk together vinegar, lime juice, mustard, chipotles, cilantro and sugar. Gradually whisk in olive oil. Season with salt and pepper.

TO GRILL FISH:

Prepare a grill. Rub fillets with oil and sprinkle lightly with salt and pepper. When the fire is medium-low, grill the fish, covered with a metal pie pan or foil. Cook the fillets for 8 to 10 minutes on the first side. Turn them over and cook, covered, about 5 minutes on the second side, or until the flesh is opaque. Remove the fillets from the grill and cut each into 2 portions. Pour the Chipotle Vinaigrette over the fillets and serve.

Serves 4.

162 CALORIES PER SERVING: 20 G PROTEIN, 8 G FAT, 2 G CARBOHYDRATE; 134 MG SODIUM; 50 MG CHOLESTEROL.

CHIPOTLE VINAIGRETTE

2 tablespoons cider vinegar

2 tablespoons fresh lime juice

2 teaspoons Dijon mustard

2 teaspoons finely chopped canned chipotle peppers

1 teaspoon chopped fresh cilantro

1 teaspoon sugar

1 tablespoon olive oil
Salt & freshly ground black pepper to taste

BLUEFISH

2 8-ounce bluefish or mackerel fillets, skinned

½ teaspoon vegetable oil
Salt & freshly ground black pepper to taste

Arugula-Stuffed Tuna Steak

This is a gorgeous and delicious dish. The lime-and-pepper marinade complements the assertiveness of the arugula, which is somewhat tamed by a brief warming. Do not be intimidated by the creation of the pocket; it is easy, and takes just a minute.

⅓ cup fresh lime juice (2 to 3 limes)

¼ cup dry white wine or water

3 tablespoons reduced-sodium soy sauce

2 teaspoons finely chopped fresh ginger

1 clove garlic, finely chopped

1 teaspoon Dijon mustard

½ teaspoon toasted sesame oil

½ teaspoon coarsely ground black pepper

1¼ pounds tuna steak (1¼-inch thick), skin removed

1 cup arugula leaves (about 1 small bunch), washed

In a small bowl, whisk together lime juice, wine or water, soy sauce, ginger, garlic, mustard, sesame oil and black pepper. Measure out 2 tablespoons and reserve. Pour the remainder into a shallow dish, add tuna and turn to coat well. Cover and marinate in the refrigerator for 30 minutes to 1 hour.

Prepare a grill or preheat the broiler. In a small bowl, toss arugula with the reserved lime-juice mixture and set aside. Remove the tuna from the marinade and reserve the marinade for basting. Place the tuna on a cutting board and, using a sharp, thin-bladed knife, make a 1-inch incision halfway through the thickness of the tuna steak, holding the knife parallel to the work surface. Insert the knife almost to the opposite edge of the steak, then move it back and forth to create a large pocket. Be careful not to cut through the top, bottom or opposite edge of the tuna, and leave about a ½-inch border around the edge.

Stuff the pocket with the arugula mixture. Grill or broil the tuna for 5 minutes, basting occasionally with the reserved marinade. Turn the tuna over and cook, no longer basting, just until the flesh is opaque, 5 to 7 minutes longer. Bring any leftover marinade to a boil and serve as a sauce. Cut the tuna steak into quarters or ¼-inch-thick slices.

Serves 4.

207 CALORIES PER SERVING: 41 G PROTEIN, 2 G FAT, 4 G CARBOHYDRATE; 605 MG SODIUM; 76 MG CHOLESTEROL.

**Arugula-Stuffed
Tuna Steak**

Aeolian Swordfish Birds (*Involtini di pesce spada*)

The breadcrumb stuffing seasoned with nuts and raisins reflects the medieval Arab influence on the cuisine of Italy's Aeolian Islands. If you like, skewer the involtini *and cook them on the grill.*

SWORDFISH

1 pound swordfish steak, about 1 inch thick, skin removed

½ teaspoon salt

1 small stalk celery

½ small onion, peeled

3 sprigs parsley

1 bay leaf

FILLING

1½-2 tablespoons fine, dry, unseasoned breadcrumbs

1-2 tablespoons canned tomato sauce

1 tablespoon freshly grated Parmesan cheese

6 green olives, pitted and finely chopped

1 tablespoon drained capers, finely chopped

1 tablespoon pine nuts, chopped

1 tablespoon golden raisins, chopped

SAUCE

¾ cup canned tomato sauce

1½ tablespoons coarsely chopped fresh basil

⅛ teaspoon ground red pepper (cayenne) or a few drops Tabasco sauce

1 teaspoon olive oil

TO PREPARE SWORDFISH:

Cut swordfish steak in two along the natural dividing line. Set one half on a cutting board; put your hand flat on top of the swordfish and, with a very sharp knife, slice through the steak keeping the knife parallel to the board to obtain four ¼-inch-thick slices. Repeat with the other piece of fish. Place each slice between 2 sheets of plastic wrap and, with a mallet or pan, pound to an ⅛-inch thickness. Trim each slice into 2 rectangles, each about 3½ by 2½ inches. Reserve the trimmings.

In a small saucepan, bring 2 cups water to a boil. Add salt, celery, onion, parsley and bay leaf; simmer for 5 minutes. With a slotted spoon, remove the vegetables and herbs. Adjust the heat so the broth simmers very gently; add the swordfish trimmings and poach for 2 minutes. Drain and place trimmings in a small bowl.

TO MAKE FILLING:

Add 1½ tablespoons breadcrumbs, 1 tablespoon tomato sauce and cheese to the swordfish trimmings and mash with a fork. (The filling should have the consistency of a very soft dough.) If necessary, thicken with additional breadcrumbs or thin with more tomato sauce. Stir in olives, capers, pine nuts and raisins.

Place a mound of the filling along a long end of each swordfish slice. Tuck in the sides and roll up. Secure the rolls with toothpicks. If the swordfish is moist enough and you can let the birds rest for 10 to 15 minutes, you will not need the toothpicks. (*The swordfish birds can be prepared ahead to this point and stored, covered, in the refrigerator for up to 8 hours.*)

TO MAKE SAUCE AND COOK SWORDFISH BIRDS:

In a small saucepan, combine tomato sauce and basil and bring to a simmer, stirring. Season with ground red pepper or

Tabasco and keep warm. In a nonstick skillet, heat oil over low heat. Swirl the pan to coat it evenly with the oil. Add the swordfish birds and cook, turning the birds gently with a fork, until the fish is firm and opaque throughout, about 5 minutes. Remove the toothpicks and transfer the birds to a serving platter. Spoon the sauce over the birds and serve.

Serves 4.

226 CALORIES PER SERVING: 25 G PROTEIN, 8 G FAT, 13 G CARBOHYDRATE; 620 MG SODIUM; 44 MG CHOLESTEROL.

Quick Cajun Catfish

Catfish farming has become a big industry in recent years and the quality of the fish is now consistently good.

Preheat the broiler. Lightly oil a wire rack large enough to hold fish in a single layer. Put the rack on a baking sheet and set aside.

In a medium bowl, whisk together buttermilk and mustard until smooth. In a shallow dish, combine cornmeal, salt, paprika, onion powder, garlic powder, thyme, ground red pepper and black pepper. Dip each fillet in the buttermilk mixture, turning to coat. Transfer to the cornmeal mixture, turning to coat completely. Place the fillets on the prepared rack; they should not touch each other.

Broil 4 inches from the heat source until the fish is opaque in the center, about 3 minutes per side. Serve hot with lemon wedges.

Serves 4.

237 CALORIES PER SERVING: 28 G PROTEIN, 7 G FAT, 15 G CARBOHYDRATE; 644 MG SODIUM; 82 MG CHOLESTEROL.

¼ cup buttermilk

2 teaspoons Dijon mustard

½ cup cornmeal

1 teaspoon salt

1 teaspoon paprika

1 teaspoon onion powder

½ teaspoon garlic powder

½ teaspoon dried thyme leaves

½ teaspoon ground red pepper (cayenne)

½ teaspoon freshly ground black pepper

4 catfish fillets (1¼ pounds total)

4 lemon wedges

Japanese Glazed Salmon with Soba & Julienned Vegetables

The contrasting colors and textures of this Japanese dish awaken the appetite. The basic Japanese ingredients called for here may be hard to find in supermarkets, but are likely to be sold in most health-food stores.

½ cup hijiki (Japanese dried seaweed)

1 pound salmon fillet, skin on, scaled, cut into 4 portions

¼ cup mirin (sweet rice wine)

3 tablespoons reduced-sodium soy sauce, plus more to taste

2 tablespoons grated fresh ginger

2 tablespoons red miso (fermented soybean paste)

5 teaspoons sugar

2 teaspoons fresh lemon juice

2 teaspoons sake (Japanese rice wine)

8 ounces dried soba noodles (Japanese buckwheat noodles)

1 teaspoon vegetable oil, preferably canola oil

1 cup snow peas, strings removed, julienned

2 carrots, julienned

1 small yellow summer squash, julienned

6 cups mung bean sprouts
   Salt & freshly ground black pepper to taste

1 cup grated daikon radish

Place hijiki in a small bowl with enough warm water to cover and soak for 30 minutes.

Meanwhile, place salmon in a shallow glass dish. In a small bowl, combine mirin, 1 tablespoon of the soy sauce, ginger, miso, 2 teaspoons of the sugar, lemon juice and sake. Pour over salmon, turn to coat well, cover with plastic wrap and refrigerate for 15 minutes or up to 1 hour, turning occasionally.

In a small saucepan, combine 4 cups water, the remaining 2 tablespoons soy sauce and the remaining 3 teaspoons sugar. Drain the hijiki and add it to the saucepan. Bring to a boil, reduce the heat to low and simmer for 15 minutes. Drain, discarding the liquid, and set aside.

Preheat the broiler; lightly oil a broiler pan. Remove the salmon from the marinade. (Discard the marinade.) Place the salmon, skin-side down, on the prepared broiler pan. Broil about 6 inches from the heat until the fish is opaque in the center, about 7 minutes (it is not necessary to turn the salmon); set aside.

In a large pot, bring 3 quarts water to a boil. Slowly add soba. When the water returns to a boil, add ½ cup cold water. Repeat the steps of returning the water to a boil and adding cold water 2 or 3 times, until the soba is just tender. (It will take 5 to 7 minutes total.)

Meanwhile, heat oil in a large skillet over medium heat. Add snow peas, carrots, squash and sprouts; cook, stirring, until tender, about 3 minutes. Season with salt, pepper and soy sauce.

Drain the soba and mound on four plates; spoon the vegetables next to the soba. Set the salmon on top. Crown the dish with a sprinkling of hijiki and daikon.

Serves 4.

525 CALORIES PER SERVING: 42 G PROTEIN, 10 G FAT, 71 G CARBOHYDRATE; 1,314 MG SODIUM; 45 MG CHOLESTEROL.

Japanese Glazed Salmon with Soba & Julienned Vegetables

Aegean Fish Stew

A simple stew of fish and vegetables, enriched with the most famous sauce of Greek cuisine:
avgolémono *(egg and lemon sauce). This is a saucy dish; serve with lots of crusty country bread.*

¼ cup all-purpose white flour

½ teaspoon salt, plus more to taste

¼ teaspoon freshly ground black pepper, plus more to taste

1 pound monkfish, halibut or sea bass fillet, trimmed of any skin and membrane and cut into 1½-inch chunks

3 teaspoons olive oil

1 large onion, chopped

2 cloves garlic, finely chopped

¾ cup dry white wine

3 cups defatted reduced-sodium chicken broth (*page 32*), fish stock (*page 121*) or 1 cup bottled clam juice diluted with 2 cups water

¾ pound yellow-fleshed potatoes (3-4 potatoes), peeled and cut into quarters or eighths lengthwise, depending on size

¾ pound carrots (about 4), peeled, cut into 2-inch-long sticks

1 large egg

3-4 tablespoons fresh lemon juice

¼ cup chopped fresh dill or fennel fronds

Combine flour, ½ teaspoon salt and ¼ teaspoon pepper in a shallow dish. Dredge fish in flour. Heat 2 teaspoons of the oil in a Dutch oven or large sauté pan. Swirl the pan to coat the bottom evenly with oil, then add the fish. Cook, turning, just until lightly browned, 2 to 3 minutes. Transfer the fish to a plate and set aside.

Add the remaining 1 teaspoon oil to the pan and reduce the heat to medium. Add onions and garlic and cook until softened, about 2 minutes. Slowly pour in wine and bring to a boil. Add chicken broth, fish stock or clam juice and water; bring to a boil. Add potatoes and carrots and return to a boil once again. Cover and cook over medium heat until the vegetables are just tender, about 20 minutes.

Return the fish to the pan, reduce the heat to low and cook, covered, until the fish is opaque in the center, 5 to 10 minutes longer. With a slotted spoon, transfer the fish and vegetables to a plate and keep warm.

Increase the heat to high and boil the cooking liquid for 5 minutes to intensify the flavors. In a medium bowl, whisk together egg, 3 tablespoons lemon juice and dill or fennel. Gradually whisk a little of the hot cooking liquid into the egg mixture, then pour the egg mixture into the remaining cooking liquid in the pan. Cook over medium heat, stirring constantly, until slightly thickened (do not boil), 1 to 2 minutes. Return the fish and vegetables to the pan and warm through. Taste and adjust seasonings, adding more lemon juice if desired.

Serves 4.

336 CALORIES PER SERVING: 22 G PROTEIN, 7 G FAT, 40 G CARBOHYDRATE; 341 MG SODIUM; 81 MG CHOLESTEROL.

Mussel & Roasted Pepper Paella

Mussels are a paella's best friend. The delicious mussel juice adds great depth of flavor to the rice.
If fresh mussels are unavailable, you can use small clams instead and cook the rice in the clam broth.

Place peppers directly over the flame of a gas burner or under a preheated broiler and roast, turning often, until they are blackened all over, about 8 to 10 minutes. Set aside to cool. Slip off the skin, cut away the stalk end, slit the peppers open vertically and remove their seeds. Chop coarsely and set aside.

In a large stockpot, combine wine, shallots, thyme, peppercorns and bay leaf and bring to a simmer over medium heat. Add mussels and cook, covered, until they have opened, about 8 to 10 minutes. (Discard any unopened mussels.) Using a slotted spoon, transfer the mussels to a large bowl, reserving the cooking liquid in the pot. Working over the pot, shell all the mussels but 10, letting their juices fall into the cooking liquid. Set aside the shelled and unshelled mussels separately in the refrigerator.

Strain the cooking liquid through a double layer of cheesecloth into a saucepan. Add clam juice and saffron and simmer for 5 minutes. Transfer the liquid to a measuring cup; pour it back into the pan along with enough water to make 3 cups total liquid.

In a deep heavy skillet or paella pan, heat oil over medium heat. Add onions and garlic and sauté until softened and browned, about 8 to 10 minutes. Add tomatoes and green peppers and cook until the liquid has evaporated, about 8 to 10 minutes. Season with salt and pepper.

Stir in rice and the reserved saffron broth. Bring to a boil, reduce the heat to low and simmer, covered, until the rice is almost tender, 20 to 30 minutes. Add the reserved shelled mussels and red peppers and simmer for 5 minutes longer. Add parsley; taste and adjust seasonings. Garnish with the unshelled cooked mussels, letting them warm up briefly, and serve.

Serves 5.

401 CALORIES PER SERVING: 29 G PROTEIN, 6 G FAT, 55 G CARBOHYDRATE; 681 MG SODIUM; 1 MG CHOLESTEROL.

2 red bell peppers

½ cup dry white wine

2 shallots, finely chopped

1 large sprig thyme or ¼ teaspoon dried thyme leaves

6 whole black peppercorns

1 bay leaf

3½-4 pounds small mussels, well scrubbed and debearded

1 8-ounce bottle clam juice

1 teaspoon crumbled saffron threads or ¼ teaspoon powdered saffron

2 teaspoons olive oil, preferably extra-virgin

2 cups finely chopped onions (2 onions)

2 cloves garlic, finely chopped

1½ cups peeled, seeded and chopped plum tomatoes or one 16-ounce can plum tomatoes, drained and chopped

1 green bell pepper, cored, seeded and chopped

Salt & freshly ground black pepper to taste

1¼ cups white rice, preferably arborio

2 tablespoons chopped fresh parsley, preferably Italian flat-leaf

Shrimp Creole

EATING WELL *contributor Steven Raichlen adapted this recipe to shrimp because conch, called for in the original, is generally unavailable in the United States. You can also use scallops.*

1½ tablespoons olive oil

1 onion, finely chopped

3 bunches chives or 12 scallions, finely chopped (2 cups)

4 shallots, finely chopped

6 cloves garlic, finely chopped (2 tablespoons)

1-2 Scotch bonnet chiles (or other very hot fresh chiles), seeded and finely chopped

2 teaspoons finely chopped fresh ginger

1½ teaspoons curry powder

3 large ripe tomatoes, peeled, seeded and diced

1 cup finely chopped fresh parsley

¼ cup chopped fresh cilantro

1 teaspoon chopped fresh thyme or ¼ teaspoon dried thyme leaves

1 bay leaf

⅓ cup dark rum

1 cup fish stock (*recipe follows*) or bottled clam juice

2 tablespoons tomato paste

18 jumbo or 24 large shrimp, peeled and deveined

2 tablespoons fresh lime juice, plus more to taste

¼ teaspoon salt, plus more to taste

¼ teaspoon freshly ground black pepper, plus more to taste

Heat oil in a large nonstick skillet over medium heat. Add onions, chives or scallions, shallots, all but 1 teaspoon of the garlic, chiles, ginger and curry powder. Cook, stirring, until just beginning to brown, 4 to 5 minutes. Stir in tomatoes, ½ cup of the parsley, cilantro, thyme and bay leaf. Increase the heat to high and cook, stirring, for 1 minute. Stir in rum and bring to a boil. Add fish stock or clam juice and tomato paste. Reduce the heat and simmer until thickened and well-flavored, about 10 minutes. Remove bay leaf. (*The onion-tomato mixture can be made ahead to this point and stored, covered, in the refrigerator for up to 1 day. Return the mixture to a simmer before proceeding.*)

Meanwhile, place shrimp in a shallow glass dish and toss with 2 tablespoons lime juice, ¼ teaspoon salt and ¼ teaspoon pepper. Cover with plastic wrap; refrigerate for 20 minutes.

Stir the marinated shrimp into the onion-tomato mixture. Gently simmer over low heat, turning occasionally, until the shrimp are curled and opaque, 3 to 5 minutes. Stir in the remaining 1 teaspoon garlic. Taste and adjust seasonings with lime juice, salt and pepper. Sprinkle with the remaining ½ cup parsley and serve at once.

Serves 6.

160 CALORIES PER SERVING: 7 G PROTEIN, 4 G FAT, 20 G CARBOHYDRATE; 295 MG SODIUM; 32 MG CHOLESTEROL.

Shrimp Creole

Fish Stock

Ask your fishmonger for heads and bones.

Rinse fish heads and bones in cold water. Place in a non-aluminum stockpot with remaining ingredients and enough cold water to cover, about 3½ quarts. Bring just to a boil. Reduce heat to low, skim off any foam and simmer, uncovered, for 30 to 35 minutes, skimming occasionally. Strain stock through a fine sieve. (*The stock can be refrigerated for 2 days or frozen for up to 6 months.*)

Makes about 3 quarts.

3 **pounds whitefish heads and bones**

2 **cups dry white wine**

2 **onions, chopped**

2 **leeks, white parts only, cleaned and chopped**

2 **stalks celery, chopped**

2 **cloves garlic, crushed**

4 **sprigs fresh parsley**

3 **sprigs fresh thyme or ½ teaspoon dried thyme leaves**

1 **bay leaf**

Aeolian Seafood Couscous (*Cuscusù*)

In the Aeolians, cuscusù *always refers to a fish couscous and is traditionally served as a first course. The final success of the* cuscusù *rests with the fish and the fish broth: the more varied the types of fish, the better. You will need firm-fleshed fish; these will simmer without falling apart. The broth requires purchasing heads and bones; they can be ordered from your fishmonger with a couple of days' notice.*

BROTH

½	pound medium shrimp
2	teaspoons olive oil
1	onion, chopped
4	cloves garlic, crushed
2	anchovy fillets, rinsed, drained and chopped
5	leaves fresh basil
3	sprigs parsley
3	bay leaves
1	teaspoon black peppercorns
1	teaspoon salt, plus more to taste
2	pounds (approximately) fish heads and bones
½	cup dry white wine
1	cup canned tomato sauce
2	tablespoons tomato paste
¼	teaspoon ground red pepper (cayenne), plus more to taste

COUSCOUS & SEAFOOD

1	teaspoon saffron threads, crumbled, or ¼ teaspoon powdered saffron
⅛	teaspoon ground cinnamon
⅛	teaspoon ground cloves
⅛	teaspoon freshly grated nutmeg
2½	cups couscous

TO MAKE BROTH:

Peel and devein shrimp, reserving the shells for the broth. Set the shrimp aside in the refrigerator. In a large soup pot, heat oil over medium-high heat. Add onions, garlic, anchovies, basil, parsley, bay leaves, peppercorns and 1 teaspoon salt; sauté for 2 minutes. Add ½ cup water and simmer until most of the water has evaporated, about 3 minutes.

Add fish heads and bones and the reserved shrimp shells. Cook, stirring, for 2 minutes. Pour in wine and simmer until it has almost evaporated, about 5 minutes. Stir in tomato sauce, tomato paste, ground red pepper and 6 cups water. Bring to a boil, stirring. Reduce the heat to low and simmer, partially covered, for 45 minutes, skimming off any froth that rises to the top. Strain the broth through a fine-meshed sieve into a bowl. (You should have about 6 cups.) Taste and add more salt and ground red pepper, if desired. The broth should be zesty. (*The broth may be prepared ahead and stored, covered, in the refrigerator for up to 8 hours.*)

TO MAKE COUSCOUS AND COOK SEAFOOD:

In a large saucepan, combine 2 cups of the fish broth, 1½ cups water, saffron, cinnamon, cloves and nutmeg; bring to a boil. Remove from the heat and stir in couscous. Cover and let stand for 5 minutes.

Meanwhile, in a large saucepan, bring the remaining 4 cups broth to a simmer. Add firm-fleshed fish, squid and the reserved shrimp; return to a simmer. Simmer very gently until the fish flesh is opaque, 3 to 5 minutes. With a slotted spoon, transfer the seafood to a platter; cover and keep warm.

To serve, fluff the couscous with a fork and stir in a ladleful (about ½ cup) of the broth. Spoon the couscous into warm soup plates. Make a hollow in the center of each portion and fill it with seafood. Pour the remaining hot broth into a soup tureen and pass for diners to add as they please.

Serves 8.

370 CALORIES PER SERVING: 31 G PROTEIN, 3 G FAT, 49 G CARBOHYDRATE; 426 MG SODIUM; 88 MG CHOLESTEROL.

1½ pounds firm-fleshed fish (preferably a combination of swordfish, monkfish, halibut, grouper, black sea bass and/or gray mullet)

½ pound squid, transparent quill removed, cut into ¼-inch-thick rings

Crispy Scallops with Soy Dipping Sauce

The scallops are delicious served with rice tossed with diced red peppers and slivered scallion greens.

Preheat oven to 450 degrees F. Lightly oil a wire rack large enough to hold scallops in a single layer. Put the rack on a baking sheet and set aside.

In a bowl, whisk together egg white, vegetable oil, sesame oil and soy sauce until creamy. In a shallow dish, stir together breadcrumbs, sesame seeds and ginger.

Add the scallops to the egg-white mixture, tossing to coat them well. Transfer the scallops to the breadcrumb mixture in two or three batches, tossing each with a spoon to coat evenly.

Place the scallops on the prepared rack; they should not touch each other. Bake for 10 minutes, or until the outsides are golden and the centers are opaque.

TO MAKE DIPPING SAUCE:

In a small bowl, stir together the sauce ingredients. Serve alongside the hot scallops.

Serves 4.

280 CALORIES PER SERVING: 32 G PROTEIN, 9 G FAT, 16 G CARBOHYDRATE; 424 MG SODIUM; 56 MG CHOLESTEROL.

1 large egg white

1 tablespoon vegetable oil, preferably canola oil

1 tablespoon toasted sesame oil

1 teaspoon reduced-sodium soy sauce

½ cup fine, dry, unseasoned breadcrumbs

2 teaspoons sesame seeds

½ teaspoon ground ginger

1¼ pounds sea scallops, sliced in half horizontally and patted dry

DIPPING SAUCE

2 tablespoons reduced-sodium soy sauce

2 tablespoons rice-wine vinegar

1 tablespoon chopped scallions

1 teaspoon honey

Shrimp & Baby Artichoke Brochettes

The choke has not yet formed in tender baby artichokes, making their preparation fast work.
This elegant, summer dish works well as an appetizer or main course.

8   baby artichokes

5   tablespoons fresh lemon juice

⅓   cup black olives, preferably Kalamata or Gaeta, pitted and chopped

⅓   cup chopped fresh parsley, preferably Italian flat-leaf

2   teaspoons olive oil, preferably extra-virgin

Freshly ground black pepper to taste

16   large shrimp (about 1 pound), peeled and deveined

If using wooden skewers for the brochettes, soak them in water for about 1 hour before grilling time.

In a large saucepan, cover artichokes with 2 quarts water, add 4 tablespoons of the lemon juice and bring to a boil. Reduce the heat and simmer for 8 to 12 minutes, or just until the artichokes are tender. Drain and refresh with cold water. Cut the artichokes in half lengthwise and trim the leaf tips with kitchen shears.

In a small bowl, combine olives, parsley, olive oil and the remaining 1 tablespoon lemon juice. Season with pepper. Set aside.

Prepare a grill. Thread the skewers alternately with shrimp and artichoke halves. Once the fire is medium-hot, grill the brochettes for 3 to 4 minutes per side, or until the shrimp are opaque. Sprinkle the olive-parsley mixture over the top and serve.

Serves 4 as a main course.

230 CALORIES PER SERVING: 27 G PROTEIN, 8 G FAT, 16 G CARBOHYDRATE; 364 MG SODIUM; 173 MG CHOLESTEROL.

Squid Salad with Ginger & Lemongrass (*Yam Pla Meuk*)

For this Thai salad, the squid is boiled whole, then sliced and tossed with cilantro and shreds of fresh
ginger and lemongrass. This whole-cooking method keeps the squid flavorful and makes it much easier
to clean after cooking. Fish sauce is available at large supermarkets and Thai grocery stores.

1   tablespoon salt

1   pound whole squid (approximately 10 squid)

¼   cup fresh lime juice

¼   cup fish sauce

½   teaspoon sugar

Bring 3 quarts of water to a rolling boil and add salt. Drop in squid and cook until opaque, 3 to 4 minutes. Drain and rinse with cold water. To clean the squid, first separate the tentacles from the pouch by gently pulling on the tentacles; the viscera will come out at the same time. Chop off the tentacles from the head below the eyes; set the tentacles aside. Slice the pouches open lengthwise and rinse thoroughly. When all squid have been cleaned, pat the tentacles and pouches dry. Slice the tentacles into 2 or 3 sections. Slice the pouches in half lengthwise, then cut into ¾-inch-wide strips. Transfer the prepared squid pieces to a bowl.

Stir together lime juice, fish sauce and sugar. Pour the mixture over the squid, tossing to coat. Add shallots, ginger, lemongrass and chiles and toss once again. (*The salad can be prepared ahead to this point and stored, covered, in the refrigerator for up to 2 hours.*)

Just before serving, add cilantro and toss well. Arrange cucumber slices and cabbage leaves around the edge of a platter. Mound the salad in the center and serve.

Serves 4.

140 CALORIES PER SERVING: 20 G PROTEIN, 2 G FAT, 11 G CARBOHYDRATE; 747 MG SODIUM; 264 MG CHOLESTEROL.

- 2 tablespoons thinly sliced shallots, separated into rings
- 1 tablespoon julienned fresh ginger
- 1 tablespoon finely chopped fresh lemongrass
- 2 bird or other fresh hot chiles, seeded and finely chopped
- ½ cup fresh cilantro, coarsely shredded
- ½ medium English cucumber, scored lengthwise with a fork and cut into ¼-inch-thick slices
- ½ small cabbage cut into wedges, cored and separated into leaves

Squid Salad with Ginger & Lemongrass (*Yam Pla Meuk*)

CHAPTER 10

Salsas&Chutneys

Sweet-Hot Tropical Salsa

Serve this refreshing mixture with simple grilled poultry or seafood or in a sandwich.
The rosy Sunrise Solo papaya is worth seeking out. For variety, add pineapple, mango and/or jícama.

Peel, seed and dice papayas and cucumber; section and dice grapefruit. Place in a serving bowl along with lime juice, 2 tablespoons mint or basil, shallots, jalapeños, vinegar, ½ teaspoon sugar and ½ teaspoon salt. Toss gently. Cover and chill for 6 to 12 hours. (Time is required to develop flavor and consistency.)

Season to taste with additional chopped jalapeños, mint or basil, sugar and salt before serving.

Makes about 4 cups.

5 CALORIES PER TABLESPOON: 0 G PROTEIN, 0 G FAT, I G CARBOHYDRATE; 17 MG SODIUM; 0 MG CHOLESTEROL.

2	small papayas
1	small cucumber
1	grapefruit
2	tablespoons fresh lime juice
2	tablespoons finely chopped fresh mint or basil, plus more to taste
1	large shallot, finely chopped
1	jalapeño pepper, seeded and finely chopped, plus more to taste
1	tablespoon distilled white vinegar
½	teaspoon sugar, plus more to taste
½	teaspoon salt, plus more to taste

Sweet-Hot Tropical Salsa

Crunchy Cucumber Kimchi (*Oisobagi*)

Kimchi is most often made with cabbage. This relatively quick cucumber version is popular in the summer in Korea. The key to making really good oisobagi *is to pour boiling water over the cucumbers after they have been salted.*

3 cucumbers (about 8 inches long), ends trimmed

1½ tablespoons salt

3 tablespoons coarsely ground Korean red chile powder or ground red pepper (cayenne)

1 small daikon radish, washed and trimmed

4 scallions, trimmed and finely chopped

4 cloves garlic, finely chopped

2 tablespoons finely chopped fresh ginger

1 tablespoon sugar

Cut each cucumber crosswise into thirds. Stand each segment on end and cut a cross down each one, almost to the base (do not separate). Gently open the cucumbers and sprinkle with salt. Set them in a bowl and cover.

In a small bowl, combine chile powder with ¼ cup water to make a paste. Set both the cucumbers and chile paste aside at room temperature for about 2 hours.

Meanwhile, cut the daikon radish into thin matchsticks about 1 inch long. (You should have about 2 cups.) Toss them in a bowl with scallions, garlic, ginger and sugar.

When the cucumbers are sufficiently salted, wipe away the excess salt and pour off any liquid that has accumulated in the bowl. Return the cucumbers to the bowl and add boiling water to cover. Drain immediately, refresh under cold, running water and wipe dry.

Stir the reserved chile paste into the radish mixture. In a deep glass container with a lid, set the cucumbers on end. Stuff the radish mixture into the slits in the cucumbers. Cover and let stand in a cool, dark place for a day, turning occasionally to distribute the liquid. (*Store in the refrigerator for up to 4 days.*) To serve, cut into small chunks and place in a pickle dish with some of the liquid.

Makes about 5 cups.

14 CALORIES PER ¼-CUP SERVING: 1 G PROTEIN, 0 G FAT, 3 G CARBOHYDRATE; 333 MG SODIUM; 0 MG CHOLESTEROL.

Cranberry-Onion Relish

Not as sweet as most cranberry relishes, this ruby-colored condiment is a perfect foil for dark turkey meat.

Preheat oven to 375 degrees F. In a shallow 2-quart baking dish, toss onions with sugar and oil. Bake, uncovered, for 1 to 1¼ hours, stirring every 15 minutes, or until the onions are very tender and golden.

Transfer the onions to a medium saucepan and add remaining ingredients. Cook, stirring, over medium heat for several minutes, or until the cranberries are tender and the mixture has thickened. Let cool. (*The relish can be prepared ahead and stored, covered, in the refrigerator for up to 1 week.*)

Makes 1 cup.

19 CALORIES PER TABLESPOON: 0 G PROTEIN, 0 G FAT, 4 G CARBOHYDRATE; 34 MG SODIUM; 0 MG CHOLESTEROL.

1	large Spanish onion, peeled, quartered and sliced
2	tablespoons sugar
1	teaspoon olive or vegetable oil
1½	cups fresh cranberries
¼	cup fresh orange juice
1	teaspoon grated orange zest
1½	teaspoons balsamic vinegar
¼	teaspoon salt

Dried Pear & Cranberry Chutney

The dried fruits in this quick chutney readily absorb the sweet, sour and spicy chutney seasonings.

Combine dried pears, dried cranberries, cider vinegar, brown sugar, ginger, garlic, red-pepper flakes, peppercorns and orange zest with ¼ cup water in a heavy medium saucepan. Bring to a simmer, stirring. Cover and simmer over low heat, stirring occasionally, until the fruit is tender, about 10 minutes.

If the chutney has not thickened sufficiently, simmer it, uncovered, for a minute or two longer. Let cool, then discard the orange zest. (*The chutney can be stored, covered, in the refrigerator for up to 1 week.*)

Makes about 1½ cups.

35 CALORIES PER TABLESPOON: 0 G PROTEIN, 0 G FAT, 10 G CARBOHYDRATE; 2 MG SODIUM; 0 MG CHOLESTEROL.

6	ounces dried pears, coarsely chopped (1 cup)
½	cup dried cranberries (cranraisins)
½	cup cider vinegar
3	tablespoons brown sugar
2	tablespoons finely chopped fresh ginger
2	cloves garlic, finely chopped
½	teaspoon red-pepper flakes
½	teaspoon crushed black peppercorns
2	strips orange zest

Basic Barbecue Sauce

Great for chicken or pork tenderloin.

¾ cup strong brewed coffee

1 cup tomato catsup

¼ cup molasses

2 tablespoons orange juice

2 tablespoons cider vinegar

1 tablespoon Worcestershire sauce

2 teaspoons Dijon mustard

2 jalapeño or serrano chiles, pierced all over with a fork

Tabasco sauce to taste

Combine coffee, catsup, molasses, orange juice, cider vinegar, Worcestershire sauce, mustard and chiles in a medium heavy saucepan; bring to a simmer, stirring. Cook over low heat until slightly thickened, 10 to 15 minutes, stirring frequently. Let cool and discard the chiles. Add Tabasco sauce to taste.

Makes about 2 cups.

16 CALORIES PER TABLESPOON: 0 G PROTEIN, 0 G FAT, 4 G CARBOHYDRATE; 97 MG SODIUM; 0 MG CHOLESTEROL.

Papaya Salsa

To accompany grilled fish, try this perky salsa.

1 ripe papaya, peeled, seeded and coarsely chopped

1 small red bell pepper, cored, seeded and sliced into short, thin strips

1 small red onion, thinly sliced

6 tablespoons fresh lime juice

¼ cup pineapple juice

¼ cup chopped fresh cilantro

1 clove garlic, finely chopped

1 jalapeño pepper, finely chopped

Salt & coarsely ground black pepper to taste

In a large bowl, combine papaya, bell peppers, onions, lime juice, pineapple juice, cilantro, garlic and jalapeños; mix well. Taste and adjust seasonings with salt and pepper. (*The salsa will keep, covered, in the refrigerator for up to 8 hours.*)

Makes about 2½ cups.

7 CALORIES PER TABLESPOON: 0 G PROTEIN, 0 G FAT, 2 G CARBOHYDRATE; 5 MG SODIUM; 0 MG CHOLESTEROL.

Corn-Tomato Salsa

A great combination for a Fourth of July cookout.

Cook the corn in boiling water for 30 seconds; refresh under cold running water and cut off the kernels. (You should have about ¾ cup of kernels.) In a bowl, combine the corn with tomatoes, lime juice, cider vinegar, cilantro, chiles and salt and pepper. Mix well. (*The salsa is best served immediately, but may be made up to 4 hours in advance and stored, covered, in the refrigerator.*)

Makes about 2 cups.

5 CALORIES PER TABLESPOON: 0 G PROTEIN, 0 G FAT, 1 G CARBOHYDRATE; 3 MG SODIUM; 0 MG CHOLESTEROL.

1	ear of corn, husked
2	vine-ripened tomatoes, cored, seeded and chopped
2	tablespoons fresh lime juice
2	tablespoons cider vinegar
2	tablespoons chopped fresh cilantro
1-2	tablespoons finely chopped fresh red or green chile pepper
	Salt & freshly ground black pepper to taste

India Spice Marinade

Marinate seafood in this spice mix for 20 minutes to 1 hour, or chicken for as long as 8 hours.

In a small dry skillet, stir cumin, coriander and mustard seeds over medium heat until fragrant, about 2 minutes. Transfer to a spice grinder or mortar and pestle and grind to a fine powder. Add paprika, ground red pepper, salt and turmeric.

In a blender or food processor, combine yogurt, lime juice, onions, garlic and ginger. Blend until smooth. Add the spices and pulse to combine.

Makes about 1⅓ cups, enough to marinate 2 pounds of fish or chicken.

9 CALORIES PER TABLESPOON: 1 G PROTEIN, 0 G FAT, 2 G CARBOHYDRATE; 58 MG SODIUM; 1 MG CHOLESTEROL.

2	teaspoons cumin seeds
1	teaspoon coriander seeds
1	teaspoon mustard seeds
1	tablespoon paprika
½	teaspoon ground red pepper (cayenne)
½	teaspoon salt
½	teaspoon turmeric
½	cup nonfat plain yogurt
2	tablespoons fresh lime juice
1	small onion, chopped
4	cloves garlic, finely chopped
1	tablespoon chopped fresh ginger

CHAPTER 11

Breakfast&Brunch

Curried Vegetables with Eggs

For entertaining, this recipe can be multiplied easily.

2   teaspoons olive oil

1   large onion, chopped

1   tablespoon curry powder

10 ounces mushrooms, trimmed and
    sliced (3 cups sliced)

1   green bell pepper, seeded and
    diced

1   yellow summer squash or
    zucchini, trimmed and diced

1   14-ounce can whole tomatoes,
    with juices

⅛   teaspoon red-pepper flakes
    (optional)

1   tablespoon tomato paste
    Salt & freshly ground black
    pepper to taste

4   large eggs

4   slices French or Italian bread,
    toasted

Preheat oven to 400 degrees F. In a large nonstick skillet, heat oil over medium heat. Add onions and sauté until softened, 3 to 5 minutes. Stir in curry powder and cook, stirring, for 1 minute. Add mushrooms, green peppers and squash or zucchini; sauté until the mushrooms are limp and release their liquid. Add tomatoes and mash with a wooden spoon. Stir in red-pepper flakes, if using, and simmer, uncovered, for 10 minutes. Stir in tomato paste and season with salt and pepper. (*The recipe can be prepared ahead to this point and stored, covered, in the refrigerator for up to 2 days. Reheat before continuing.*)

Spread the vegetable mixture evenly over the bottom of a shallow 3-quart baking dish. Make 4 wells in the vegetable mixture and break an egg into each one. Season the eggs with salt and pepper. Bake for 12 to 15 minutes, or until the eggs are set. With a large spoon, gently transfer the eggs to plates and surround with the vegetable mixture. Serve with toasted bread.

Serves 4.

251 CALORIES PER SERVING: 13 G PROTEIN, 8 G FAT, 33 G CARBOHYDRATE;
420 MG SODIUM; 213 MG CHOLESTEROL.

Curried Vegetables with Eggs

Spinach & Feta Soufflé

Inspired by Greek spinach pie, spanakopita, *this soufflé is light but satisfying.*

2   tablespoons fine, dry, unseasoned breadcrumbs

8   cups fresh spinach (½ pound), stemmed and washed

1½   teaspoons vegetable oil, preferably canola oil

1   onion, finely chopped

1   clove garlic, finely chopped

1½   cups low-fat milk

⅓   cup cornstarch

2   large egg yolks

½   cup crumbled feta cheese (2 ounces)

2   tablespoons chopped fresh mint or dill

1   teaspoon salt

½   teaspoon freshly ground black pepper

6   large egg whites

Position rack in the lower third of the oven; preheat to 375 degrees F. Lightly oil a 2-quart soufflé dish or coat it with nonstick cooking spray. Sprinkle with breadcrumbs, tapping out excess.

Heat a large skillet over medium heat. Add spinach with the water still clinging to the leaves and cook, stirring, just until wilted. Transfer to a colander to drain. Squeeze out the excess liquid and chop.

Wipe out the skillet, add oil and heat over medium heat. Add onions and garlic; cook, stirring, until softened, about 5 minutes. Add the chopped spinach and cook, stirring, until heated through and quite dry, about 2 minutes. Set aside.

Heat 1 cup of the milk in a heavy saucepan until steaming. In a small bowl, stir cornstarch into the remaining ½ cup cold milk. Add to the hot milk and cook, whisking constantly, until thickened and smooth, 2 to 3 minutes. Remove from the heat and let cool slightly. Add egg yolks, one at a time, whisking until incorporated. Stir in the reserved spinach mixture, feta, mint or dill, ½ teaspoon salt and pepper. Set aside.

In a large mixing bowl, beat egg whites with an electric mixer on medium speed until foamy and opaque. Add the remaining ½ teaspoon salt; gradually increase the speed to high and beat until stiff (but not dry) peaks form.

Whisk about one-third of the beaten egg whites into the spinach mixture to lighten it. Using a rubber spatula, fold the spinach mixture back into the remaining whites. Turn into the prepared dish and smooth the top with a spatula.

Bake until puffed and the top feels firm to the touch, about 35 minutes. Serve immediately.

Serves 4.

240 CALORIES PER SERVING: 16 G PROTEIN, 9 G FAT, 25 G CARBOHYDRATE; 670 MG SODIUM; 123 MG CHOLESTEROL.

Good Egg Casserole

A very hearty dish with a surprisingly low amount of fat, this casserole makes enough for 12 people.

Position rack in the top third of the oven; preheat to 350 degrees F. Lightly oil a 9-by-13-inch baking dish or coat it with nonstick cooking spray.

In a large nonstick skillet over medium heat, cook sausage until no longer pink, breaking it up with a wooden spoon; transfer to a paper towel to drain, blotting the top with a second paper towel.

Wipe the skillet clean and add oil; heat over medium-high heat. Add potatoes and sauté until tender and browned, 10 to 12 minutes. (Reduce the heat if the potatoes are browning too quickly.) Let cool slightly.

In a large bowl, whisk together eggs and egg whites. Add cottage, Cheddar and Parmesan cheeses, chiles, flour, baking powder, salt and pepper and whisk to mix thoroughly. Add the cooked sausage, crumbling up any large pieces, and the potatoes; mix well. Pour into the prepared dish. Bake for 30 to 35 minutes, or until golden on top and set in the center.

Serves 12.

213 CALORIES PER SERVING: 19 G PROTEIN, 9 G FAT, 13 G CARBOHYDRATE; 857 MG SODIUM; 118 MG CHOLESTEROL.

½ pound bulk turkey sausage

1 teaspoon vegetable oil, preferably canola oil

3 medium Yukon Gold or red potatoes (1 pound), peeled, quartered and thinly sliced

5 large eggs

7 large egg whites

1 pint 1% cottage cheese, preferably small-curd

4 ounces sharp Cheddar cheese, grated (1¼ cups)

2 ounces Parmesan cheese, grated (1 cup)

2 4-ounce cans green chiles, drained and chopped

⅓ cup all-purpose white flour

1 teaspoon baking powder

½ teaspoon salt

½ teaspoon freshly ground black pepper

Tomato & Spinach Strata

This layered egg-cheese-bread dish has been around since the turn of the century, but has had many names over the years including Oven Fondue, Savory Cheese Pudding and even Christmas Morning Lifesaver. The name "strata" turned up in the '70s and is probably one cook's bit of whimsy that stuck. The strata is assembled and refrigerated overnight before it is baked.

TOMATO SAUCE

1½   teaspoons olive oil

1   onion, coarsely chopped

3   cloves garlic, finely chopped

2   28-ounce cans plum tomatoes, drained

1   bay leaf

½   teaspoon dried thyme or oregano

2   tablespoons chopped fresh parsley

Salt & freshly ground black pepper to taste

STRATA

1   tablespoon olive oil

2   onions, chopped

¾   pound mushrooms, trimmed and thinly sliced (4 cups)

½   teaspoon salt

½   teaspoon freshly ground black pepper

2   pounds nonfat cottage cheese

2   10-ounce packages chopped frozen spinach, thawed and squeezed dry, or 3 pounds fresh spinach, cooked, squeezed dry and chopped

¼   teaspoon freshly grated nutmeg

TO MAKE TOMATO SAUCE:

Heat olive oil in a large heavy (preferably nonstick) saucepan over medium heat. Add onions and cook, stirring, until softened, 3 to 5 minutes. Add garlic and stir 2 minutes longer. Add tomatoes, bay leaf and thyme or oregano. Cook over medium-high heat, stirring and breaking up the tomatoes well with a fork or wooden spoon, until thickened, 15 to 20 minutes. Remove the bay leaf. Stir in parsley and season with salt and pepper. Let cool. (*The sauce can be made ahead and stored, covered, in the refrigerator for up to 2 days.*)

TO MAKE STRATA:

Lightly brush two 8-by-12-inch or similar shallow 2-quart baking dishes with vegetable oil, or coat them with nonstick cooking spray. Heat 1½ teaspoons of the olive oil in a large nonstick skillet over medium-high heat. Add onions and sauté for 2 to 3 minutes. Lower the heat to medium and cook until the onions are softened but not browned, 3 to 5 minutes longer. Transfer the onions to a bowl.

Add the remaining 1½ teaspoons olive oil to the skillet; raise the heat to medium-high. Add mushrooms and sauté until the moisture has evaporated, 4 to 5 minutes. Transfer to the bowl with the onions and season the mixture with ¼ teaspoon of the salt and ¼ teaspoon of the pepper.

Line a medium bowl with a double thickness of cheesecloth and spoon cottage cheese into the center. Gather up the cheesecloth and squeeze; discard all the liquid from the cottage cheese. In the bowl, combine the pressed cottage cheese, spinach, nutmeg, the remaining ¼ teaspoon salt and ¼ teaspoon pepper.

Spoon about one-quarter of the tomato sauce into the bottom of one of the prepared baking dishes. Arrange one-quarter of the bread slices over the tomato sauce. Spoon half of the spinach mixture over the bread. Arrange another layer of bread over the spinach mixture. Scatter half of the onion-mushroom mixture over the bread. Top with half of the mozzarella cheese. Spoon another quarter of the tomato sauce over top. Repeat these steps in assembling the second strata.

In a small bowl, whisk together eggs, egg whites and milk. Pour half of the egg mixture slowly over each casserole, poking the bread gently with the tip of a knife until the mixture has been absorbed. Cover and refrigerate overnight.

Preheat oven to 375 degrees F. Bake the stratas, uncovered, for 40 minutes. Sprinkle with Parmesan and bake for 10 minutes longer, or until puffed and golden brown. Let stand for 10 minutes. Sprinkle with parsley, cut into squares and serve hot.

Serves 12.

375 CALORIES PER SERVING: 33 G PROTEIN, 8 G FAT, 43 G CARBOHYDRATE; 911 MG SODIUM; 90 MG CHOLESTEROL.

1	1-pound loaf best-quality Italian bread (preferably day-old), sliced into ¼-inch-thick slices
½	pound part-skim mozzarella cheese, thinly sliced
4	large eggs
4	large egg whites
2	cups skim milk
⅓	cup freshly grated Parmesan cheese
2	tablespoons chopped fresh parsley

Huevos Rancheros

*As the name implies, this dish makes a breakfast suitable for any cowboy, but for those with
a less physically demanding occupation, it is perfect for a hearty breakfast or brunch.*

2   teaspoons olive oil

1   7-ounce jar roasted red peppers,
    drained, rinsed and sliced

1   tomato, seeded and chopped

2   cloves garlic, finely chopped

1   15-ounce can black beans,
    drained and rinsed

1   tablespoon distilled white vinegar

3-5 dashes Tabasco sauce

2   tablespoons chopped fresh
    cilantro

    Salt & freshly ground black
    pepper to taste

2   corn tortillas

2   medium eggs

2   tablespoons prepared salsa

¼   cup grated Cheddar cheese

1   scallion, trimmed and chopped

Preheat the broiler. Heat 1 teaspoon of the oil in a nonstick
skillet over medium heat. Add red peppers, tomatoes and garlic;
cook, stirring, until the tomatoes have softened, about 4 minutes. Add black beans, vinegar and Tabasco; cook, stirring, for
3 minutes. Stir in cilantro and season with salt and pepper.

Soften tortillas by heating them directly on a stovetop burner
for about 30 seconds, turning frequently. Place the tortillas side
by side on a heatproof dish. Spoon half of the bean mixture
over each tortilla.

Wipe out the skillet, brush with the remaining 1 teaspoon oil
and heat over medium heat. Crack eggs into the skillet and
break the yolks with a fork. Cook over medium heat until the
whites are set, about 1 minute. Flip the eggs and cook until desired doneness. Place an egg on each tortilla. Top with salsa and
cheese and broil until the cheese melts. Garnish with scallions
and serve immediately.

Serves 2.

402 CALORIES PER SERVING: 21 G PROTEIN, 17 G FAT, 59 G CARBOHYDRATE;
273 MG SODIUM; 228 MG CHOLESTEROL.

Artichoke & Swiss Chard Pie

Swiss chard and artichokes are the perfect pairing in this phyllo pie.

FILLING

2   lemons, cut in half

8   artichokes

1   bunch Swiss chard (1½ pounds),
    tough stems removed, washed

TO MAKE FILLING:

Squeeze the juice of 3 lemon halves into a big bowl of cold
water; keep the remaining half handy. Peel away the outer leaves
of the artichokes, snapping them off at the base, until you reach
the pale yellow leaves with darker green tops. Slice off the green

tops. Rub each artichoke with the lemon half. With a paring knife, trim the base where you snapped off the leaves, removing any fibrous green portions. Rub with the lemon half. Trim the bottom ¼ inch off the stem and pare away the tough outer skin. Rub with the lemon half. With a melon baller or knife, remove the fuzzy choke. Drop the trimmed artichokes into the lemon water as you work.

Set a large pot over medium heat. Add Swiss chard with water still clinging to the leaves and cook, stirring, until wilted, about 2 minutes. Add 1 teaspoon salt, cover, and cook the chard until tender, about 2 minutes more. Drain well in a colander, pressing out any excess moisture. Coarsely chop and set aside.

Cut the trimmed artichokes lengthwise into thin wedges. Heat oil in a large nonstick skillet over medium-high heat. Add onions and the artichokes; cook, stirring, until the artichokes begin to soften, about 5 minutes. Reduce the heat to medium and add the reserved chard. Cover and cook until the mixture becomes quite dry, about 3 minutes. Remove from the heat and set aside.

In a small bowl, soak bread slices in milk. Squeeze the excess milk from the bread and shred into the artichoke mixture. Add marjoram and mix well. Let cool slightly. Stir in Parmesan and season with salt and pepper; set aside. (*The filling can be made up to a day ahead and stored, covered, in the refrigerator.*)

TO PREPARE CRUST:

Preheat oven to 350 degrees F. Lightly oil a 10-inch springform pan or coat it with nonstick cooking spray.

In a small bowl, whisk together egg whites, oil and salt. Set aside. Unwrap sheets of phyllo and lay one sheet in the prepared springform pan so that the edges hang over the sides. (Cover the remaining phyllo with a damp kitchen towel.) With a pastry brush, brush the sheet with egg-white mixture. Sprinkle with about 1 teaspoon of the breadcrumbs. Lay another sheet of phyllo, at a 90-degree angle, over the first. Brush with egg-white mixture and sprinkle with another 1 teaspoon of the breadcrumbs. Repeat with 3 more sheets of phyllo. Spread the reserved filling evenly over the phyllo layer. Top with 2 additional

1 teaspoon salt
2 teaspoons olive oil
1 onion, chopped
2 ½-inch-thick slices day-old Italian bread, crusts removed
⅓ cup skim milk
½ teaspoon dried marjoram
¾ cup freshly grated Parmesan cheese
   Salt & freshly ground black pepper to taste

CRUST

2 large egg whites
3 tablespoons olive oil
¼ teaspoon salt
8 sheets phyllo pastry (14x18 inches)
2 tablespoons (approximately) fine, dry, unseasoned breadcrumbs

phyllo layers, brushing with egg-white mixture and sprinkling with breadcrumbs. Lay the remaining phyllo sheet on top. With scissors, trim the excess phyllo at the top of the pan. Press the phyllo edges lightly down into the sides of the pan. Brush the top of the pie with egg-white mixture.

Bake for 30 to 35 minutes, or until the phyllo is browned and the filling is heated through. Serve hot or at room temperature.

Serves 8.

257 CALORIES PER SERVING: 14 G PROTEIN, 10 G FAT, 34 G CARBOHYDRATE; 893 MG SODIUM; 8 MG CHOLESTEROL.

Pumpkin Waffles

Brush the waffle iron lightly with oil to prevent sticking and give the waffles a crisp exterior.

1½ cups all-purpose white flour
1½ teaspoons baking powder
 ½ teaspoon ground cinnamon
 ½ teaspoon baking soda
 ½ teaspoon salt
 ¼ teaspoon ground cloves
1¼ cups buttermilk
 ¾ cup canned pumpkin puree
 2 large eggs, separated
 2 tablespoons brown sugar
 1 tablespoon vegetable oil, preferably canola oil, plus extra for oiling waffle iron

In a large bowl, stir together flour, baking powder, cinnamon, baking soda, salt and cloves.

In a separate bowl, whisk together buttermilk, pumpkin puree, egg yolks, brown sugar and oil until well blended. Add the wet ingredients to the dry ingredients and fold in just until moistened.

Beat egg whites until stiff but not dry. Fold into the pumpkin mixture. (Do not overmix.)

Preheat waffle iron. Lightly oil it and cook waffles, filling the waffle iron about two-thirds full each time.

Serves 4.

314 CALORIES PER SERVING: 11 G PROTEIN, 7 G FAT, 51 G CARBOHYDRATE; 635 MG SODIUM; 109 MG CHOLESTEROL.

Overnight French Toast with Cinnamon Syrup

The beauty of this dish is that you assemble it in the evening and quickly cook it the following morning.

TO PREPARE FRENCH TOAST:

In a medium bowl, whisk together egg, egg whites, milk, sugar, vanilla, cinnamon and baking powder until well blended.

Place bread slices in a large, shallow baking dish and pour the egg mixture over the top; turn to coat evenly. Press a piece of wax paper directly on the bread to cover it, then cover dish with plastic wrap. Refrigerate overnight.

TO MAKE CINNAMON SYRUP:

In a small saucepan, stir together sugar, corn syrup, cinnamon and ¼ cup water. Bring the mixture to a boil over medium-high heat, stirring constantly. Boil for 2 minutes. Remove from the heat and stir in evaporated skim milk. Let cool; transfer to a small pitcher. (*The syrup can be stored, covered, in the refrigerator for up to 1 week. If desired, warm before serving.*)

TO COOK FRENCH TOAST:

Heat 1 teaspoon of the oil and ½ teaspoon of the butter in a 12-inch nonstick skillet over medium-high heat. Add four of the soaked bread slices to the pan and cook until golden on both sides, 2 to 3 minutes per side. Transfer the toast to a platter and keep warm in a warm oven. Cook the remaining slices in the same manner, using the remaining 1 teaspoon oil and ½ teaspoon butter. Serve with cinnamon syrup.

Serves 4.

432 CALORIES PER SERVING: 12 G PROTEIN, 5 G FAT, 84 G CARBOHYDRATE; 423 MG SODIUM; 57 MG CHOLESTEROL.

1 large egg
2 large egg whites
¾ cup skim milk
2 tablespoons sugar
1 teaspoon pure vanilla extract
¼ teaspoon ground cinnamon
⅛ teaspoon baking powder
8 ½-inch-thick slices Italian bread
2 teaspoons vegetable oil, preferably canola oil
1 teaspoon butter

CINNAMON SYRUP

½ cup sugar
¼ cup dark corn syrup
¼ teaspoon ground cinnamon
¼ cup evaporated skim milk

Crackle-Topped Rhubarb Coffee Cake

Chunks of rhubarb accent this moist, tender cake.

CAKE

- 2 cups all-purpose white flour
- 1 cup sugar
- 4 teaspoons baking powder
- 1 teaspoon ground cinnamon
- ½ teaspoon salt
- 1 large egg
- 1 cup buttermilk
- ¼ cup vegetable oil, preferably canola oil
- 2 teaspoons pure vanilla extract
- ½ pound rhubarb, trimmed and cut into ½-inch pieces (2 cups)

TOPPING

- ¼ cup sugar
- ½ teaspoon ground cinnamon

TO MAKE CAKE:

Preheat oven to 350 degrees F. Lightly oil an 8-inch square baking pan or coat it with nonstick cooking spray. Sift flour, sugar, baking powder, cinnamon and salt into a medium bowl.

In a large bowl, whisk together egg, buttermilk, oil and vanilla. Add the flour mixture and stir with a rubber spatula or wooden spoon just to blend. Stir in rhubarb. Turn the batter into the prepared pan, spreading evenly.

TO MAKE TOPPING & BAKE CAKE:

In a small bowl, stir together sugar and cinnamon. Sprinkle evenly over the top of the cake. Bake for 45 to 50 minutes, or until the top is brown and crackled and a cake tester inserted in the center comes out clean. Let the cake cool in the pan on a wire rack for 15 minutes. Serve warm.

Serves 9.

294 CALORIES PER SERVING: 5 G PROTEIN, 7 G FAT, 53 G CARBOHYDRATE; 303 MG SODIUM; 25 MG CHOLESTEROL.

Cranberry Streusel Coffee Cake

Cake flour produces a tender crumb for this easy treat.

STREUSEL

- ½ cup packed brown sugar
- ⅔ cup all-purpose white flour
- ½ teaspoon ground cinnamon
- 2 tablespoons frozen apple-juice concentrate, thawed
- 1 tablespoon vegetable oil, preferably canola oil

TO MAKE STREUSEL:

In a bowl, stir together brown sugar, flour and cinnamon. Sprinkle in apple-juice concentrate and oil. Blend with a fork or your fingers until crumbly. Set aside.

TO MAKE CAKE:

In a food processor or blender, puree pears. Transfer to a wide saucepan and cook over medium-low heat, stirring almost constantly, until reduced to ½ cup, 8 to 10 minutes. Transfer to a large bowl and let cool completely.

Preheat oven to 350 degrees F. Lightly oil a 9-by-13-inch baking dish or coat it with nonstick cooking spray.

In a small saucepan, melt butter over medium heat. Cook, swirling the pan, until the butter turns a light nutty brown, about 60 seconds. Whisk into the pear puree. Add sugar, egg, egg white, oil and vanilla, whisking until smooth.

Sift together flour, baking powder, baking soda and salt; add to the pear mixture alternately with yogurt or sour cream.

Spread half of the batter in the bottom of the prepared pan. Top with cranberries, then with the remaining batter. Sprinkle the streusel over the top. Bake for 40 to 45 minutes, or until a cake tester inserted in the center comes out clean. Serve warm.

Serves 12.

284 CALORIES PER SERVING: 5 G PROTEIN, 4 G FAT, 59 G CARBOHYDRATE; 225 MG SODIUM; 21 MG CHOLESTEROL.

CAKE

- 1 16-ounce can pears packed in light syrup, drained
- 1 tablespoon butter
- 1 cup sugar
- 1 large egg
- 1 large egg white
- 1 tablespoon vegetable oil, preferably canola oil
- 1 tablespoon pure vanilla extract
- 2¼ cups cake flour (unsifted)
- 1 teaspoon baking powder
- 1 teaspoon baking soda
- ½ teaspoon salt
- 1 cup nonfat plain yogurt or nonfat sour cream
- 1 12-ounce package fresh cranberries (3 cups)

Cranberry Streusel Coffee Cake

Apple Jonnycake

*Cornmeal pancakes, also known as jonnycakes, were a staple at all meals in Colonial times.
In this takeoff, a pan of corn bread is turned upside down to reveal a layer of maple syrup-glazed apples.
Serve this for breakfast or brunch. For best results, choose apples that hold their shape during cooking.*

APPLE TOPPING

1 tablespoon unsalted butter

2 tablespoons pure maple syrup

2 large apples, such as Golden
Delicious or Newtown Pippin,
peeled, cored and sliced ¼ inch
thick

BUTTERMILK CORN BREAD

¾ cup cornmeal

¾ cup all-purpose white flour

1 teaspoon baking powder

½ teaspoon salt

¼ teaspoon baking soda

1 large egg, lightly beaten

1 cup buttermilk, or ½ cup nonfat
plain yogurt and ½ cup skim
milk

¼ cup pure maple syrup, plus more
for serving, if desired

2 tablespoons vegetable oil,
preferably canola oil

TO MAKE TOPPING:

Preheat oven to 375 degrees F. In a 10-inch, heavy, ovenproof skillet (cast iron is traditional and good), heat butter and maple syrup over medium-high heat. Add apple slices and sauté, tossing occasionally, until softened slightly, 5 to 7 minutes. Remove the pan from the heat. Use two spoons to arrange the apple slices in a neat pattern in the skillet, fanning them out from the center.

TO MAKE CORN BREAD:

In a mixing bowl, combine cornmeal, flour, baking powder, salt and baking soda. In a separate bowl, whisk together egg, buttermilk (or yogurt and skim milk), maple syrup and oil. Make a well in the center of the dry ingredients, pour in the egg mixture and stir together just until combined.

Spread the batter gently over the apples. Bake for 30 to 35 minutes, or until a knife inserted in the center of the corn bread comes out clean. Cool in the skillet on a wire rack for about 5 minutes. Invert onto a serving platter, rearranging any apples that stick to the pan. Serve immediately, passing additional maple syrup at the table, if you like.

Serves 8.

211 CALORIES PER SERVING: 4 G PROTEIN, 6 G FAT, 36 G CARBOHYDRATE; 260 MG SODIUM; 32 MG CHOLESTEROL.

Baked Pancake with Apple-Raspberry Compote

Really an overgrown popover, this baked pancake makes an easy, delicious breakfast for company.

TO MAKE APPLE-RASPBERRY COMPOTE:

In a large nonstick skillet, melt butter over medium heat. Add apples and sauté for 2 minutes. Stir in sugar, apple cider or apple juice and lemon juice. Reduce the heat to low and simmer, stirring occasionally, until the apples are tender but still hold their shape, 5 to 7 minutes. (*The compote can be prepared ahead to this point and stored, covered, in the refrigerator for up to 2 days. Warm gently before continuing.*) Stir in raspberries.

TO MAKE PANCAKE:

Preheat oven to 425 degrees F. Place an ovenproof 10-inch nonstick skillet in the oven to heat for 10 to 15 minutes.

In a large bowl, whisk eggs and egg whites. Add flour, sugar and salt and whisk until smooth. Gradually whisk in milk and vanilla. Pour into the hot skillet and bake for 15 to 20 minutes, or until the pancake is puffed and golden. Loosen the edges and slide the pancake onto a serving platter. Dust with confectioners' sugar and serve with apple-raspberry compote.

Serves 6.

260 CALORIES PER SERVING: 7 G PROTEIN, 5 G FAT, 49 G CARBOHYDRATE; 175 MG SODIUM; 112 MG CHOLESTEROL.

APPLE-RASPBERRY COMPOTE

- 2 teaspoons butter
- 4 flavorful apples, such as McIntosh, peeled, cored and thinly sliced
- ½ cup sugar
- ¼ cup apple cider or apple juice
- 2 tablespoons fresh lemon juice
- 1 cup fresh raspberries

PANCAKE

- 3 large eggs
- 2 large egg whites
- ½ cup all-purpose white flour
- 2 tablespoons sugar
- ¼ teaspoon salt
- 1 cup low-fat milk
- 2 teaspoons pure vanilla extract
  Confectioners' sugar for dusting

Citrus Platter with Frosted Rosemary Sprigs

A very festive presentation. The fruit is a light, healthful counterpoint to an egg casserole, such as the Tomato & Spinach Strata (page 136). Pumpkin Gingerbread Muffins (page 162) complete the brunch.

7-8   oranges, preferably blood oranges

12   tangerines or tangelos

1   cup sugar

3   pink or ruby-red grapefruit

2   tablespoons Grand Marnier or Cointreau (optional)

FROSTED ROSEMARY SPRIG GARNISH

4-5   fresh rosemary sprigs
      Approximately ¼ cup sugar
      Approximately ¼ cup fresh lemon juice

Scrub 3 of the oranges and 2 of the tangerines or tangelos. With a zester, remove the zest in long thin strips. (If you do not have a zester, use a vegetable peeler to remove strips of zest, then cut them into fine julienne with a chef's knife.) Put the zest in a small saucepan and add cold water to cover; bring to a boil over high heat and blanch for 4 minutes. Drain.

In a heavy saucepan, combine sugar with 1½ cups water and bring to a boil, stirring to dissolve the sugar. Add the blanched zest and simmer gently until translucent, 8 to 10 minutes. Remove from the heat and let the zest cool in the syrup. (*The candied zest in syrup can be stored, covered, in the refrigerator for up to 2 days.*)

Working over a bowl to catch the juices, use a sharp paring knife to cut the peel and white pith from all of the citrus fruits, discarding the peels. Slice the fruits into rounds about ⅜ inch thick, removing any seeds, and arrange the fruit on a serving platter. Pour the collected juices over the fruit. Sprinkle with Grand Marnier or Cointreau, if using. Cover loosely with plastic wrap and refrigerate for at least 2 hours. (*The fruit platter and the candied zest in syrup can be prepared ahead and stored separately, covered, in the refrigerator overnight.*)

TO MAKE FROSTED ROSEMARY SPRIG GARNISH:

Leave rosemary sprigs whole or break them into 2-inch lengths. Spread sugar on a plate. Dip each rosemary sprig in lemon juice, then dredge in the sugar, turning it over gently with 2 forks until the sprigs are coated. Place on a sheet of wax paper.

Just before serving time, drain the candied zest, reserving the syrup. Scatter the zest over the fruit and drizzle a little of the syrup over the top. Garnish with the frosted rosemary sprigs.

Serves 12.

151 CALORIES PER SERVING: 2 G PROTEIN, 0 G FAT, 39 G CARBOHYDRATE; 1 MG SODIUM; 0 MG CHOLESTEROL.

Citrus Platter with Frosted Rosemary Sprigs and Pumpkin Gingerbread Muffins (page 162)

Layered Mango Fruit Mélange

*The velvety texture and brilliant color of mango puree turn even simple fruit desserts
into something special. For a different approach, cut long, thin slices of pineapple and mango,
arrange on the plate with berries, then drizzle with mango puree.*

2 medium-large mangoes (about 1 pound each), cubed

¼ cup fresh orange juice

About 3 tablespoons sugar

Fresh lime juice

2 pints strawberries, rinsed and hulled

1 pineapple, peeled, cored and cut into thin wedges (about 3 cups)

1 tablespoon rum or orange liqueur

¼ teaspoon pure vanilla extract

3 tablespoons shredded coconut, toasted (optional)

Combine half of the cubed mango with orange juice in a food processor or blender and process until smooth. Add about 1 tablespoon of the sugar and lime juice to taste and continue processing to dissolve the sugar, about 30 seconds.

Chop the remaining mango coarsely and set aside. Reserve several strawberries for garnish and thinly slice the remainder. Sprinkle the sliced berries with 1 tablespoon of the sugar and set aside. Toss pineapple wedges with the remaining 1 tablespoon sugar, rum or orange liqueur, and vanilla.

In a 1½-quart glass dish, preferably straight-sided, layer the sliced strawberries, then the chopped mango, followed by the pineapple. Spoon the mango puree evenly over the top. Cover and refrigerate until serving time, not more than several hours.

To serve, sprinkle with coconut, if desired, and garnish with the reserved strawberries.

Serves 6.

146 CALORIES PER SERVING: 1 G PROTEIN, 1 G FAT, 35 G CARBOHYDRATE; 3 MG SODIUM; 0 MG CHOLESTEROL.

Mango-Buttermilk *Batido*

Mangoes turn into a smooth breakfast drink, snack or light dessert when pureed. This fruity, creamy quaff is based on the Hispanic batido, a fresh fruit shake. For fullest flavor, refrigerate for several hours.

In a food processor or blender, puree mango with maple syrup and nutmeg or cinnamon. Add 1 cup of the buttermilk and 4 ice cubes and process until smooth. Taste and add more maple syrup and/or citrus juice, if desired. With the motor running, gradually add more buttermilk to obtain the desired consistency. Transfer to a pitcher and chill for several hours for a richer flavor or serve the frothy mixture immediately. Dust with additional nutmeg or cinnamon, if desired.

Makes about 3½ cups, serves 4.

98 CALORIES PER SERVING: 3 G PROTEIN, 1 G FAT, 21 G CARBOHYDRATE; 108 MG SODIUM; 3 MG CHOLESTEROL.

1	medium-large mango (about 1 pound), cubed
2	tablespoons pure maple syrup, plus more to taste
	Pinch of freshly grated nutmeg or ground cinnamon
1-1½	cups buttermilk
	Fresh orange juice or lemon juice to taste

Cantaloupe Smoothie

If on a hurried morning you have nothing but this smoothie, you will still be doing your body a favor. The drink packs a powerful punch of potassium, calcium, vitamin C and beta carotene.

Place unpeeled banana in the freezer overnight or for up to 3 months. Remove the banana from the freezer and let it sit for 2 minutes, or until the skin begins to soften. With a paring knife, remove the skin. (Don't worry if a little fiber remains.) Cut the banana into chunks and put in a blender or food processor. Add cantaloupe, yogurt, dry milk, orange-juice concentrate, honey and vanilla. Blend until smooth.

Serves 1.

427 CALORIES PER SERVING: 12 G PROTEIN, 1 G FAT, 86 G CARBOHYDRATE; 290 MG SODIUM; 8 MG CHOLESTEROL.

1	ripe banana
¼	ripe cantaloupe, seeded and cut into chunks
½	cup nonfat or low-fat plain yogurt
2	tablespoons nonfat dry milk powder
1½	tablespoons orange-juice concentrate
2	teaspoons honey
½	teaspoon pure vanilla extract

CHAPTER 12

Breads, Muffins & Biscuits

Rum-Raisin Rolls

These make a great contribution to a potluck, though everyone will complain that you should have made more.

2	cups raisins
½	cup dark rum
1½	cups skim milk
½	cup packed dark brown sugar
2	teaspoons active dry yeast
8-9	cups unbleached all-purpose or bread flour
1	tablespoon salt
½	cup whole-wheat flour
1	large egg white

In a saucepan, combine raisins and rum; gently warm over low heat, stirring. Transfer to a bowl, cover and set aside to soak for at least 2 hours or overnight.

Meanwhile, in another saucepan, heat milk until steaming. Pour into a large bowl, add brown sugar and stir. Add 1½ cups cold water and cool to lukewarm. Sprinkle yeast over the milk mixture and stir until it has dissolved.

One cup at a time, stir in 4 cups of the white flour. Stir the batter 100 times in the same direction (for 1 minute). Cover with plastic wrap and let stand for 30 minutes or up to 2 hours.

Uncover, sprinkle with the rum-soaked raisins and salt; stir gently. Stir in whole-wheat flour. One cup at a time, mix in the remaining white flour until the dough becomes too difficult to stir. Turn the dough onto a well-floured work surface and knead, gradually incorporating more flour as necessary to prevent sticking, until smooth and slightly elastic, about 8 minutes.

Place the dough in a large, oiled bowl, turn to coat, and cover with plastic wrap. Let rise until doubled in volume, 2 to 3 hours or as long as 8 hours.

Lightly oil a 12-by-18-inch baking sheet or 2 smaller sheets that will fit side by side in your oven.

Rum-Raisin Rolls

Gently punch down the dough and transfer to a lightly floured work surface. With a sharp knife, cut the dough into 2 equal pieces, then cut each in 2 again. Cover 3 of these with plastic wrap and set aside. Cut the remaining piece into 8 equal pieces.

Cup the palm of your hand over one piece and gently press it downward. Keeping pressure downward, begin moving the dough clockwise 10 to 15 times in a short, circular motion. Place on the baking sheet, rounded-side up. Repeat with remaining dough, placing rolls ½ inch apart on the baking sheet. Keep the rolls covered with plastic wrap as you work. Cover and let rise until almost doubled in volume, about 45 minutes.

Meanwhile, position rack in the upper third of the oven; preheat to 400 degrees F. In a small bowl, whisk the egg white with 1 tablespoon water. Brush rolls with the egg-white mixture just before placing in the oven. Bake until golden brown and the bottoms sound hollow when tapped, 20 to 25 minutes. Transfer the rolls to a wire rack to cool slightly.

Makes 32 rolls.

173 CALORIES PER ROLL: 4 G PROTEIN, 0 G FAT, 37 G CARBOHYDRATE; 210 MG SODIUM; 1 MG CHOLESTEROL.

Potato-Buttermilk Bread

Potato breads tend to be light, but moist and slightly sweet, and they are good keepers.

1 **pound potatoes (4 medium), peeled and coarsely chopped**

1 **cup buttermilk**

1 **teaspoon sugar**

1 **teaspoon active dry yeast**

4 **cups whole-wheat flour**

1½ **tablespoons salt**

5-6 **cups unbleached all-purpose or bread flour**

Place potatoes in a medium saucepan with 1 cup water. Cover and bring to a boil. Reduce heat to low and cook, covered, until potatoes are soft, about 10 minutes. Transfer potatoes and cooking liquid to a blender or food processor and puree. You should have 3 cups of puree. (Add water if necessary to make 3 cups.) Transfer the puree to a large bowl. Stir in buttermilk and let cool to lukewarm.

In a measuring cup or small bowl, stir together 1 cup lukewarm water and sugar. Sprinkle with yeast and stir until it has dissolved, about 5 minutes. Stir into the potato mixture.

One cup at a time, mix in whole-wheat flour. Stir 100 times in the same direction (for 1 minute) to properly develop the gluten. Cover with plastic wrap and let stand for 30 minutes or up to 2 hours.

Uncover, sprinkle with salt, and stir gently. One cup at a time, stir in white flour until the dough becomes too difficult to stir. Turn the dough onto a well-floured work surface and knead, gradually incorporating more flour as necessary to prevent sticking, until the dough becomes smooth and slightly elastic, about 10 minutes. (The dough will feel quite soft and sticky at first because of the potatoes.)

Place the dough in a large, oiled bowl, turn to coat, and cover with plastic wrap. Let rise until doubled in volume, 2 to 3 hours.

Lightly oil a large baking sheet. Gently punch down the dough. Transfer to a lightly floured work surface and cut into two equal pieces. Working with one piece at a time, knead the dough briefly, then shape into a high, round mound about 8 inches in diameter. Repeat with the other piece of dough. Place the dough mounds on the baking sheet, leaving ½ inch between the loaves and the rim and 1 inch between the loaves. Generously dust the top of each loaf with flour. Cover with plastic wrap and let rise until almost doubled, about 30 minutes.

Meanwhile, position rack in the lower third of the oven; preheat to 400 degrees F.

Using a thin, sharp knife, slash the tops of the loaves in a crisscross pattern, making two ¾-inch-deep parallel slashes 2 inches apart in each direction. Use a spritzer to liberally mist the loaves with water just before placing in the oven. Bake for 5 minutes. Lower heat to 375 degrees F and bake until the loaves are golden and sound hollow when tapped on the bottom, another 35 to 40 minutes. Transfer the loaves to wire racks to cool.

Makes 2 loaves, about 32 slices.

135 CALORIES PER SLICE: 5 G PROTEIN, 1 G FAT, 29 G CARBOHYDRATE; 310 MG SODIUM; 1 MG CHOLESTEROL.

Slow-Rise Family Loaf

This bread uses very little yeast and should be left to rise overnight. The long rise gives the dough time to sour slightly. The bread has a flavorful, feather-light crumb dotted with flecks of rye flour, and the crust is firm and toothsome.

1	teaspoon sugar
½	teaspoon active dry yeast
7½-8½	cups unbleached all-purpose or bread flour
1	cup rye flour
1	tablespoon salt
2	tablespoons sesame seeds

In a large bowl, stir together 3 cups lukewarm water and sugar. Sprinkle with yeast and stir until dissolved. One cup at a time, mix in 3 cups of the white flour and the rye flour. Stir the batter 100 times in the same direction (for 1 minute) to properly develop the gluten. Cover with plastic wrap and let stand for 30 minutes or up to 2 hours.

Uncover, sprinkle with salt and stir gently. One cup at a time, stir in the remaining white flour until the dough becomes too difficult to stir. Turn the dough out onto a well-floured work surface and knead, gradually incorporating more flour as necessary to prevent sticking, until the dough is smooth and slightly elastic, about 10 minutes.

Place the dough in a large, oiled bowl, turn to coat, and cover with plastic wrap. Let rise until doubled in volume, 8 to 12 hours.

Lightly oil a large baking sheet, sprinkle with 1 tablespoon of the sesame seeds and set aside.

Gently punch down the dough and transfer to a lightly floured work surface. Knead briefly, then press the dough into a rectangle about ½ inch thick.

Starting at one long side, tightly roll up the dough to form a loaf about 16 to 18 inches long. Pinch the ends and all along the seam to seal. (*Alternatively, divide the dough in half to make two ½-inch-thick rectangles. Then form into two 8- to 9-inch loaves.*) Place the loaf or loaves on the baking sheet, seam-side down. Cover with plastic wrap and let rise until almost doubled, 30 to 45 minutes.

Meanwhile, position rack in the lower third of the oven; preheat to 400 degrees F.

Sprinkle the bread with the remaining 1 tablespoon sesame seeds, and with a thin, very sharp or serrated knife, make several parallel diagonal slashes across the top. Use a spritzer to liberally mist the bread with water before placing in the oven.

Bake for 10 minutes. Lower the heat to 375 degrees F and bake until the bread sounds hollow when tapped on the bottom, 25 to 35 minutes for the smaller loaves, or 30 to 40 minutes for the larger loaf. Transfer the bread to a wire rack to cool.

Makes 1 large or 2 smaller loaves, about 36 slices.

110 CALORIES PER SLICE: 3 G PROTEIN, 1 G FAT, 23 G CARBOHYDRATE; 178 MG SODIUM; 0 MG CHOLESTEROL.

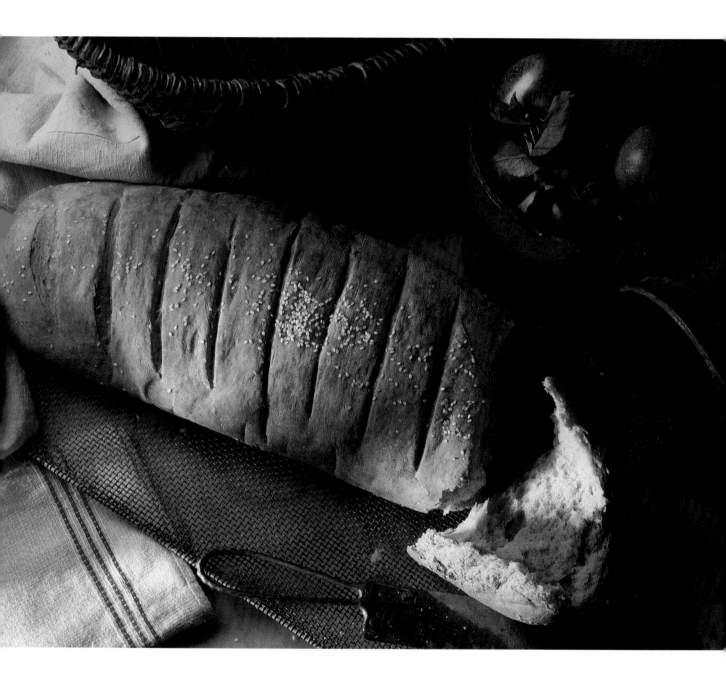

Crusty Rolls

With their flour-dusted tops, these rolls have an appealing rustic look.

1　teaspoon brown sugar

1　package active dry yeast

5½　cups (approximately) unbleached all-purpose or bread flour

¼　cup nonfat dry milk

1　tablespoon salt

　　Cornmeal for dusting baking sheets

In a large mixing bowl, combine 2½ cups lukewarm water and brown sugar; sprinkle yeast on top and let stand for 5 minutes. Gradually stir in 3 cups of the flour, stirring in the same direction for 3 minutes. Stir in nonfat dry milk and salt. Then gradually add more flour until the dough is too difficult to stir.

Turn the dough out onto a lightly floured surface and knead, gradually incorporating more flour as needed to prevent sticking, until smooth and elastic, about 10 minutes.

Place the dough in a lightly oiled bowl, turn to coat, and cover with plastic wrap. Let rise until almost tripled in volume, 2½ to 3 hours. Punch the dough down; cover and let rise until doubled, about 1½ hours.

Lightly oil 2 baking sheets; sprinkle with cornmeal. Punch the dough down, turn out onto a lightly floured surface and knead into a ball. Divide the dough into 16 portions. Shape each portion into a ball, then roll to make a slight oval. Place the rolls at least 2 inches apart on the prepared baking sheets. Sprinkle the rolls with flour and rub it gently over the surfaces. Cover with a towel and let rise until almost doubled, about 1 hour.

Thirty minutes before baking, place a baking stone or an inverted baking sheet on the center rack of a cold oven. Place a metal cake pan on the bottom rack; preheat to 425 degrees F. Just before baking, pour 1 cup water into the cake pan. Working with one batch at a time, cut a ¼-inch-deep slash with a serrated knife across the top of each roll. Place the baking sheet on the baking stone or inverted baking sheet and bake for 15 to 20 minutes, or until the rolls are golden brown and sound hollow when tapped. Transfer to a wire rack and let cool. Add more water to the cake pan, slash the remaining rolls, and bake.

Makes 16 rolls.

163 CALORIES PER SERVING: 5 G PROTEIN, 0 G FAT, 34 G CARBOHYDRATE; 406 MG SODIUM; 1 MG CHOLESTEROL.

Round Italian Bread (*Pagnotta*)

This old-fashioned loaf was originally made with rendered pork or chicken fat; today's version uses olive oil.

In a glass measuring cup, stir together ¼ cup lukewarm water, yeast, ¼ cup of the white flour and sugar. Let stand for about 20 minutes, or until bubbly.

In a large bowl, stir together the remaining 2¼ cups white flour, whole-wheat flour and salt. Add the yeast mixture, ¾ cup lukewarm water and oil. Stir with a wooden spoon until the ingredients come together. The dough should be medium-soft but not sticky. Adjust the consistency with more water or flour as needed. Turn out onto a floured surface and knead for 8 to 10 minutes, or until the dough is smooth and elastic.

Place the dough in a lightly oiled bowl, turning the dough over to coat with oil. Cover with plastic wrap and let rise in a draft-free place for 1 to 1½ hours, or until doubled in bulk. (*You can also let the dough rise overnight in the refrigerator.*)

Punch the dough down and form into a ball. Place on a lightly oiled baking sheet, cover with plastic wrap and let rise in a draft-free place for about 1 hour, or until almost doubled in bulk.

Preheat oven to 375 degrees F. With a sharp knife, cut 4 shallow slashes in the surface of the loaf, forming a crisscross pattern. Brush the loaf lightly with cold water and bake for about 40 minutes, or until the top is golden and the bottom sounds hollow when tapped. Transfer to a rack and let cool completely before slicing.

Makes one 1½-pound loaf, about 12 slices.

133 CALORIES PER SLICE: 4 G PROTEIN, 2 G FAT, 26 G CARBOHYDRATE; 356 MG SODIUM; 0 MG CHOLESTEROL.

1½	teaspoons active dry yeast
2½	cups unbleached all-purpose or bread flour
1	teaspoon sugar
¾	cup whole-wheat flour
2	teaspoons salt, preferably kosher
1	tablespoon olive oil

Whole-Wheat Walnut Bread

When working with an entirely whole-wheat bread, remember to knead well—
a good dough will require a full 10 minutes.

2 tablespoons brown sugar, honey or malt syrup

1 teaspoon active dry yeast

4-5 cups whole-wheat flour

2 teaspoons salt

1 tablespoon walnut or olive oil

¾ cup chopped walnuts or walnut pieces (3 ounces)

In a large bowl, stir together 2 cups lukewarm water and brown sugar, honey or malt syrup. Sprinkle with yeast and stir until it has dissolved. Gradually mix in 2½ cups of the flour. Stir the batter 100 times in the same direction (for 1 minute). Cover with plastic wrap and let stand for 30 minutes or up to 2 hours.

Uncover, sprinkle with salt and stir gently. Stir in oil. Then stir in the remaining flour, ½ cup at a time, until the dough becomes too difficult to stir. Turn the dough out onto a well-floured work surface and knead, gradually incorporating more flour as necessary to prevent sticking, until the dough is smooth and slightly elastic, 10 to 12 minutes.

Place the dough in a large, oiled bowl, turn to coat, and cover with plastic wrap. Let rise until doubled in volume, 2 to 3 hours.

In a small dry skillet, stir walnuts over medium heat until golden and fragrant, 3 to 4 minutes. Lightly oil a 9-by-5-inch loaf pan or coat it with nonstick cooking spray. Set aside.

Gently punch down the dough and transfer to a lightly floured work surface. Press the dough with your hands into a 10-by-8-inch oval. Sprinkle evenly with the walnuts, then press them lightly into the dough. Starting at one narrow edge, tightly roll up the dough to form a loaf. Pinch the edges all along the seam to seal. Place in the bread pan, seam-side down, and cover with plastic wrap. Let rise until almost doubled, 45 to 55 minutes.

Meanwhile, position rack in the lower third of the oven; preheat to 400 degrees F. Bake for 10 minutes. Reduce the heat to 350 degrees F and bake until the bread sounds hollow when tapped on the bottom, another 40 to 50 minutes. Transfer the loaf to a wire rack to cool.

Makes 1 loaf, about 18 slices.

133 CALORIES PER SLICE: 5 G PROTEIN, 4 G FAT, 22 G CARBOHYDRATE; 239 MG SODIUM; 0 MG CHOLESTEROL.

Whole-Wheat Walnut Bread

Anadama Bread

The often-told story of anadama bread is about the beleaguered Yankee husband whose indolent wife, Anna, deserted him, leaving behind nothing more than the usual cornmeal gruel. In a burst of curses, he added flour and molasses and a new American bread was born. This updated anadama is made faster with the use of quick-rising yeast and a food processor. You can knead this dough by hand but the temperature of the cornmeal mixture should be a little hotter: 125 to 130 degrees F.

¼ cup yellow cornmeal, preferably stone-ground, plus additional for preparing baking sheet

¼ cup unsulfured molasses

3 cups unbleached all-purpose or bread flour

1 package quick-rising yeast

1½ teaspoons salt

1 egg white beaten with 2 teaspoons water, for glazing bread

In a saucepan, bring 1⅓ cups water to a boil. Pour into a large glass measuring cup and stir in cornmeal and molasses. Let stand for 5 minutes or longer to soften the cornmeal and to cool the liquid to between 105 and 115 degrees F.

In a food processor, combine flour, yeast and salt. Pulse to mix. With the motor running, gradually pour the cornmeal mixture through the feed tube until a ball forms. Process for about 45 seconds to "knead" the dough. (The dough will be sticky.) Turn the dough out onto a lightly floured surface. Cover with plastic wrap and let rest for 10 minutes.

Lightly oil a baking sheet. Dust with cornmeal, shaking off excess. Punch down the dough and form into a round loaf. Place on the prepared baking sheet. Cover lightly with plastic wrap and let rise until doubled in bulk, 40 to 45 minutes.

Meanwhile, position rack in the center of the oven; preheat to 425 degrees F. Just before baking, place a shallow pan of hot water on the lowest rack in the oven.

Brush the risen loaf lightly with egg-white glaze, taking care not to let it drip onto the pan. Use a sharp knife to make two slashes, ½ inch deep, in a crisscross pattern on top.

Bake for 10 minutes. Brush again with the glaze and rotate the pan 180 degrees. Lower oven temperature to 400 degrees and bake for 10 to 15 minutes more, or until the loaf is golden and the bottom sounds hollow when tapped. Transfer the loaf to a rack to cool. Serve within 6 hours of baking.

Makes 1 loaf, about 12 slices.

128 CALORIES PER SLICE: 4 G PROTEIN, 0 G FAT, 27 G CARBOHYDRATE; 272 MG SODIUM; 0 MG CHOLESTEROL.

Parmesan Bread

The warm aroma of this cheese-rich bread will draw eager tasters to your kitchen.

In a large bowl, dissolve yeast in 1¼ cups lukewarm water. Stir in nonfat dry milk, 1 cup cheese, whole egg, oil, sugar, salt, ground red pepper and 3 cups of the flour. Beat well with a wooden spoon. Gradually stir in enough of the remaining flour until the dough pulls away from the side of the bowl.

Turn out onto a lightly floured work surface and knead for 5 minutes, adding additional flour as necessary, until the dough is smooth, elastic and only slightly sticky. (*Alternatively, the dough can be mixed and kneaded in a stand-up electric mixer fitted with a dough hook.*) Place the dough in a lightly oiled bowl, turn to coat, and cover with plastic wrap. Let rise in a warm place until doubled in volume, about 1½ hours.

Punch down the dough and turn it out onto a floured work surface; divide it in half and shape each half into a ball. Place the balls on an oiled baking sheet, cover loosely with plastic wrap and let rise until doubled, 30 to 40 minutes.

Meanwhile, preheat oven to 350 degrees F. Brush the risen loaves with egg-white glaze. With a sharp knife, make three ½-inch-deep slashes in each loaf. Sprinkle the loaves with the remaining 1 tablespoon cheese. Bake for 25 to 35 minutes, or until the loaves sound hollow when tapped on the bottom. Cool on a wire rack.

Makes two 6-inch loaves, 8 slices each.

170 CALORIES PER SLICE: 8 G PROTEIN, 3 G FAT, 27 G CARBOHYDRATE; 147 MG SODIUM; 19 MG CHOLESTEROL.

2	packages active dry yeast (4½ teaspoons)
⅔	cup nonfat dry milk
1	cup plus 1 tablespoon freshly grated Parmesan cheese
1	large egg, lightly beaten
1	tablespoon olive oil
2	teaspoons sugar
1½	teaspoons salt
½	teaspoon ground red pepper (cayenne)
3¾-4	cups all-purpose white flour
1	egg white, lightly beaten, for glazing bread

Pumpkin Gingerbread Muffins with Nutmeg Glaze

Dark and spicy, the muffins are pretty when baked in mini-Bundt pans (see photograph on page 147).

½ cup chopped pitted dates

½ cup currants or raisins

¼ cup finely chopped crystallized ginger

3 tablespoons rum, brandy or cider

2½ cups all-purpose white flour

2 tablespoons ground ginger

1 teaspoon ground allspice

1 teaspoon freshly grated nutmeg

½ teaspoon ground cinnamon

½ teaspoon ground cloves

2 teaspoons baking soda

½ teaspoon salt

¼ teaspoon freshly ground black pepper

1½ cups canned pumpkin puree

1 cup buttermilk

1 teaspoon pure vanilla extract

2 large eggs

2 large egg whites

1⅓ cups packed light brown sugar

¾ cup molasses

3 tablespoons butter, melted

3 tablespoons vegetable oil, preferably canola oil

NUTMEG GLAZE

1½ cups confectioners' sugar

2 tablespoons skim milk

1½ tablespoons rum, brandy or cider

½ teaspoon freshly grated nutmeg

Preheat oven to 375 degrees F. Brush 12 mini-Bundt molds or 24 muffins cups (3-inch size) with vegetable oil or coat them with nonstick cooking spray. In a small bowl, soak dates, currants or raisins and crystallized ginger in rum or brandy or apple cider, stirring from time to time, while preparing the batter.

Sift flour, ginger, allspice, nutmeg, cinnamon, cloves, baking soda, salt and pepper together onto a sheet of wax paper or into a bowl. In a small bowl, whisk together pumpkin, buttermilk and vanilla; set aside.

In a large mixing bowl, beat eggs and egg whites with an electric mixer at medium speed until foamy. Gradually add brown sugar and beat until light and frothy, about 1 minute. Add molasses and beat well. Add half of the flour mixture and beat on low speed until just combined, stopping to scrape the bowl as necessary. Pour in melted butter and oil and beat until just mixed. Add the remaining flour mixture and beat until just mixed. Stir in the pumpkin mixture and beat until just combined. Stir in the dried fruit mixture and soaking liquid. Pour into the prepared pans, using about ⅔ cup batter for each mini-Bundt pan or ⅓ cup batter for each muffin cup. (If necessary, let the batter stand while you bake consecutive batches.)

Bake for 15 to 20 minutes, or until a toothpick inserted in the center comes out clean. Cool the muffins in the pan on a rack for 2 minutes, then turn out onto the rack.

TO MAKE NUTMEG GLAZE:

In a small bowl, stir together confectioners' sugar, milk, rum or brandy or apple cider and nutmeg until smooth. Drizzle the glaze over the muffins, letting the glaze drip down the sides.

Makes 12 mini-Bundt muffins or 24 medium muffins.

190 CALORIES FOR EACH OF 24: 3 G PROTEIN, 4 G FAT, 37 G CARBOHY-DRATE; 151 MG SODIUM; 22 MG CHOLESTEROL.

Morning Glory Bran Muffins

Thick, naturally sweet apple butter is rich in pectin and other soluble fibers, making it a suitable replacement for much of the fat in these wholesome muffins. Use dried fruits of your choice.

Position rack in the upper third of the oven; preheat to 425 degrees F. Coat 12 muffin cups with nonstick cooking spray.

In a large bowl, stir together bran, flours, baking powder, baking soda and salt. Stir in raisins, dates and dried apricots.

In a separate bowl, whisk together buttermilk, molasses, apple butter, egg white, oil, lemon juice, lemon zest and vanilla. Stir into the flour mixture just until the dry ingredients are moistened; do not overmix.

Divide the batter among the prepared muffin cups. (They will be nearly full.) Bake for 15 to 20 minutes, or until a cake tester inserted in the center comes out clean. Turn the muffins out onto a rack and let cool for 5 minutes before serving.

Makes 12 muffins.

182 CALORIES PER MUFFIN: 4 G PROTEIN, 4 G FAT, 36 G CARBOHYDRATE; 145 MG SODIUM; 1 MG CHOLESTEROL.

¾	cup wheat bran
¾	cup all-purpose white flour
½	cup whole-wheat flour
1½	teaspoons baking powder
½	teaspoon baking soda
¼	teaspoon salt
½	cup golden raisins
½	cup chopped pitted dates
½	cup chopped dried apricots
1	cup buttermilk
⅓	cup molasses
⅓	cup apple butter
1	large egg white
3	tablespoons vegetable oil, preferably canola oil
1	tablespoon fresh lemon juice
1½	teaspoons grated lemon zest
1	teaspoon pure vanilla extract

Orange-Date Pumpkin Muffins

A whole orange pulverized in the food processor gives a wonderful intense flavor to these nutrient-rich muffins.

1½ cups all-purpose white flour

½ cup whole-wheat flour

2 teaspoons baking powder

1 teaspoon baking soda

1 teaspoon salt

½ teaspoon ground cinnamon

1 large seedless orange, scrubbed and cut into 8 sections

1 large egg

1 large egg white

⅔ cup canned pumpkin puree

½ cup packed brown sugar

¼ cup honey or corn syrup

3 tablespoons vegetable oil, preferably canola oil

¾ cup chopped pitted dates

3 tablespoons chopped walnuts or pecans

Preheat oven to 400 degrees F. Line 12 muffin cups with paper liners or coat them with nonstick cooking spray.

In a large bowl, whisk together flours, baking powder, baking soda, salt and cinnamon; set aside.

Place orange sections in a food processor and puree. Add egg, egg white, pumpkin, brown sugar, honey or corn syrup and oil; process until mixed.

Make a well in the center of the dry ingredients and add the orange mixture and dates; stir with a rubber spatula just to moisten the dry ingredients. Spoon into the prepared muffin cups and sprinkle with nuts. Bake for 18 to 20 minutes, or until the tops spring back when touched lightly.

Makes 12 muffins.

220 CALORIES PER MUFFIN: 4 G PROTEIN, 5 G FAT, 41 G CARBOHYDRATE; 314 MG SODIUM; 18 MG CHOLESTEROL.

Blueberry Corn Muffins

Yellow cornmeal adds a delicious flavor and golden hue to these moist muffins. If you can get them, the tiny, lowbush berries are wonderful here. If using frozen blueberries, do not thaw them. Simply rinse off the ice crystals, then pat them dry completely on paper towels. Toss separately with about 3 tablespoons of the flour, then stir in after the liquid is added.

1⅓ cups all-purpose white flour

⅔ cup yellow cornmeal, preferably stone-ground

Preheat oven to 400 degrees F. Spray a muffin tin with nonstick cooking spray or lightly brush it with oil.

In a large bowl, stir or whisk together the flour, cornmeal, baking powder, cinnamon and salt. Add blueberries and toss to coat with the flour mixture. In a smaller bowl, lightly beat egg. Add milk, honey and oil, whisking until well combined. Add the liquid mixture to the dry ingredients and stir until just combined. Do not overmix.

Divide the batter equally among 12 muffin cups, filling each about two-thirds full. Sprinkle the tops with sugar. Bake for 18 to 22 minutes, until well-risen and golden. Turn out onto a rack to cool.

Makes 12 muffins.

169 CALORIES PER MUFFIN: 3 G PROTEIN, 4 G FAT, 30 G CARBOHYDRATE; 143 MG SODIUM; 18 MG CHOLESTEROL.

1	tablespoon baking powder
1	teaspoon ground cinnamon
¼	teaspoon salt
1	cup blueberries
1	egg
⅔	cup skim milk
½	cup honey
3	tablespoons vegetable oil, preferably canola oil
1	teaspoon sugar

Sage-Scented Cornmeal Biscuits

If you are preparing a large meal, the biscuit dough can be mixed and formed about an hour before baking and set aside in the refrigerator. (Photograph on page 80.)

Preheat oven to 425 degrees F. Lightly oil a baking sheet or coat it with nonstick cooking spray.

In a mixing bowl, stir together flour, cornmeal, sage, baking powder, sugar, baking soda and salt. With 2 knives or your fingers, cut in cream cheese and butter until you have lumps the size of peas. Stir in buttermilk until just combined. Do not overmix or the biscuits will be tough.

Turn the dough out onto a floured surface and pat into a circle about 9 inches in diameter. Cut into 12 wedges with a sharp knife.

Transfer the wedges to the prepared baking sheet. Brush the tops lightly with some egg glaze. Bake for 10 to 12 minutes, or until they are firm to the touch and very lightly browned. Serve warm.

Makes 12 biscuits.

118 CALORIES PER BISCUIT: 4 G PROTEIN, 4 G FAT, 18 G CARBOHYDRATE; 223 MG SODIUM; 26 MG CHOLESTEROL.

1½	cups all-purpose white flour
½	cup yellow cornmeal, preferably stone-ground
1	tablespoon chopped fresh sage or 1 teaspoon dried rubbed sage
1	tablespoon baking powder
1	teaspoon sugar
½	teaspoon baking soda
¼	teaspoon salt
3	tablespoons reduced-fat cream cheese
2	tablespoons cold butter, cut into small pieces
1	cup buttermilk
1	large egg, lightly beaten with 1 tablespoon water for glaze

Ginger-Lemon Scones

After researching and writing a cookbook on Scottish, Irish and Welsh baked goods, EATING WELL contributor Deborah Krasner was an expert on scones—of the high-fat variety. Her Americanized, low-fat versions are equally good. She suggests working the dough as lightly as possible to keep them tender.

Preheat oven to 350 degrees F. Lightly oil a baking sheet or coat it with nonstick cooking spray.

Sift together flour, ¼ cup of the sugar, baking soda, cream of tartar and salt into a mixing bowl. Stir in ginger and lemon zest. Combine buttermilk and oil and add to the dry ingredients, stirring just until blended. (The dough will be slightly sticky.)

Turn the dough out onto a lightly floured work surface and pat to a thickness of ½ inch. Using a floured 4-inch round cutter, cut out the dough. Cut each circle in half to make half-moons. Reroll and cut the scraps, handling the dough as little as possible. Transfer to the prepared baking sheet.

Brush the tops with egg glaze. Sprinkle with the remaining 1 tablespoon sugar. Bake for 15 to 20 minutes, or until the tops are golden and firm to the touch. Serve warm.

Makes about 16 scones.

110 CALORIES PER SCONE: 2 G PROTEIN, 1 G FAT, 21 G CARBOHYDRATE; 139 MG SODIUM; 14 MG CHOLESTEROL.

- 2 cups all-purpose white flour
- ¼ cup plus 1 tablespoon sugar
- 1 teaspoon baking soda
- 1 teaspoon cream of tartar
- ½ teaspoon salt
- ¼ cup finely chopped crystallized ginger
- 2 teaspoons grated lemon zest
- 1 cup buttermilk
- 1 tablespoon vegetable oil, preferably canola oil
- 1 large egg, lightly beaten with 1 tablespoon water for glaze

Currant & Caraway Scones

For a whimsical touch, cut these with a heart-shaped cutter.

Preheat oven to 350 degrees F. Lightly oil a baking sheet or coat it with nonstick cooking spray.

Combine currants and Marsala in a small saucepan. Bring to a simmer over low heat and stir until liquid is absorbed, about 3 minutes. Set aside to cool.

Currant & Caraway Scones and Ginger-Lemon Scones

- ¾ cup currants
- ¼ cup sweet Marsala wine
- 2 cups all-purpose white flour
- ¼ cup sugar
- 1 teaspoon baking soda
- 1 teaspoon cream of tartar

½   teaspoon salt

1   tablespoon caraway seeds

1   tablespoon grated orange zest

1   cup buttermilk

1   tablespoon vegetable oil,
    preferably canola oil

1   large egg, lightly beaten with 1
    tablespoon water for glaze

Sift together flour, sugar, baking soda, cream of tartar and salt into a mixing bowl. Stir in caraway seeds and orange zest. Combine buttermilk, oil and the reserved currants and Marsala. Add to the dry ingredients and stir just until blended. (The dough will be slightly sticky.)

Turn the dough out onto a lightly floured work surface and pat into a circle that is ½ inch thick. Cut the dough into 12 wedges and transfer to the prepared baking sheet.

Brush the tops with egg glaze. Bake for 15 to 20 minutes, or until the tops are golden and firm to the touch. Serve warm.

Makes 12 scones.

145 CALORIES PER SCONE: 3 G PROTEIN, 1 G FAT, 28 G CARBOHYDRATE; 273 MG SODIUM; 19 MG CHOLESTEROL.

Pumpkin Popovers

Preheating the muffin pan before baking makes these reduced-fat popovers rise to dramatic heights.

¼   cup canned pumpkin puree

3   large eggs

3   large egg whites

2   cups skim milk

2   tablespoons vegetable oil,
    preferably canola oil

2   cups all-purpose white flour

½   teaspoon salt

¼   teaspoon pumpkin-pie spice

⅛   teaspoon ground red pepper
    (cayenne)

Preheat the oven to 400 degrees F. Place a 12-cup muffin pan or popover pan on a baking sheet in the oven to preheat. In a bowl, whisk together pumpkin puree, eggs, egg whites, skim milk and oil until smooth. In a large bowl, combine flour, salt, pie spice and ground red pepper. Add the pumpkin mixture to the dry ingredients and whisk until smooth.

Remove the muffin pan from the oven and lightly oil it. Pour in batter. Bake the popovers until they are puffed and browned, about 25 minutes. Remove from the oven and reduce the oven temperature to 350 degrees. With a small knife cut small slits into the sides of the popovers, 3 to 4 per popover. Bake an additional 7 to 10 minutes. Serve hot.

Makes 12 popovers.

135 CALORIES PER POPOVER: 6 G PROTEIN, 4 G FAT, 19 G CARBOHYDRATE; 140 MG SODIUM; 54 MG CHOLESTEROL.

Cherry-Fig Tea Loaf

Brew some of your favorite tea and pause to enjoy this fruity quick bread.
If you cannot find dried cherries, substitute dried cranberries.

Preheat oven to 350 degrees F. Lightly oil a 9-by-5-inch loaf pan or spray it with nonstick cooking spray. Dust the pan with flour, shaking out excess, and set aside.

In a saucepan, combine cherries, figs and 1 cup water. Bring to a simmer over low heat. Simmer, covered, for 5 minutes. Strain, reserving ⅓ cup of the fruit-cooking liquid. Set the fruit and liquid aside in separate bowls.

In a large bowl, stir together flour, sugar, wheat bran, lemon zest, baking powder, baking soda and salt. In another large bowl, whisk together egg, egg whites, buttermilk, oil, vanilla and the reserved ⅓ cup fruit-cooking liquid; beat until smooth. Add to the flour mixture and stir with a rubber spatula until just combined. Fold in the reserved fruit. Turn the batter into the prepared pan.

Bake for 45 to 55 minutes, or until the top is golden and a cake tester inserted in the center of the loaf comes out clean. Let cool in the pan on a rack for 10 minutes. Loosen the edges and invert the loaf onto the rack to cool. Serve warm or at room temperature.

Makes 1 loaf, about 12 slices.

260 CALORIES PER SLICE: 5 G PROTEIN, 5 G FAT, 53 G CARBOHYDRATE; 245 MG SODIUM; 18 MG CHOLESTEROL.

1   cup dried tart cherries
1   cup chopped dried figs
2   cups all-purpose white flour
⅔   cup sugar
¼   cup wheat bran
2   teaspoons grated lemon zest
2   teaspoons baking powder
1   teaspoon baking soda
½   teaspoon salt
1   large egg
2   large egg whites
⅔   cup buttermilk
3   tablespoons vegetable oil, preferably canola oil
1   teaspoon pure vanilla extract

Cranberry-Orange Tea Loaf

*Leftover slices of cranberry-orange tea loaf are also delicious toasted and spread
with orange marmalade, such as the one that follows.*

1 cup all-purpose white flour
½ cup whole-wheat flour
1 cup sugar
½ cup yellow cornmeal, preferably stone-ground
1½ teaspoons baking powder
½ teaspoon baking soda
½ teaspoon salt
1½ cups fresh or frozen cranberries
1 tablespoon grated orange zest
¾ cup fresh orange juice
1 large egg white
1 tablespoon vegetable oil, preferably canola oil
Confectioners' sugar for dusting

Preheat oven to 350 degrees F. Lightly oil an 8-by-4-inch loaf pan or coat it with nonstick cooking spray.

In a mixing bowl, whisk together both flours, sugar, cornmeal, baking powder, baking soda and salt. Add cranberries and orange zest. Stir to coat with the dry ingredients.

In a small bowl, whisk together orange juice, egg white and oil. Pour into the dry ingredients and stir just until blended. Do not overmix or the tea loaf will be tough.

Scrape the batter into the prepared pan and bake for 50 to 60 minutes, or until a cake tester inserted in the center of the loaf comes out clean. Cool in the pan on a rack for 5 minutes. Turn the loaf out onto the rack and let cool. Dust the top with confectioners' sugar before slicing.

Makes 1 loaf, about 12 slices.

170 CALORIES PER SLICE: 2 G PROTEIN, 2 G FAT, 38 G CARBOHYDRATE; 171 MG SODIUM; 0 MG CHOLESTEROL.

Iris's Orange Marmalade

Toronto food writer Iris Raven makes this classic marmalade every January.

5 **large Seville oranges, scrubbed**
1 **lemon, scrubbed**
7½ **cups sugar**

In a large wide saucepan or Dutch oven, combine whole oranges, whole lemon and 6 cups water. Cover and bring to a simmer. Simmer very gently over low heat for 2 hours.

Remove the pan from the heat. With a slotted spoon, remove the fruit and let cool for 5 minutes. (Do not discard the liquid in the pan.) Cut the fruits in half; scoop out pulp, pith and seeds and add to the pan. Reserve the orange shells and discard the lemon shells. Bring the fruit mixture to a boil and boil for 5 minutes.

Strain the fruit mixture through a colander lined with dampened cheesecloth into a bowl. Gather the ends of the cheesecloth and twist out any remaining juice. Add water, if necessary, to make 6 cups. Return the juice to the pan.

Slice the reserved orange shells into thin strips and add to the juice in the pan. Stir in sugar and cook over low heat, stirring, until sugar dissolves. Increase the heat to medium and boil, stirring occasionally to prevent scorching, until the jelling point is reached, about 25 minutes.

To test for jelling, place a spoonful of the mixture on a chilled plate and refrigerate for 2 minutes. The jelling point has been reached if the marmalade is firm enough to remain divided when a finger is drawn through it and there is no watery edge. Continue cooking and testing as necessary.

Remove the marmalade from the heat and stir for 5 minutes, skimming off any foam. Ladle into hot jars, leaving ¼ inch of headspace. Seal with canning lids and process for 5 minutes in a boiling-water bath. Store in a cool, dry place.

Makes about six 8-ounce jars.

60 CALORIES PER TABLESPOON: 0 G PROTEIN, 0 G FAT, 16 G CARBOHYDRATE; 0 MG SODIUM; 0 MG CHOLESTEROL.

CHAPTER 13

Pies, Tarts & Cakes

Rustic Plum-Walnut Tart

There is nothing like the sight of bushels of late-summer fruit piled high at the farmstand under a clear September sky to inspire a pie. For this French free-form plum tart, the plums are arranged over a bed of ground walnuts, sugar and flour, which absorbs the delicious plummy juices and helps keep the pastry crust crisp.

CRUST

1½	cups all-purpose white flour
2	tablespoons plus 1 teaspoon sugar
½	teaspoon salt
⅓	cup walnut oil or vegetable oil
1	tablespoon skim milk

FILLING

2	tablespoons chopped walnuts or pecans
2	pounds plums, such as Santa Rosa or Queen Ann (12-16 plums)
¼	cup all-purpose white flour
3	tablespoons Grape-Nuts cereal
½	cup sugar
3	tablespoons red currant jelly

TO MAKE CRUST:

Position oven rack at the lowest level; preheat to 425 degrees F. Coat a large baking sheet (12 by 17 inches) with nonstick cooking spray or brush it lightly with oil.

In a mixing bowl, stir together flour, 2 tablespoons sugar and salt. Using a fork, slowly stir in oil until the mixture is crumbly. Stir in enough ice water, about 3 to 6 tablespoons, so that the dough will hold together in a ball. (The dough should be wetter than traditional pastry doughs.) Press the dough into a flattened disk.

Place two 14-inch sheets of plastic wrap on the work surface, overlapping them to make a square about 24 by 24 inches. Place pastry in the center and cover with two more overlapping sheets of plastic wrap. Roll the dough into a rough circle, 14 to 15 inches in diameter and approximately 1/16 inch thick, patching where necessary. Remove the top sheets and invert the dough onto the prepared baking sheet. Refrigerate, covered, while you prepare the filling.

TO MAKE FILLING AND BAKE TART:

Spread nuts on a pie plate and bake for 5 minutes, or until fragrant. Let cool.

Rustic Plum-Walnut Tart

Meanwhile, quarter plums, discarding pits. Place flour, cereal, ¼ cup of the sugar and the toasted nuts in a food processor or blender; process until nuts and cereal are finely ground.

Spread the nut mixture over the pastry, leaving a 1½-inch border around the edge. Arrange the plums, resting on their sides, in concentric circles, over the nut mixture. Sprinkle with the remaining ¼ cup sugar. Fold the pastry border halfway over the outer circle of plums to form a rim. Brush milk over the pastry rim and sprinkle with the remaining 1 teaspoon sugar.

Bake for 15 minutes, reduce the heat to 375 degrees and bake for 30 to 40 minutes longer, or until the crust is golden and the juices are bubbling. Using a long metal spatula, slide the tart onto a serving platter and let cool. Before serving, heat jelly over low heat until melted, then brush over the plums. Serve with Vanilla Cream.

Serves 10.

281 CALORIES PER SERVING: 3 G PROTEIN, 8 G FAT, 53 G CARBOHYDRATE; 124 MG SODIUM; 0 MG CHOLESTEROL.

Vanilla Cream

An easy topping provides the final flourish for pies. It also adds a bit of low-fat decadence to Ginger-Lemon Scones and Currant & Caraway Scones (page 167).

1½ cups low-fat vanilla yogurt
½ cup light whipping cream
1 tablespoon confectioners' sugar
1 tablespoon orange liqueur, such as Grand Marnier

Line a sieve with cheesecloth and set it over a bowl. (*Alternatively, use a coffee filter lined with filter paper.*) Spoon in yogurt and let it drain in the refrigerator until reduced to 1 cup, about 1 hour.

In a chilled mixing bowl with chilled beaters, whip cream to soft peaks. Add the drained yogurt, sugar and orange liqueur; fold gently to mix. Serve immediately or refrigerate, covered, for up to 8 hours.

Makes about 2 cups.

50 CALORIES FOR 2 TABLESPOONS: 1 G PROTEIN, 3 G FAT, 5 G CARBOHYDRATE; 16 MG SODIUM; 10 MG CHOLESTEROL.

Pumpkin Pie

With a fraction of the fat, this lighter pumpkin pie has the rich, subtle spices
of the classic and a delicate, faintly sweet crust.

TO MAKE CRUST:

In a bowl, stir together flour, sugar and salt. In a small saucepan, melt butter over low heat. Cook for about 30 seconds, swirling the pan, until the butter is light brown. Transfer to a small bowl to cool. Stir in oil. Using a fork, slowly stir the butter-oil mixture into the dry ingredients until the dough is crumbly. Gradually stir in enough ice water, about 1 to 2 tablespoons, so that the dough will hold together. Press the dough into a flattened disk.

Place two sheets of plastic wrap on the work surface, overlapping them by 2 inches. Place the dough in the center and cover with 2 more overlapping sheets of plastic wrap. With a rolling pin, roll the dough into a circle about 12 inches in diameter. Remove the top sheets and invert the dough over a 9-inch pie plate. Remove the remaining plastic wrap. Fold the edges under at the rim and crimp. Chill the pastry while you prepare the filling.

TO MAKE FILLING:

Position rack in the lower third of the oven; preheat to 425 degrees F. In a mixing bowl, whisk together pumpkin, eggs, evaporated skim milk and vanilla. In a small bowl, mix brown sugar, cornstarch, cinnamon, ginger, nutmeg and salt. Rub through a sieve into pumpkin mixture and whisk until incorporated.

Pour the filling into the prepared crust and bake for 12 minutes. Reduce the heat to 350 degrees and bake for 35 to 40 minutes longer, or until the filling is set and a knife inserted in the center comes out clean. During baking, cover the edges with foil if they are browning too quickly. Cool on a rack.

Serves 8.

283 CALORIES PER SERVING: 8 G PROTEIN, 8 G FAT, 45 G CARBOHYDRATE;
212 MG SODIUM; 60 MG CHOLESTEROL.

CRUST

1   cup all-purpose white flour
1   tablespoon sugar
⅛   teaspoon salt
1   tablespoon butter
3   tablespoons vegetable oil, preferably canola oil

FILLING

1   cup canned pumpkin puree
2   large eggs, lightly beaten
2   cups evaporated skim milk
1   teaspoon pure vanilla extract
¾   cup packed dark brown sugar
1   tablespoon cornstarch
1   teaspoon ground cinnamon
1   teaspoon ground ginger
¼   teaspoon freshly grated nutmeg
¼   teaspoon salt

Rhubarb Custard Pie

If there is no rhubarb in your garden, look for it at farmers' markets.

CRUST

- 1 cup all-purpose white flour
- 1 tablespoon sugar
- ⅛ teaspoon salt
- 1 tablespoon butter
- 3 tablespoons vegetable oil, preferably canola oil

FILLING

- ¾ cup sugar
- 1 tablespoon butter, softened
- 1 large egg
- 2 large egg whites
- ¼ cup skim milk
- 1 teaspoon pure vanilla extract
- 1½ pounds rhubarb, trimmed and cut into ¼-inch pieces (5 cups)
- 2 tablespoons all-purpose white flour

MERINGUE

- 3 large egg whites
- ¼ teaspoon cream of tartar
- ½ cup sugar

TO MAKE CRUST:

Position oven rack at the lowest level; preheat to 375 degrees F. Lightly oil a 9-inch glass pie plate or coat it with nonstick cooking spray.

In a bowl, stir together flour, sugar and salt. In a small saucepan, melt butter over low heat, swirling it in the pan for about 30 seconds, until light brown. Pour into a small bowl and let cool. Stir in oil. Using a fork, slowly stir the butter-oil mixture into the dry ingredients until the mixture is crumbly. Gradually stir in enough ice water, 1 to 2 tablespoons, so that the dough will hold together. Press the dough into a flattened disk.

Place two sheets of plastic wrap on the work surface, overlapping them by 2 inches. Place the pastry in the center and cover with two more overlapping sheets of plastic wrap. With a rolling pin, roll the dough into a circle about 12 inches in diameter. Remove the top sheets and invert the dough over the prepared pie plate. Carefully peel away the remaining plastic wrap. Fold the edges under at the rim and crimp. Chill the pastry while you prepare the filling.

TO MAKE FILLING:

In a mixing bowl, beat together sugar and butter until fluffy. Beat in egg, egg whites, milk and vanilla until well blended. In another bowl, toss rhubarb with flour. Stir the rhubarb into the egg mixture. Turn the filling into the crust-lined pan, spreading evenly. Bake for about 1¼ hours, or until the filling is firm. Let cool to room temperature before topping with meringue.

TO MAKE MERINGUE:

Position rack in the center of the oven; preheat to 375 degrees F. In a large mixing bowl, beat egg whites with an electric mixer

Rhubarb Custard Pie

on medium speed until frothy. Add cream of tartar and beat on high speed just until soft peaks form. While continuing to beat egg whites, gradually add sugar. Beat until stiff and glossy.

Spread the meringue over the cooled pie, making sure that it touches the edge of the crust all the way around. Bake for 12 to 15 minutes, or until the top is lightly browned. Let cool on a rack for 1 hour before serving.

Serves 8.

294 CALORIES PER SERVING: 6 G PROTEIN, 9 G FAT, 50 G CARBOHYDRATE; 213 MG SODIUM; 34 MG CHOLESTEROL.

Very Lemon Pie

Lemon zest, pulp and juice are combined with eggs and sugar in a wonderful custard.

CRUST

1	cup all-purpose white flour
1	tablespoon sugar
⅛	teaspoon salt
1	tablespoon butter
3	tablespoons vegetable oil, preferably canola oil

FILLING

3	lemons
2	cups sugar
½	teaspoon salt
2	large eggs
3	large egg whites
	Confectioners' sugar for dusting

TO MAKE CRUST:

Lightly oil a 9-inch pie plate or coat it with nonstick cooking spray. In a mixing bowl, stir together flour, sugar and salt. In a small saucepan over low heat, melt butter, swirling it in the pan for about 30 seconds, until light brown. Pour into a small bowl and let cool. Stir in oil. Using a fork, slowly stir the butter-oil mixture into the dry ingredients until the dough is crumbly. Gradually stir in enough ice water, about 1 to 2 tablespoons, so that the dough will hold together. Press the dough into a flattened disk.

Place two sheets of plastic wrap on the work surface, overlapping them by 2 inches. Place the pastry in the center and cover with 2 more overlapping sheets of plastic wrap. With a rolling pin, roll the dough into a 12-inch circle. Remove the top sheets and invert the dough over the prepared pie plate. Carefully peel away the remaining plastic wrap. Fold the edges under at the rim and crimp. Chill the pastry while you prepare the filling.

TO MAKE FILLING:

Position oven rack at the lowest level; preheat to 350 degrees F. Grate the zest from the lemons into a saucepan; set aside. With a sharp knife, cut the white pith from the lemons and discard. Working over the saucepan to catch the juice, cut the lemon segments from their surrounding membranes, letting them drop into the saucepan and discarding any seeds. Squeeze any remaining juice from the membranes into the saucepan. Stir in sugar and salt. Bring to a simmer over medium heat, stirring, until the sugar dissolves. Remove from the heat.

In a mixing bowl, whisk together eggs and egg whites. Slowly whisk the hot lemon-sugar mixture into the eggs. Pour into the pie shell and bake for 20 to 25 minutes, or until the filling is set. Let cool. Before serving, dust with confectioners' sugar.

Serves 8.

332 CALORIES PER SERVING: 5 G PROTEIN, 8 G FAT, 64 G CARBOHYDRATE; 219 MG SODIUM; 57 MG CHOLESTEROL.

Triple Cherry Pie

Three cherries wins the jackpot in a slot machine; this pie is a sure winner as well.
Serve with vanilla frozen yogurt.

2 cups tart cherries (about ¾ pound), pitted

2 cups sweet cherries (about ¾ pound), pitted

½ cup dried tart cherries

½ cup sugar

1 tablespoon quick-cooking tapioca

2 teaspoons grated lemon zest

2 tablespoons butter

2 tablespoons vegetable oil, preferably canola oil

1 large egg white

6 sheets phyllo pastry (14x18 inches), thawed in the refrigerator overnight if frozen

4 teaspoons fine dry breadcrumbs
Confectioners' sugar for dusting

Position oven rack at the lowest level; preheat to 400 degrees F. Place a baking sheet in the oven to heat. Lightly oil a 9-inch pie plate or coat it with nonstick cooking spray.

In a large bowl, combine tart cherries, sweet cherries, dried cherries, sugar, tapioca and lemon zest. Toss well to mix and set aside.

In a small saucepan, melt butter over low heat. Cook until it begins to turn light brown, 1½ to 2 minutes. (Be careful not to burn the butter.) Pour into a small bowl and let cool. Add oil and egg white and stir briskly with a fork.

Unwrap phyllo and lay one sheet in the prepared pie plate so that the edges hang over the sides. (Cover the remaining phyllo with a kitchen towel.) With a pastry brush, brush the phyllo with the egg-white mixture. Sprinkle with 1 teaspoon breadcrumbs. Lay another sheet of phyllo at an angle over the first. Brush with the egg-white mixture and sprinkle with 1 teaspoon breadcrumbs. Repeat with 2 more sheets of phyllo. Lay the fifth sheet on top and brush with the egg-white mixture.

Spoon the cherries into the phyllo-lined pie plate. Lift one corner of overhanging phyllo, give it a quick twist and set it on the fruit filling. Repeat with the remaining overhanging corners to form a circle of ruffles around the edge. Brush the ruffled phyllo with the egg-white mixture. Cut the remaining sheet of phyllo in half lengthwise, then crosswise. Lift each quarter from underneath, bunch it together at the center to form a ruffle and set it on the exposed fruit in the pie's center, to give the entire tart a ruffled top. (Do not worry if some fruit is still visible; small holes will serve as steam vents.) Brush the center ruffles with the egg-white mixture.

Place the pie plate on the baking sheet in the oven and bake for 10 minutes. Reduce the heat to 350 degrees and bake for 40 to 50 minutes longer, or until the pastry is golden and the fruit mixture is bubbling. Set the pie on a rack and let cool to room temperature. Just before serving, dust with confectioners' sugar. (*The pie is best served the day it is made. If the phyllo ruffles become soft, reheat the pie in a 350-degree oven to re-crisp.*)

Serves 8.

169 CALORIES PER SERVING: 2 G PROTEIN, 7 G FAT, 27 G CARBOHYDRATE; 53 MG SODIUM; 8 MG CHOLESTEROL.

Mango Tart

Garnish this glorious tropical tart with sliced carambola or strawberries, or toasted unsweetened coconut shreds if desired.

TO MAKE ALMOND MERINGUE CRUST:

Preheat oven to 300 degrees F. Line a baking sheet with parchment paper. Using a 10-inch cake pan or plate as a guide, draw a circle on the paper. Turn the paper over; the line will show through. (*Alternatively, line the baking sheet with aluminum foil, coat with nonstick cooking spray and dust with flour, shaking off excess. Trace the circle with your fingertip.*)

Spread almonds in a pie plate and bake for 8 to 12 minutes, or until lightly toasted. Let cool, then put them in a food processor along with ⅓ cup of the sugar and cornstarch; process until the nuts are coarsely ground; set aside.

In a clean mixing bowl, beat egg whites with an electric mixer at low speed for 20 seconds. Add cream of tartar and gradually increase speed to high. When the whites begin to form soft peaks, gradually add the remaining ⅓ cup sugar and vanilla; continue beating until the meringue is glossy and stiff peaks form. Sprinkle the almond-sugar mixture over the meringue and fold in with a rubber spatula just until mixed.

Spoon about 1 cup of the meringue into a piping bag fitted with a ½-inch open-star tip. Spread the remaining meringue

ALMOND MERINGUE CRUST
- ⅓ cup slivered or chopped blanched almonds
- ⅔ cup sugar
- 1½ tablespoons cornstarch
- 3 large egg whites, at room temperature
- ¼ teaspoon cream of tartar
- ½ teaspoon pure vanilla extract

MANGO TOPPING
- 3 ripe mangoes (¾-1 pound each)
- 1 tablespoon sugar
- ½ teaspoon grated lime zest
- 1 teaspoon unflavored gelatin
- 2 tablespoons fresh lime juice
- ¼ cup whipping cream
- ¼ cup guava jelly or strained apricot preserves

inside the traced circle. Pipe the reserved meringue on the outside edge to form a rim.

Reduce the oven temperature to 250 degrees F. Bake the meringue crust until golden and firm to the touch, 50 to 70 minutes. Let cool on the baking sheet on a rack. Carefully peel off the paper or foil. (*The meringue crust can be prepared up to 3 days in advance and stored in an airtight container.*)

TO MAKE MOUSSE:

About 3 hours before serving, cube 1 of the mangoes and place in a food processor or blender, along with sugar. Process until smooth. To remove any fibers, press the puree through a fine sieve set over a bowl. (You should have about ½ cup of puree.) Stir in lime zest; set aside.

Sprinkle gelatin over lime juice in a small heatproof bowl; let stand until softened, about 1 minute. Set the bowl over barely simmering water until the gelatin has melted, or microwave on high for 20 to 40 seconds. Whisk into the mango mixture. Refrigerate, stirring occasionally with a rubber spatula, until slightly thickened and beginning to set, about 20 minutes. Whip cream in a chilled bowl just until it forms soft peaks. Gently fold into the mango mixture.

TO ASSEMBLE TART:

Set the meringue crust on a serving plate. In a small saucepan, melt guava jelly or apricot preserves over low heat. Brush a thin coat of guava jelly or apricot preserves over the crust, using about 2 tablespoons. (Set the saucepan aside.) Spread the mango mousse inside the crust. Cover loosely and refrigerate until the mousse has set, about 2 hours. Not more than 1 hour before serving, peel and thinly slice the remaining 2 mangoes. Fan the slices on top of the mango mousse. Rewarm the jelly or preserves and brush over the mangoes. Refrigerate the tart until serving time.

Serves 8.

224 CALORIES PER SERVING: 7 G PROTEIN, 5 G FAT, 41 G CARBOHYDRATE; 32 MG SODIUM; 8 MG CHOLESTEROL.

Mango Tart

Died-and-Went-to-Heaven Chocolate Cake

Originally featured in EATING WELL'*s* Rx *for Recipes column and on CNN's
"On the Menu" program, this foolproof cake has turned out to be one of our most popular recipes.
Dutch-process cocoa is preferred here for its deep chocolate flavor.*

1¾ cups all-purpose white flour

1 cup white sugar

¾ cup unsweetened Dutch-process cocoa powder

1½ teaspoons baking soda

1½ teaspoons baking powder

1 teaspoon salt

1¼ cups buttermilk

1 cup packed light brown sugar

2 large eggs, lightly beaten

¼ cup vegetable oil, preferably canola oil

2 teaspoons pure vanilla extract

1 cup hot strong black coffee

ICING

1 cup confectioners' sugar

½ teaspoon pure vanilla extract

1-2 tablespoons buttermilk or low-fat milk

Preheat oven to 350 degrees F. Lightly oil a 12-cup Bundt pan or coat it with nonstick cooking spray. Dust the pan with flour, shaking out the excess.

In a large mixing bowl, whisk together flour, white sugar, cocoa powder, baking soda, baking powder and salt. Add buttermilk, brown sugar, eggs, oil and vanilla; beat with an electric mixer on medium speed for 2 minutes. Whisk in hot coffee until completely incorporated. (The batter will be quite thin.)

Pour the batter into the prepared pan. Bake for 35 to 40 minutes, or until a cake tester inserted in the center comes out clean. Cool the cake in the pan on a rack for 10 minutes; remove from the pan and let cool completely.

TO MAKE ICING:

In a small bowl, whisk together confectioners' sugar, vanilla and enough of the buttermilk or milk to make a thick but pourable icing. Set the cake on a serving plate and drizzle the icing over the top.

Serves 16.

222 CALORIES PER SERVING: 3 G PROTEIN, 4 G FAT, 43 G CARBOHYDRATE; 274 MG SODIUM; 27 MG CHOLESTEROL.

Carrot Cake

Do not be put off by the prunes in this recipe, which are pureed. The puree's rich flavor melds beautifully with the spiced cake. It also helps cut most of the fat from a traditional carrot cake recipe.

TO MAKE CAKE:

Preheat oven to 350 degrees F. Coat two 9-inch round layer-cake pans with nonstick cooking spray. Line the bottoms with wax paper and set aside.

Spread pecans in a pie plate and bake for 8 to 10 minutes, or until fragrant. Let cool and chop coarsely. Meanwhile, in a food processor, combine prunes with 6 tablespoons hot water; process until smooth. Set aside.

In a medium bowl, whisk together flour, cinnamon, baking powder, baking soda and salt. In a large bowl, whisk together eggs, egg whites, sugar, oil and the reserved prune puree. Add the dry ingredients to the egg mixture and stir with a rubber spatula until blended. Stir in carrots, pineapple and the toasted pecans.

Divide the batter between the prepared pans and bake for 25 to 30 minutes, or until a cake tester inserted in the center comes out clean. Loosen the edges and invert the cakes onto racks. Peel off the wax paper and let cool completely.

TO MAKE FROSTING:

In a mixing bowl, combine Neufchatel cheese, Marshmallow Fluff or Creme and lemon juice; beat with an electric mixer until smooth and creamy.

TO ASSEMBLE CAKE:

Place a cake layer on a serving plate. Spread a scant ⅓ cup of the frosting over the bottom layer. Top with the other cake layer and spread the remaining frosting over the top and sides.

Serves 12.

411 CALORIES PER SERVING: 7 G PROTEIN, 13 G FAT, 70 G CARBOHYDRATE; 447 MG SODIUM; 50 MG CHOLESTEROL.

CAKE

- ¼ cup pecans
- 1 cup pitted prunes
- 2½ cups sifted cake flour
- 2 teaspoons ground cinnamon
- 2 teaspoons baking powder
- 1½ teaspoons baking soda
- 1 teaspoon salt
- 2 large eggs
- 2 large egg whites
- 1½ cups sugar
- ⅓ cup vegetable oil
- 2 cups grated carrots (5-6 small carrots)
- 1 8-ounce can crushed pineapple, thoroughly drained

FROSTING

- 1 8-ounce package Neufchatel cheese (reduced-fat cream cheese), softened
- 1 cup Marshmallow Fluff or Marshmallow Creme
- ½ teaspoon lemon juice

Cherry-Almond Upside-Down Cake

Cherry pits have an almondy taste; perhaps this explains why the flavor combination works so well here.

TOPPING

3½   cups tart cherries (about 1¼ pounds), pitted

2   tablespoons sugar

2   tablespoons kirsch or brandy

1   tablespoon cornstarch

CAKE

½   cup whole unblanched almonds (3 ounces)

⅔   cup sifted cake flour

1   teaspoon baking powder

¼   teaspoon salt

2   large egg whites

⅔   cup sugar

2   large eggs

1½   teaspoons pure vanilla extract

TO MAKE TOPPING:

Preheat oven to 350 degrees F. Lightly oil a 9-inch cake pan or coat it with nonstick cooking spray.

In a bowl, toss cherries with sugar, kirsch or brandy and cornstarch. Spoon into the prepared pan, arranging the cherries in a single layer; set aside.

TO MAKE CAKE:

Spread almonds in a pie plate and bake for about 10 minutes, or until fragrant. Let cool slightly, about 5 minutes.

In a food processor or blender, combine the almonds, flour, baking powder and salt; process until the almonds are ground to a fine meal.

In a large mixing bowl, beat the 2 egg whites with an electric mixer until soft peaks form. Gradually beat in ⅓ cup of the sugar, continuing until the whites are stiff and glossy. Set aside.

In a separate mixing bowl, with an electric mixer, beat the whole eggs and the remaining ⅓ cup sugar until thickened and pale, about 5 minutes. Blend in vanilla.

Whisk one-quarter of the beaten egg whites into the whole-egg mixture. Sprinkle half of the dry ingredients over the top and, with a rubber spatula, fold until just blended. Fold in the remaining beaten whites, then the remaining dry ingredients.

Spread the batter over the cherries in the prepared pan and bake for 30 minutes, or until the top springs back when touched lightly and a cake tester inserted into the center of the cake comes out clean. Let cool in the pan for 5 minutes, then invert onto a cake plate. Serve warm or at room temperature.

Serves 10.

176 CALORIES PER SERVING: 4 G PROTEIN, 4 G FAT, 30 G CARBOHYDRATE; 80 MG SODIUM; 43 MG CHOLESTEROL.

**Cherry-Almond
Upside-Down Cake**

Lemon Meringue Cake

Beneath swirls of golden meringue lies a sponge cake filled with a light lemon center.
Serve the cake cold or at room temperature.

LEMON FILLING

1 cup sugar

1 large egg, lightly beaten

½ cup fresh lemon juice

2 teaspoons grated lemon zest

2 tablespoons cornstarch, mixed with ¼ cup water

SPONGE CAKE

¾ cup plus 2 tablespoons cake flour

1 teaspoon baking powder

¼ teaspoon freshly grated nutmeg

2 large eggs

2 large egg whites

1 cup sugar

2 teaspoons fresh lemon juice

2 teaspoons pure vanilla extract

⅓ cup skim milk, heated to steaming

MERINGUE TOPPING

¾ cup sugar

4 large egg whites

½ teaspoon cream of tartar

TO PREPARE LEMON FILLING:

In a small saucepan, combine sugar, egg, lemon juice, lemon zest and ½ cup water. Heat over low heat, whisking constantly, until the sugar dissolves. Increase the heat to medium-high and whisk in the cornstarch mixture. Bring to a boil, whisking, and boil for 30 seconds. The filling should be thick and clear. Transfer to a small bowl, cover and chill until cool, 45 minutes to 1 hour.

TO BAKE AND FILL CAKE:

Preheat oven to 350 degrees F. Line the bottom of a 9-inch round layer cake pan with wax paper. Lightly oil the paper and the pan or coat it with nonstick cooking spray.

Sift flour, baking powder and nutmeg into a small bowl; set aside. In the bowl of an electric mixer, beat eggs and egg whites on low speed until frothy. Add sugar and beat on medium speed until the eggs are fluffy and a light creamy yellow color, about 3 minutes. Reduce the speed to low; add lemon juice, vanilla and the reserved dry ingredients and mix just until the flour is incorporated. Mix in hot milk.

Pour the batter into the prepared pan. Bake for 23 to 25 minutes, or until a cake tester inserted into the center of the cake comes out clean. Let cool in the pan for 5 minutes. Run a knife around the inside of the pan to loosen the cake. Turn the cake out onto a rack to cool completely.

To hollow out the cake for the meringue filling, use a small serrated knife to mark a circle on the top of the cake ½ inch in from the edge. Cutting about ½ inch deep into the cake, with a sawing motion, cut at an angle toward the center. (Take care to keep the bottom of the cake intact.) Lift out the cake center and set it aside. Spread the prepared lemon filling in the cake bottom. Replace the cake center. Brush off any loose crumbs. Set the cake on a large ovenproof plate.

TO PREPARE MERINGUE:

Preheat oven to 350 degrees F. In a small saucepan, combine sugar and ¼ cup water. Cover and cook over medium-low heat, stirring occasionally, until the sugar dissolves. Uncover and increase the heat to medium-high. Boil until the syrup reaches 240 degrees F and is at the soft-ball stage (when a bit of syrup dropped into ice water forms a pliable ball). Brush the pan with a brush dipped in water to dissolve any sugar crystals that have formed.

Meanwhile, as the syrup begins to boil, start beating the egg whites and cream of tartar in a small bowl at low speed. When frothy, increase the mixer speed to medium and beat until the whites are shiny and form soft peaks.

When the syrup reaches 240 degrees, decrease the mixer speed to low. Slowly pour the hot syrup in a thin stream onto the egg whites as they are beaten. (If the syrup reaches 240 degrees before the egg whites are beaten, remove the syrup from the heat for a few seconds and finish beating the egg whites.) Increase the mixer speed to medium. Beat until the bottom of the bowl is lukewarm and the meringue is firm, about 5 minutes.

Cover the top and outside of the cake with meringue. Mound the meringue toward the center of the cake and swirl with the tip of a spatula. Bake for 15 minutes, or until the meringue is golden. Let cool to room temperature, about 1 hour. Cover carefully and refrigerate for up to 8 hours.

Serves 10.

281 CALORIES PER SERVING: 5 G PROTEIN, 2 G FAT, 64 G CARBOHYDRATE; 90 MG SODIUM; 64 MG CHOLESTEROL.

Prune & Armagnac Cake

Bring a cup of coffee and a slice of this moist, rustic cake over by the fire for a perfect end to a winter's dinner.

1 cup pitted prunes, quartered

½ cup Armagnac or Cognac

½ cup yellow cornmeal, plus more for preparing pan

¼ cup all-purpose white flour

1 teaspoon baking powder
Pinch of salt

½ cup sugar

2 tablespoons vegetable oil, preferably canola oil

1 tablespoon butter, softened

1 large egg

1 large egg white

¼ cup nonfat plain yogurt

2 teaspoons pure vanilla extract

Combine prunes and Armagnac or Cognac in a small bowl and macerate for 2 hours, stirring occasionally. Drain, reserving the liquid.

Preheat oven to 350 degrees F. Lightly oil an 8-inch round cake pan or coat it with nonstick cooking spray. Line the bottom of the pan with a circle of parchment or wax paper. Lightly oil the paper or coat it with nonstick cooking spray and dust the pan with a little cornmeal, shaking out the excess.

In a small bowl, combine cornmeal, flour, baking powder and salt. In a large mixing bowl, whisk together sugar, oil and butter until well combined. Add egg and egg white, whisking until just combined. Stir in yogurt, vanilla and 1 tablespoon of the reserved prune-soaking liquid. (Set aside the remainder for brushing the top of the cake.) Fold in the dry ingredients until just combined.

Pour the batter into the prepared pan and scatter the reserved prunes over the top. Bake for 20 to 25 minutes, or until the cake is golden and a toothpick inserted in the center comes out clean.

Cool for 10 minutes on a rack. Invert the cake, peel off the paper, and place right-side up on a serving plate. Brush the top of the cake with the remaining prune-soaking liquid and serve warm.

Serves 8.

232 CALORIES PER SERVING: 3 G PROTEIN, 6 G FAT, 35 G CARBOHYDRATE; 79 MG SODIUM; 31 MG CHOLESTEROL.

Prune & Armagnac Cake

Dried-Apple Gingerbread Stack Cake

One of the most unusual and interesting of traditional American cakes, stack cakes are found in the Appalachians and throughout the Midwest, wherever apples were (and are) dried for storage.

DRIED-APPLE FILLING

- 3 cups dried apples (about 6½ ounces)
- 3 cups apple cider, plus more if needed
- ¼ cup sugar, or to taste

GINGERBREAD

- 1⅔ cups packed brown sugar
- 2 tablespoons ground ginger
- 1½-2 tablespoons finely chopped crystallized ginger
- 1 tablespoon grated lemon zest (1 lemon)
  Pinch of ground allspice
  Pinch of ground cinnamon
  Pinch of freshly ground black pepper
- 2 large eggs
- 3 large egg whites
- ¾ cup unsulfured molasses
- 2 cups sifted all-purpose white flour (sift before measuring)
- ⅓ cup vegetable oil, preferably canola oil
- ¾ cup buttermilk
- 1 teaspoon baking soda
  Confectioners' sugar for dusting

TO MAKE FILLING:

In a large saucepan, combine dried apples and 3 cups cider; cook, covered, over medium-low heat, mashing occasionally, until the apples are very tender and form a chunky puree, 20 to 30 minutes. Check the apples occasionally as they cook; if they become too dry, add a little more cider or water. Sweeten the apples with sugar to taste and set aside to cool. (*The apple filling can be made up to 3 days ahead and stored, covered, in the refrigerator.*)

TO MAKE GINGERBREAD:

Preheat oven to 350 degrees F. Lightly oil a 12-cup Bundt pan or coat it with nonstick cooking spray.

In a small bowl, stir together brown sugar, ground and crystallized gingers, lemon zest, allspice, cinnamon and black pepper; set aside.

In a large mixing bowl, beat eggs and egg whites with an electric mixer at medium-high speed until light and frothy, about 5 minutes. Beat in molasses. Gradually add the sugar-and-spice mixture until well blended.

Lower the mixer speed slightly. Add about one-third of the flour, then the oil, then another third of the flour. Quickly stir together the buttermilk and baking soda and add to the batter, mixing gently. Add the remaining flour, mixing just until evenly blended. Pour the batter into the prepared pan.

Bake the gingerbread for 45 to 55 minutes, or until a toothpick inserted in the cake comes out clean. If the gingerbread is browning too quickly, cover it loosely with aluminum foil halfway through the baking time. Cool the gingerbread in the pan on a wire rack for 15 minutes; then invert onto a rack and cool completely.

TO ASSEMBLE CAKE:

With a long serrated knife, split the gingerbread into 3 even
layers. Place the bottom layer on a serving platter. Spread half
of the dried-apple filling on the cake and place the middle layer
over the filling. Spread the remaining filling over the cake and
top with the third layer. Cover the cake with plastic wrap and let
it stand for 30 minutes to 1 hour to allow the flavors to blend.
Dust with confectioners' sugar before serving.

    Serves 16.

295 CALORIES PER SERVING: 4 G PROTEIN, 6 G FAT, 60 G CARBOHYDRATE;
110 MG SODIUM; 27 MG CHOLESTEROL.

Black Ginger Cake

The color of this cake depends both on the type of the molasses (blackstrap makes the darkest cake) and the strength of the coffee. It is a perfect cake to accompany afternoon tea.

2 cups all-purpose white flour
½ cup sugar
1½ teaspoons ground cinnamon
1½ teaspoons ground ginger
½ teaspoon salt
¼ cup finely chopped crystallized ginger
1½ teaspoons baking soda
⅔ cup strong hot coffee
1 cup molasses
1 large egg white
1 tablespoon vegetable oil, preferably canola oil
  Confectioners' sugar for dusting

Preheat oven to 350 degrees F. Lightly oil an 8-inch square baking pan or coat it with nonstick cooking spray. Line the bottom of the pan with a square of parchment or wax paper; oil or coat the paper with cooking spray.

Sift flour, sugar, cinnamon, ginger and salt into a mixing bowl. Add crystallized ginger and stir to coat.

In another bowl, stir baking soda into hot coffee. Whisk in molasses, egg white and oil and pour into the dry ingredients; stir just until blended. Do not overmix or the cake will be tough.

Scrape the batter into the prepared pan and bake for 30 to 40 minutes, or until a cake tester inserted in the center of the cake comes out clean. Cool in the pan on a rack for 5 minutes. Turn the cake out onto a wire rack and let cool to lukewarm.

Sprinkle the cake with confectioners' sugar or, for a decorative touch, lay a stencil or a paper doily on the cake, sprinkle confectioners' sugar over all and carefully remove the stencil.

Serves 9.

285 CALORIES PER SERVING: 3 G PROTEIN, 2 G FAT, 64 G CARBOHYDRATE; 269 MG SODIUM; 0 MG CHOLESTEROL.

Glazed Cheesecake with Fruit

Directions for yogurt cheese, a key ingredient in this recipe, are in "The Well-Stocked Kitchen" (page 248).

TO MAKE CRUST:

Preheat oven to 350 degrees F. Coat a 9- or 10-inch springform pan with nonstick cooking spray. In a small bowl, stir together crumbs, cereal and oil. Press into the bottom of the prepared pan and set aside.

TO MAKE FILLING:

Put the pressed cottage cheese in a food processor and process until smooth. Add yogurt cheese, cream cheese, sugar, eggs, egg whites, cornstarch, vanilla, lemon zest and lemon juice; process until smooth. Spoon the mixture over the crust. Set the pan on a baking sheet and bake until just set, 40 to 45 minutes for a 10-inch cake or 50 to 55 minutes for a 9-inch cake. Remove from the oven and cool for 15 minutes. Keep oven temperature at 350 degrees.

TO MAKE TOPPING:

In a small bowl, stir together yogurt cheese, sugar and vanilla. Spoon over the baked cheesecake, starting at the center and extending to within ½ inch of the edge. Return the cheesecake to the oven and bake for 5 minutes longer. Cool on a rack. Cover and refrigerate for at least 12 hours or for up to 3 days.

TO GLAZE CHEESECAKE:

Using a sharp knife, remove the skin and white pith from oranges and discard. Cut the segments away from their surrounding membranes and reserve. In a small saucepan, melt apricot preserves over low heat. Remove from the heat and stir in orange liqueur. With a pastry brush, brush about half of the apricot preserves onto the chilled cheesecake. Arrange kiwi fruit, orange segments and strawberries decoratively over the top. Brush with the remaining apricot preserves.

Serves 16.

322 CALORIES PER SERVING: 17 G PROTEIN, 6 G FAT, 52 G CARBOHYDRATE; 271 MG SODIUM; 36 MG CHOLESTEROL.

CRUST

- ½ cup graham cracker crumbs
- ½ cup Grape-Nuts cereal
- 2 tablespoons vegetable oil, preferably canola oil

FILLING

- 2 cups nonfat cottage cheese, pressed to yield 1 cup
- 2 cups yogurt cheese, made from 6 cups nonfat plain yogurt
- 1 8-ounce package reduced-fat cream cheese, softened
- 1¼ cups sugar
- 2 large eggs
- 2 large egg whites
- 1 tablespoon cornstarch
- 1 tablespoon pure vanilla extract
- 2 teaspoons grated lemon zest
- 1 teaspoon lemon juice

TOPPING

- 2 cups yogurt cheese, made from 6 cups nonfat plain yogurt
- ⅓ cup sugar
- 2 teaspoons pure vanilla extract

FRUIT & GLAZE

- 4 navel oranges
- ¼ cup apricot preserves
- 2 tablespoons orange liqueur, such as Grand Marnier
- 4 kiwi fruit, peeled and sliced
- 1 pint strawberries, hulled

Sunny Citrus Chiffon Cake

Flavored with orange, lemon and lime, this big, beautiful cake is a fitting ending to a springtime garden party. Just three egg yolks give the cake a golden hue and a texture richer than angel food.

TO MAKE CAKE:

Preheat oven to 350 degrees F. Sift flour, ¾ cup of the sugar, baking powder and salt into a small bowl; set aside.

In the bowl of an electric mixer, beat egg whites and cream of tartar just until soft peaks form. Beat in the remaining ¾ cup sugar, 2 tablespoons at a time, until the whites are shiny and form soft peaks.

In a small bowl, whisk together egg yolks, Grand Marnier, orange, lemon and lime zests, lemon and lime juices, and vanilla. Pour over the whites and fold together with a rubber spatula.

Resift the reserved dry ingredients over the beaten egg whites in four parts, folding in gently after each addition. Spoon the batter into an ungreased 10-inch angel food cake pan with a removable bottom. Smooth the top and run a knife or spatula through the batter to remove any air bubbles.

Bake for 45 to 50 minutes, or until the top is golden and a long skewer inserted into the cake comes out clean. Invert the pan over the neck of a bottle and let cool completely.

TO PREPARE CITRUS GLAZE:

Use a citrus zester to remove long threads of zest from the orange, lemon and lime. Squeeze 4 teaspoons of juice from each of the fruits. In a small bowl, whisk the juices into the confectioners' sugar to make a smooth glaze.

With a knife, loosen the edges of the cake and invert onto a cake plate. Spoon the glaze over the top, allowing it to drip down the sides. Sprinkle the top of the cake with the julienned zest. Let the cake stand at least 30 minutes for the glaze to set.

Serves 12.

243 CALORIES PER SERVING: 5 G PROTEIN, 1 G FAT, 54 G CARBOHYDRATE; 120 MG SODIUM; 53 MG CHOLESTEROL.

CAKE

- 1½ cups cake flour
- 1½ cups sugar
- 1 teaspoon baking powder
- ¼ teaspoon salt
- 10 large egg whites, at room temperature
- ½ teaspoon cream of tartar
- 3 large egg yolks
- 2 tablespoons Grand Marnier or other orange liqueur
- 2 tablespoons grated orange zest
- 2 teaspoons grated lemon zest
- 2 teaspoons grated lime zest
- 1 tablespoon fresh lemon juice
- 1 tablespoon fresh lime juice
- 1 teaspoon pure vanilla extract

CITRUS GLAZE

- 1 large orange, scrubbed
- 1 lemon, scrubbed
- 1 lime, scrubbed
- 2 cups confectioners' sugar

Strawberry Patch Cake

The neat rows of shiny strawberries bring to mind the local strawberry patch. When making this cake,
keep in mind that the yogurt used in the filling needs to drain for 4 hours ahead of time.

BUTTERMILK POUND CAKE

- 1½ cups cake flour
- ½   teaspoon salt
- ½   teaspoon baking powder
- ¼   teaspoon baking soda
- 1   16-ounce can pear halves in light syrup, drained
- 1   tablespoon butter
- ¾   cup plus 2 tablespoons sugar
- ½   cup buttermilk
- 1   tablespoon vegetable oil, preferably canola oil

TO MAKE CAKE:

Preheat oven to 350 degrees F. Lightly oil a 9-inch square pan or coat it with nonstick cooking spray. Dust with flour, shaking out the excess.

Sift cake flour, salt, baking powder and baking soda into a bowl and set aside.

In a food processor or blender, puree pears. Transfer to a large bowl. In a small saucepan, melt butter over medium heat. Cook, swirling the pan, until the butter turns a light brown, about 1 minute. Add to the pears, along with ¾ cup sugar, buttermilk, oil, vanilla, lemon zest and egg yolk; whisk until smooth. Set aside.

In the bowl of an electric mixer, beat the 2 egg whites until

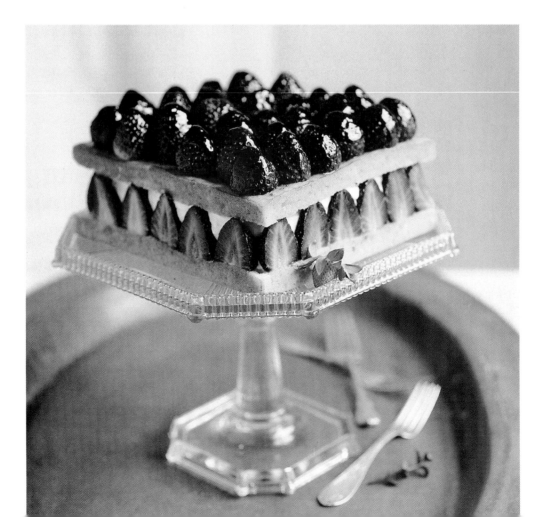

soft peaks form. Continue beating and slowly add the remaining 2 tablespoons sugar. Beat until stiff but not dry peaks form.

With a rubber spatula, gently fold the reserved dry ingredients into the pear mixture alternately with the beaten egg whites, making three additions of the dry ingredients and two of the beaten whites. Pour the batter into the prepared pan. Bake for about 30 minutes, or until a cake tester inserted in the center of the cake comes out clean. Let cool in the pan for 5 minutes, then turn out onto a rack to cool, right-side up.

TO MAKE FILLING AND ASSEMBLE CAKE:

In a food processor or blender, puree ricotta until smooth. Add the drained yogurt, orange zest and confectioners' sugar; blend to mix.

In a small saucepan, melt strawberry preserves over low heat. Strain into a small bowl and set aside.

Use a large serrated knife to slice the cake horizontally into 2 layers. Put the bottom layer on a cake plate, cut-side up. Spread a thin layer of ricotta filling (about ½ cup) over the bottom layer. Set aside 2 pints of strawberries to garnish the cake. Cut the remaining berries in half lengthwise.

Place a row of strawberry halves, points up and cut sides facing out, on the edge of the bottom layer. (Choose smaller strawberries that are the same height. Trim the base of the strawberries, if needed, to make them all of equal height.) Fill the center with strawberry halves, cut sides facing down. Spread the remaining ricotta filling evenly over the strawberries in the center of the cake.

Set the top layer, cut-side down, on the filled cake. Press gently on the cake to level it. Brush a thin layer of strained preserves over the cake. Arrange whole strawberries in rows on top of the cake. Brush the strawberries with the strained preserves. (*The cake can be made in advance and kept, covered, in the refrigerator for up to 24 hours.*)

Serves 9.

319 CALORIES PER SERVING: 8 G PROTEIN, 6 G FAT, 59 G CARBOHYDRATE; 272 MG SODIUM; 36 MG CHOLESTEROL.

1½ teaspoons pure vanilla extract

1½ teaspoons grated lemon zest

1 large egg, separated

1 large egg white

ORANGE-RICOTTA FILLING

1 cup part-skim ricotta cheese

1 cup nonfat vanilla yogurt, drained for 4 hours in a cheesecloth-lined sieve in the refrigerator

1½ teaspoons grated orange zest

2 tablespoons confectioners' sugar

½ cup strawberry preserves

4 pints small strawberries, hulled

CHAPTER 14

Cookies

Oatmeal Lace Cookies with Dried Tart Cherries

EATING WELL *recipe developer Susanne Davis fondly remembers her Swedish grandmother's oatmeal lace cookies. Susanne adapted the recipe, reducing the butter and incorporating dried cherries.*

1   cup rolled oats
⅓   cup corn syrup
1   tablespoon vegetable oil, preferably canola oil
2   tablespoons butter
1   large egg
⅓   cup sugar
1   teaspoon pure vanilla extract
2   tablespoons all-purpose white flour
1   teaspoon baking powder
¼   teaspoon salt
⅓   cup chopped dried tart cherries

Position rack in the center of the oven; preheat to 400 degrees F. Lightly oil 3 baking sheets or coat them with nonstick cooking spray, and dust them with flour, shaking off the excess.

In a mixing bowl, combine oats, corn syrup and oil. In a small saucepan, melt butter over low heat. Cook until it begins to turn a light, nutty brown, 1 to 1½ minutes. (Be careful not to burn the butter.) Pour into the oat mixture and stir to combine. Set aside.

In large bowl, beat egg and sugar with an electric mixer until thick and pale, about 5 minutes. Blend in vanilla.

In a small bowl, stir together flour, baking powder and salt; fold into the egg mixture. Add the oat mixture and dried cherries; stir gently to combine.

Drop the batter by teaspoonfuls, about 2 inches apart, onto the prepared baking sheets. Bake, one sheet at a time, for about 4 minutes, or until the cookies are golden and lacy. Let cool on the baking sheet for 2 minutes, then carefully remove the cookies from the baking sheet and cool on a flat surface (not a rack). (*The cookies can be stored in an airtight container with parchment or wax paper between the layers for up to 4 days.*)

Makes about 2½ dozen cookies.

36 CALORIES PER COOKIE: 1 G PROTEIN, 2 G FAT, 5 G CARBOHYDRATE; 39 MG SODIUM; 9 MG CHOLESTEROL.

Oatmeal Lace Cookies with Dried Tart Cherries

Lemon Slices

Fresh lemon zest and frozen lemonade concentrate enhance these mild, crunchy, crisp wafers.
Pine nuts simulate the seeds of a lemon for a little culinary trompe l'oeil.

COOKIE DOUGH

2¼	cups all-purpose white flour
⅓	cup cornstarch
1	teaspoon baking powder
¼	teaspoon salt
⅛	teaspoon baking soda
¾	cup sugar
½	cup light corn syrup
3	tablespoons unsalted butter, slightly softened
2½	tablespoons vegetable oil, preferably canola oil
1	large egg white
3	tablespoons frozen lemonade concentrate
1	tablespoon grated lemon zest
2	teaspoons pure vanilla extract
2½	tablespoons pine nuts (1 ounce)
	About 2 tablespoons yellow decorating sugar crystals

LEMON ICING

1½	cups confectioners' sugar
5	tablespoons frozen lemonade concentrate, thawed

TO MAKE COOKIES:

Position rack in upper third of oven; preheat to 375 degrees F. Lightly oil 3 baking sheets or coat with nonstick cooking spray.

In a bowl, thoroughly combine flour, cornstarch, baking powder, salt and baking soda. In a large mixing bowl, beat ½ cup of the sugar, corn syrup, butter and oil with an electric mixer on medium speed until smooth. Beat in egg white, lemonade concentrate, lemon zest and vanilla. With the mixer on low speed, beat in about half of the dry ingredients until just mixed. Stir in the remaining dry ingredients.

Place the remaining ¼ cup sugar in a pie plate. Roll the dough into 1-inch balls. Roll in the sugar and place on baking sheets about 2 inches apart. Rub the bottom of a wide glass or custard cup lightly with oil and dip into sugar. Flatten the balls with the glass to make 2½-inch cookies, dipping the glass into the sugar after each cookie. Press about 5 pine nuts randomly onto each cookie and sprinkle with yellow decorating sugar.

Bake for 8 to 12 minutes, or until the cookies are light golden. While the cookies are still warm, cut each cookie in half and quickly transfer to a wire rack to cool.

TO ICE COOKIES:

Sift confectioners' sugar into a bowl and stir in lemonade concentrate. If the mixture is too thick to pipe, add a few more drops of lemonade concentrate. Transfer to a pastry bag fitted with a fine round tip. Pipe the outline of 4 or 5 lemon sections onto each cookie. Let the cookies stand until the icing sets, about 1 hour. (*The cookies can be stored in an airtight container, with wax paper between the layers, for up to 1 week.*)

Makes about 6 dozen cookies.

39 CALORIES PER COOKIE: 1 G PROTEIN, 0 G FAT, 9 G CARBOHYDRATE; 15 MG SODIUM; 0 MG CHOLESTEROL.

Mocha-Almond Biscotti

In this pretty marbled cookie, half of the dough is almond-flavored and the other half is chocolate/coffee-flavored.

Preheat oven to 325 degrees F. Spread almonds on a baking sheet and bake for 12 to 14 minutes, or until lightly toasted. Set aside. Line a second baking sheet with parchment paper or coat it with nonstick cooking spray.

In a mixing bowl, stir together flour, sugar, baking powder, baking soda and salt. In another bowl, whisk together eggs, egg whites and vanilla, and add to the dry ingredients; mix just until smooth. The batter will be sticky. In a small bowl, combine cocoa, instant coffee and 4 teaspoons water. Divide the dough in half. To one half, add the cocoa mixture and melted chocolate. Mix just until incorporated. To the other half, stir in almond extract and the almonds.

Place half of the almond dough on a well-floured work surface. Pat into a 4-by-8-inch rectangle. Top with half of the chocolate dough. Roll up into a cylinder, then roll the cylinder back and forth to form a 14-inch log, 1½ inches thick. Repeat with the remaining dough halves.

Place the logs on the prepared baking sheet. Bake for 20 to 25 minutes, or until firm to the touch. Transfer the logs to a rack to cool. Reduce the oven temperature to 300 degrees.

Cut the logs diagonally into ½-inch-thick slices. Stand the slices upright on the baking sheet and bake for 40 minutes. Let cool before storing. (*The biscotti can be stored in an airtight container for up to 1 month.*)

Makes about 4 dozen biscotti.

48 CALORIES PER BISCOTTO: 1 G PROTEIN, 1 G FAT, 8 G CARBOHYDRATE; 32 MG SODIUM; 9 MG CHOLESTEROL.

½ cup whole unblanched almonds

2 cups all-purpose white flour

1 cup sugar

1 teaspoon baking powder

½ teaspoon baking soda

¼ teaspoon salt

2 large eggs

2 large egg whites

1 teaspoon pure vanilla extract

1 tablespoon unsweetened cocoa powder

2 teaspoons instant coffee powder

1 ounce unsweetened chocolate, melted

½ teaspoon pure almond extract

Hamantashen

The traditional cookie for the Jewish holiday of Purim, hamantashen *is Yiddish for "Haman's pockets." They are meant to recall the story of Haman, a wicked Persian prince who wished to destroy the Jews but was foiled by Mordecai and Esther.*

TO MAKE FILLING:

In a saucepan, combine prunes, raisins and ½ cup water. Simmer over low heat until the liquid has been absorbed, about 10 minutes. In a food processor, combine the prune mixture, apples, walnuts, sugar, lemon juice and lemon zest; process until smooth. Transfer to a small bowl and set aside. (*The filling can be made up to 2 days ahead and kept, covered, in the refrigerator.*)

TO MAKE COOKIES:

In a mixing bowl, using an electric mixer on medium speed, cream sugar, oil and butter until smooth. Add egg and beat until smooth. Add vanilla and beat until blended. In another bowl, sift together flour, baking powder and salt. Stir the dry ingredients into the sugar mixture until just combined. Gather the dough together into a ball, wrap with plastic wrap and flatten slightly. Refrigerate for 2 to 3 hours or overnight.

Line 2 baking sheets with parchment or coat them with non-stick cooking spray. Set aside. Preheat oven to 350 degrees F.

Divide the dough in half. (Refrigerate the other half.) Roll out on a lightly floured surface to a thickness of ⅛ inch. Using a 2½-inch cookie cutter, cut the dough into circles. Place ½ teaspoon of the filling in the center of each circle. Bring the edges together to partially cover the filling, forming a 3-cornered cookie. Pinch the corners together to seal.

Place cookies about 1½ inches apart on the prepared baking sheets. Bake for 10 to 15 minutes, or until the tops are golden. Transfer to racks to cool. Repeat with the remaining dough. (*The hamantashen can be stored in an airtight container for up to 3 days.*)

Makes about 4 dozen cookies.

58 CALORIES PER COOKIE: 1 G PROTEIN, 2 G FAT, 6 G CARBOHYDRATE; 13 MG SODIUM; 9 MG CHOLESTEROL.

Mandelbrot (page 206) and Hamantashen

FILLING

¾ cup pitted prunes

⅓ cup raisins

⅓ cup coarsely chopped apple

¼ cup walnut pieces

2 tablespoons sugar

2 tablespoons fresh lemon juice

1 teaspoon grated lemon zest

COOKIE DOUGH

½ cup sugar

¼ cup vegetable oil, preferably canola oil

2 tablespoons butter or margarine, at room temperature

1 large egg

1 teaspoon pure vanilla extract

2 cups all-purpose white flour

1 teaspoon baking powder

Pinch of salt

Mandelbrot

Mandelbrot is Yiddish for almond bread, and the almond-rich dough in this recipe is shaped like a loaf and baked. Like Italian biscotti, the loaf is then sliced and the slices are rebaked into crisp cookies.

½ cup sliced almonds

¾ cup sugar

2 tablespoons butter or margarine, at room temperature

2 tablespoons vegetable oil, preferably canola oil

2 large eggs, lightly beaten

1 large egg white, lightly beaten

¼ cup whiskey or brandy

2 tablespoons nonfat yogurt or applesauce

1 teaspoon pure vanilla extract

⅛ teaspoon pure almond extract (optional)

2 cups all-purpose white flour

2 teaspoons baking powder

½ teaspoon salt

½ cup raisins

Preheat oven to 350 degrees F. Lightly oil 2 loaf pans or coat them with nonstick cooking spray. Dust with flour, shaking out the excess. Set aside. Put almonds in a pie plate and toast in the oven until golden, 5 to 7 minutes. Set aside.

In a mixing bowl, using an electric mixer on medium speed, cream sugar, butter or margarine and oil. Add eggs, egg white, whiskey or brandy, yogurt or applesauce, vanilla and almond extract, if using; mix until smooth. In a large bowl, stir together flour, baking powder and salt. Using a wooden spoon, stir in the wet ingredients until incorporated. Add raisins and the toasted almonds.

Divide the batter evenly between the two prepared pans. Bake for 25 to 30 minutes, or until the tops are golden and a toothpick inserted in the center comes out clean. Cool in the pan for 10 minutes.

Remove from the pans, slice into ½-inch-thick slices and arrange in a single layer on 2 baking sheets. Return to the oven and bake for 10 to 12 minutes, or until light brown, switching the baking sheets midway through baking. Turn off the oven, and leave the mandelbrot in the oven until crisp, about 45 minutes. (*The mandelbrot can be stored in an airtight container for up to 1 month.*)

Makes about 30 slices.

93 CALORIES PER SLICE: 2 G PROTEIN, 3 G FAT, 14 G CARBOHYDRATE; 73 MG SODIUM; 16 MG CHOLESTEROL.

Chocolate Meringue Kisses

Although these are very low in fat, they offer plenty of satisfaction for chocolate lovers.
They are crispy on the outside, chewy-soft on the inside.

Position racks in the center and upper positions of the oven; preheat to 325 degrees F. Line 2 baking sheets with parchment paper.

Pulverize cocoa powder and chocolate in a food processor for about 30 seconds, or until the chocolate is ground to a fine powder. Stir (do not process) confectioners' sugar and cornstarch into the chocolate-cocoa mixture until evenly incorporated; set aside.

In a grease-free mixing bowl, combine egg whites and coffee powder; let stand for 5 minutes. With an electric mixer on medium speed, beat the egg white-coffee mixture until frothy. Increase the mixer speed to high and beat until soft peaks start to form. Gradually add granulated sugar, about 2 tablespoons at a time, until all of the sugar is incorporated. Add vanilla. Beat until mixture is stiff and glossy, about 90 seconds. Fold in the pulverized chocolate and cocoa until evenly incorporated but not overmixed.

Spoon the mixture into a piping bag fitted with a ½-inch open-star tip and pipe kisses about 1 inch in diameter on the prepared baking sheets, spacing the kisses about 1½ inches apart. (*Alternatively, drop the mixture by rounded teaspoonfuls.*)

Bake the cookies for 14 to 18 minutes, switching the baking sheets halfway through; the cookies should be almost firm to the touch. (Bake all the cookies at once; the batter does not hold.) Remove the sheets to cooling racks and let the cookies stand for a minute or two. Then slide the parchment from the baking sheet to a flat surface and let the cookies stand until completely cooled. Carefully peel the cookies from the parchment. (*The cookies can be stored in an airtight container for up to 4 days.*)

Makes about 3½ dozen cookies.

20 CALORIES PER COOKIE: 0 G PROTEIN, 0 G FAT, 4 G CARBOHYDRATE; 4 MG SODIUM; 0 MG CHOLESTEROL.

3½ tablespoons unsweetened cocoa powder (American-style or Dutch-process)

1 ounce unsweetened chocolate, chopped

¼ cup sifted confectioners' sugar

1½ tablespoons cornstarch

3 large egg whites

½ teaspoon instant coffee powder or granules

⅔ cup granulated sugar

1 teaspoon pure vanilla extract

Hickory Nut Cookies

Shagbark hickory trees are a common sight in Wisconsin, where this recipe originates. Shelling the nuts is a labor of love, however—they are one of the hardest nuts to crack. You may substitute pecans, which are members of the hickory family. These helix-shaped cookies are easy to form; if you prefer round cookies, drop the batter by heaping teaspoonfuls onto the baking sheet.

2 tablespoons butter

¼ cup chopped hickory nuts (1 ounce)

¼ cup white sugar

¼ cup packed light brown sugar

2 large egg whites

6 tablespoons all-purpose white flour

2 teaspoons pure vanilla extract

Preheat oven to 300 degrees F. Lightly oil 3 baking sheets or coat them with nonstick cooking spray. (Or use 1 baking sheet and wash and respray it between batches.)

In a small saucepan, melt butter over medium heat. Add nuts and stir until the butter is lightly browned, about 1 minute. Transfer to a mixing bowl. Stir in white and brown sugars. Add egg whites, flour and vanilla; whisk until combined.

Working with one baking sheet at a time, spoon a heaping teaspoon of batter to make a line about 8 inches long and ¾ inch wide. Repeat to make 8 lines on the sheet, spacing them about 1 inch apart. Bake for 8 to 10 minutes, or until the cookies are well-browned on the edges.

Working quickly using a metal spatula, remove a cookie and wrap it around a ¾-inch-thick wooden dowel or fat wooden spoon handle. Once the cookie stiffens, slide it off and repeat with the next cookie.

If the unshaped cookies begin to harden and stick to the baking sheet, return the baking sheet to the oven for about 30 seconds to soften them. Bake and shape the remaining batter in the same manner. (*The cookies may be stored in an airtight container for up to 4 days.*)

Makes about 2 dozen cookies.

45 CALORIES PER COOKIE: 1 G PROTEIN, 2 G FAT, 6 G CARBOHYDRATE; 16 MG SODIUM; 3 MG CHOLESTEROL.

Hickory Nut Cookies

Date Pinwheel Icebox Cookies

These homey icebox cookies have a mild, pleasing aroma and an appealing chewy-crisp texture. The pinwheel logs may be held in the freezer for several weeks; slicing and baking the cookies takes only a few minutes.

FILLING

2⅓ cups chopped pitted dates (12 ounces)

½ cup sweet orange marmalade (not Seville)

½ cup fresh orange juice

1 teaspoon grated orange zest

½ teaspoon ground cinnamon

DOUGH

3¼ cups all-purpose white flour

¾ teaspoon baking powder

½ teaspoon ground cinnamon

¼ teaspoon salt

⅛ teaspoon baking soda

⅔ cup white sugar

⅔ cup packed dark brown sugar

¼ cup unsalted butter, slightly softened

3 tablespoons vegetable oil, preferably canola oil

3 large egg whites

2 teaspoons grated orange zest

1½ teaspoons pure vanilla extract

TO MAKE FILLING:

In a saucepan, combine dates, marmalade, orange juice, orange zest and cinnamon. Bring to a simmer over medium heat. Cook, stirring frequently, until the dates are soft and most of the liquid has been absorbed, 2 to 3 minutes. Cover and set aside until cooled to room temperature. (*The filling can be stored, covered, up to 48 hours in the refrigerator.*)

TO MAKE DOUGH:

In a large bowl, combine flour, baking powder, cinnamon, salt and baking soda. In a large mixing bowl, combine white and brown sugars, butter, oil, egg whites, zest and vanilla and beat with electric mixer on medium speed until smooth. With the mixer speed on low, beat in half of the dry ingredients just until incorporated. Stir in the remaining dry ingredients by hand.

Divide the dough in half. Shape each half into a rough log about 6 inches long. Place one log on a sheet of wax paper; cover with a second sheet of wax paper. With a rolling pin, roll the log into an 11-inch square of even thickness. Flip the dough once or twice and smooth out any wrinkles that form in the paper. Also, patch the dough as necessary to keep the square's sides straight. Repeat with the remaining dough. Stack the squares on a baking sheet with wax paper between them. Refrigerate until fairly firm, at least 30 minutes or overnight.

TO MAKE PINWHEELS:

Working with one square of dough at a time, place the dough on a flat work surface. Peel off the top sheet of wax paper. Spread half of the date filling evenly over the entire surface of the dough; the filling layer will be thin. Peeling off the second sheet of paper as you work, tightly roll up the dough as you would a jelly roll. Gently stretch out the center slightly to yield an evenly thick roll. Wrap the roll in wax paper. Repeat the process with the second square of dough. Freeze the rolls for at least 2 hours, or until firm enough to slice.

Position rack in the upper third of the oven; preheat to 350 degrees F. Brush several baking sheets with oil or coat them with nonstick cooking spray. Using a large, sharp knife, cut the rolls crosswise into scant ¼-inch-thick slices and carefully transfer to the prepared baking sheets, spacing the slices about 1 inch apart.

Bake for 10 to 15 minutes, or until edges are browned. Reverse pan from front to back halfway through baking to ensure even browning. With a spatula, carefully transfer cookies to wire racks to cool. (*The cookies can be stored in an airtight container for up to 1 week.*)

Makes about 5½ dozen cookies.

67 CALORIES PER COOKIE: 1 G PROTEIN, 1 G FAT, 13 G CARBOHYDRATE; 23 MG SODIUM; 2 MG CHOLESTEROL.

Pistachio-Ginger Thins

These cookies make a fine accompaniment to a fruit compote.

Preheat oven to 300 degrees F. Lightly oil 2 baking sheets or coat them with nonstick cooking spray.

In a saucepan over medium heat, melt butter. Add pistachios and stir until the butter is lightly browned, about 1 minute. Transfer the mixture to a bowl. Whisk in sugar. Add flour, egg whites and ginger and whisk until smooth.

Drop the batter by heaping teaspoonfuls, about 2 inches apart, onto the prepared baking sheets. Bake, one sheet at a time, for 12 to 15 minutes, or until golden. With a spatula, immediately transfer the cookies to a rack to cool. If the cookies begin to stick before all are removed, return the pan briefly to the oven. (*The thins can be stored in an airtight container for up to 1 week.*)

Makes 2 dozen cookies.

40 CALORIES PER COOKIE: 1 G PROTEIN, 2 G FAT, 6 G CARBOHYDRATE; 14 MG SODIUM; 3 MG CHOLESTEROL.

2 tablespoons butter

¼ cup chopped skinned pistachios, rinsed if salted

½ cup sugar

6 tablespoons all-purpose white flour

2 large egg whites

¼ teaspoon ground ginger

Chewy Oatmeal Raisin Cookies

Creating a truly satisfying low-fat cookie has been one of the EATING WELL *Test Kitchen's greatest challenges. This oatmeal cookie is a great success.*

3 cups rolled oats

⅓ cup chopped walnuts or pecans

1 cup raisins

1½ cups sugar

½ cup apple butter

2 large eggs

¼ cup vegetable oil, preferably canola oil

1 teaspoon pure vanilla extract

2 cups all-purpose white flour

1 teaspoon baking soda

½ teaspoon baking powder

½ teaspoon salt

½ teaspoon ground cinnamon

½ teaspoon ground cloves

Preheat oven to 375 degrees F. Spread oats and nuts on an ungreased baking sheet and bake for 5 to 7 minutes, or until lightly toasted; set aside. Line 2 baking sheets with parchment paper or coat them with nonstick cooking spray.

In a small saucepan, combine raisins with 1 cup water. Bring to a simmer over low heat and cook until the raisins are plumped, about 10 minutes. Drain, discarding the liquid, and set aside.

In a large mixing bowl, beat sugar, apple butter, eggs, oil and vanilla with an electric mixer until light and fluffy, about 5 minutes. Sift flour, baking soda, baking powder, salt, cinnamon and cloves into another bowl; stir the dry ingredients into the wet ingredients with a spoon. Stir in the reserved oats, nuts and raisins; mix well.

Drop the dough by rounded teaspoonfuls, about 2 inches apart, onto the prepared baking sheets. Bake, one sheet at a time, for 8 to 10 minutes, or until lightly browned. Transfer the cookies to racks and let cool. The cookies are best when eaten within a day or two of when they are made, or stored in the freezer.

Makes about 4 dozen cookies.

114 CALORIES PER COOKIE: 3 G PROTEIN, 3 G FAT, 21 G CARBOHYDRATE; 46 MG SODIUM; 9 MG CHOLESTEROL.

Chocolate Chip Cookies

These cookies have a third as much fat as traditional chocolate chip cookies.

Preheat oven to 375 degrees F. Line 2 baking sheets with parchment paper or coat them with nonstick cooking spray.

In a small bowl, stir together flour, baking soda and salt; set aside. Melt butter in a small saucepan over low heat. Cook, swirling the pan, until the butter turns nutty brown, about 1 minute. Pour into a large mixing bowl. Add cream cheese, brown sugar and white sugar. Beat with an electric mixer on low speed until smooth. Add egg, egg white and vanilla; beat until well incorporated. Add the reserved dry ingredients and chocolate chips and stir with a wooden spoon just until combined. (The batter will be runny.)

Drop the batter by rounded tablespoonfuls, 2 inches apart, onto the prepared baking sheets. Bake, one sheet at a time, for 12 to 15 minutes, or until golden. Transfer the cookies to racks and let cool.

Makes about 2½ dozen cookies.

63 CALORIES PER COOKIE: 1 G PROTEIN, 2 G FAT, 10 G CARBOHYDRATE; 73 MG SODIUM; 10 MG CHOLESTEROL.

1	cup all-purpose white flour
½	teaspoon baking soda
½	teaspoon salt
2	tablespoons unsalted butter
2	ounces reduced-fat cream cheese
6	tablespoons packed light brown sugar
6	tablespoons white sugar
1	large egg
1	large egg white
1	teaspoon pure vanilla extract
½	cup semisweet chocolate chips, coarsely chopped

Chewy Oatmeal Raisin Cookies (page 212) and Chocolate Chip Cookies

Chocolate Crinkles

Very dark and chocolaty, these sugar-coated rounds are remarkably low in fat—a mere 2 grams per cookie.
A tin of Chocolate Crinkles is the perfect gift for the chocoholic who is trying to cut back on fat.

2 cups all-purpose white flour

2½ cups confectioners' sugar

½ cup unsweetened cocoa powder (not Dutch-process)

2½ teaspoons baking powder

¼ teaspoon salt

3½ ounces unsweetened chocolate, coarsely chopped

3½ tablespoons vegetable oil, preferably canola oil

1½ cups packed light brown sugar

⅓ cup light corn syrup

1½ tablespoons pure vanilla extract

4 large egg whites

Sift flour, 1½ cups of the confectioners' sugar, cocoa, baking powder and salt together into a large bowl.

In a heavy saucepan, combine chocolate and oil; warm over very low heat, stirring frequently, until just melted and smooth. Be very careful that chocolate does not scorch. Remove from the heat and let cool slightly. Stir in brown sugar, corn syrup and vanilla until well blended. Using a whisk, beat egg whites into chocolate mixture until no lumps of brown sugar remain. With a spoon, gently stir the chocolate mixture into the dry ingredients just until smooth. Cover the dough and refrigerate until firm enough to shape into balls, at least 2½ hours and up to 8 hours.

Preheat oven to 350 degrees F. Lightly oil 2 baking sheets or coat them with nonstick cooking spray.

Put the remaining 1 cup confectioners' sugar in a shallow bowl. Dusting your hands with additional confectioners' sugar, roll portions of dough into 1-inch balls between your palms. Dredge each ball in confectioners' sugar until heavily coated. Arrange the cookies on baking sheets, about 1½ inches apart.

Bake for 8 to 10 minutes, or until the tops are almost firm when tapped. Let the cookies stand until they firm up slightly, about 2 minutes. With a spatula, transfer the cookies to wire racks to cool. (*The crinkles can be stored in an airtight container for up to 3 days.*)

Makes about 4 dozen cookies.

92 CALORIES PER COOKIE: 1 G PROTEIN, 2 G FAT, 18 G CARBOHYDRATE; 35 MG SODIUM; 0 MG CHOLESTEROL.

Molasses Cookies

A great little cookie with only 1 gram of fat in each.

Position rack in the center of the oven; preheat to 350 degrees F. Line 2 baking sheets with parchment paper or coat them with nonstick cooking spray.

In a small bowl, cover prunes with ¼ cup hot water; let steep for 5 minutes to soften.

Meanwhile, in a large bowl, stir together flour, cinnamon, ginger, baking soda and salt. Set aside.

Place the prunes and steeping liquid in a food processor and blend until smooth, about 1 minute. Add 1 cup sugar, oil and molasses; blend well. Add to the dry ingredients, along with egg whites, and stir just to combine.

Spoon some sugar into a shallow dish. Form the dough into 1-inch balls. Roll the balls in the sugar and place on the prepared baking sheets, spacing them about 2 inches apart. Gently flatten the balls to a ¼-inch thickness.

Bake, one sheet at a time, for 8 to 10 minutes, or until the bottoms are browned and the tops are crackled. Transfer the cookies to racks and let cool. (*The cookies can be stored in an airtight container for up to 1 week.*)

Makes about 4 dozen cookies.

50 CALORIES PER COOKIE: 1 G PROTEIN, 1 G FAT, 9 G CARBOHYDRATE; 44 MG SODIUM; 0 MG CHOLESTEROL.

5   pitted prunes

2   cups all-purpose white flour

1   tablespoon ground cinnamon

2   teaspoons ground ginger

1   teaspoon baking soda

½   teaspoon salt

1   cup sugar, plus extra for rolling

¼   cup vegetable oil, preferably canola oil

¼   cup unsulfured molasses (not blackstrap)

2   large egg whites, lightly beaten with a fork

CHAPTER 15

Puddings & Other Desserts

Rhubarb Fool

Choose the reddest rhubarb stalks you can find for this fool.

Tie cinnamon stick, cloves and lemon zest together in a cheese-cloth bag. In a large saucepan, combine rhubarb, sugar and the spice bag. Bring to a boil over medium-high heat. Cook, stirring occasionally, until the mixture has the consistency of applesauce, 6 to 8 minutes. Discard the spice bag. Chill the rhubarb mixture about 1 hour.

Meanwhile, line a colander with cheesecloth and set it over a bowl. Spoon in yogurt and let it drain in the refrigerator until it measures 1½ cups, 45 minutes to 1 hour.

Place the drained yogurt in a mixing bowl. Add the rhubarb mixture and fold lightly, leaving some swirls. In a chilled bowl, whip cream and swirl it into the fool. Spoon into individual dishes. Cover and refrigerate for at least 1 hour or up to 6 hours.

Serves 8.

216 CALORIES PER SERVING: 5 G PROTEIN, 5 G FAT, 41 G CARBOHYDRATE; 55 MG SODIUM; 18 MG CHOLESTEROL.

1	cinnamon stick
3	whole cloves
1	2-inch-long strip lemon zest
2¼	pounds rhubarb, trimmed and cut into ½-inch pieces (8 cups)
1¼	cups sugar
2	cups nonfat vanilla yogurt
½	cup whipping cream

Rhubarb Fool

Summer Pudding

*Although red currants are classic in summer pudding, other combinations of berries,
such as raspberries and blackberries or blueberries, can be used. Just be sure that at least half of
the berries are red for the pudding to have the nicest color.*

1 pint red currants

1 pint loganberries

⅔-¾ cup sugar, depending on sweetness of fruit

¼ cup pure seedless raspberry or strawberry spread or jam

1 tablespoon crème de cassis or eau-de-vie de framboise

1 teaspoon fresh lemon juice

7-9 slices firm white sandwich bread, crusts trimmed

1 cup nonfat vanilla yogurt

In a large heavy saucepan, combine currants, loganberries, sugar and 1 tablespoon water. Bring to a simmer, stirring. Simmer over medium-low heat for 2 minutes. Remove from the heat, stir in berry spread or jam, liquor and lemon juice. Let cool completely.

Line a 1-quart pudding basin or soufflé dish with plastic wrap, leaving a 4-inch overhang all around. Cut bread slices in half diagonally, then fit them in the bottom and sides of the bowl, trimming further to fit snugly if needed. (You will have extra slices to be used for the top.)

Spoon the berry mixture into the bread-lined bowl; trim bread slices level with the top. Use the remaining bread slices to cover the top. Fold the plastic wrap over the top of the pudding, then top with a plate slightly smaller than the diameter of the bowl. Weight the plate with a heavy can. Refrigerate for at least 8 hours or up to 24 hours.

To serve, remove the weight and plate, then fold back the overlap of plastic wrap. Set a rimmed serving plate over the bowl, then invert the pudding onto the plate. Remove the bowl and plastic wrap. Carefully cut wedges with a serrated knife and serve each portion with a dollop of yogurt.

Serves 6.

277 CALORIES PER SERVING: 5 G PROTEIN, 1 G FAT, 62 G CARBOHYDRATE; 164 MG SODIUM; 1 MG CHOLESTEROL.

Apple Roly-Poly

A tender, gingery biscuit dough is spiraled around a spiced apple filling and baked in a hot cider bath. Golden Delicious, Cortland or Rome apples are good choices.

Preheat oven to 375 degrees F.

In a small bowl, stir together cider, brown sugar and 1 tablespoon of the lemon juice and pour into four 10-ounce custard cups. Set the cups on a baking sheet and place them in the oven to heat the syrup while you prepare the filling and dough.

Combine apples, currants, cinnamon, allspice and the remaining 1 tablespoon lemon juice. Set aside.

To make the biscuit dough, whisk together flour, baking powder, baking soda, ginger and salt in a bowl. Cut butter into the dry ingredients with two forks until the mixture resembles coarse meal. With a fork, gradually stir in just enough of the buttermilk to make a soft dough.

On a well-floured surface, pat the dough into an 8-inch square. Distribute the grated-apple mixture evenly over the surface. Roll up the dough and filling like a jelly roll. Slice the roll into 4 pieces.

Carefully remove the syrup-filled cups from the oven. Place a roly-poly piece cut-side down in each cup, pressing on the dough to flatten it slightly. (As the roly-polys bake, they expand to fill the dishes and absorb most of the syrup.) Bake for 15 to 20 minutes, or until the dough is baked through to the center. Serve immediately.

Serves 4.

358 CALORIES PER SERVING: 5 G PROTEIN, 7 G FAT, 72 G CARBOHYDRATE; 397 MG SODIUM; 16 MG CHOLESTEROL.

1   cup apple cider
½   cup packed light brown sugar
2   tablespoons fresh lemon juice
2   large apples, peeled and grated (1½ cups)
¼   cup currants
1   teaspoon ground cinnamon
¼   teaspoon ground allspice
1   cup all-purpose white flour
1½ teaspoons baking powder
½   teaspoon baking soda
½   teaspoon ground ginger
⅛   teaspoon salt
2   tablespoons cold butter, cut into pieces
½   cup buttermilk

Chocolate-Cinnamon Bread Pudding

While American-style cocoa certainly works in this recipe, Dutch-process cocoa produces a deeper color and richer flavor.

4 slices whole-wheat or white bread, torn into small pieces

2 large eggs

12 ounces evaporated skim milk

¾ cup packed light brown sugar

¼ cup cocoa powder, preferably Dutch-process

2 teaspoons pure vanilla extract

1 teaspoon ground cinnamon

1 ounce semisweet chocolate, chopped

3 cups nonfat vanilla or coffee frozen yogurt

Preheat oven to 350 degrees F. Lightly oil an 8-inch square baking dish or coat it with nonstick cooking spray. Spread bread in the dish in an even layer.

In a mixing bowl, whisk eggs. Add evaporated skim milk, brown sugar, cocoa, vanilla and cinnamon; whisk until the sugar and cocoa dissolve. Pour the cocoa mixture over the bread. With a fork, mix in any unsoaked bread pieces. Sprinkle chocolate over the top and let stand for 10 minutes.

Bake for 35 to 40 minutes, or until puffed and set in the center. Serve warm, with a scoop of frozen yogurt on top. (The pudding is also good cold.)

Serves 6.

332 CALORIES PER SERVING: 14 G PROTEIN, 4 G FAT, 62 G CARBOHYDRATE; 271 MG SODIUM; 76 MG CHOLESTEROL.

Tiramisù

The low-fat version of this ultra-high-fat Italian dessert is exceedingly good.

8 ounces ladyfingers (60 ladyfingers)

4 tablespoons brandy

1 tablespoon instant coffee (preferably espresso) granules

3 large egg whites

1 cup plus 2 tablespoons sugar

¼ teaspoon cream of tartar

4 ounces mascarpone cheese (½ cup)

If ladyfingers are the soft variety, toast them in a 350-degree F oven for 6 to 8 minutes.

In a small bowl, stir together 3 tablespoons of the brandy, coffee granules and 1 cup water. Brush over the flat side of the ladyfingers. Set aside.

Bring about 1 inch of water to a simmer in the bottom of a large saucepan. Combine egg whites, sugar, cream of tartar and 3 tablespoons cold water in a heatproof mixing bowl that will fit over the saucepan. Set the bowl over the simmering water and beat with a hand-held mixer at low speed until an instant-read or candy thermometer registers 140 degrees F, 4 to 5 minutes. Increase speed to high and continue beating over the heat for 3 minutes. (The mixture should form a ribbon trail.) Remove the bowl from the heat and beat until cool and fluffy, about 4 minutes. Set aside.

In a large bowl, beat mascarpone and cream cheese until creamy. Add about 1 cup of the beaten whites and the remaining 1 tablespoon brandy and beat until smooth, scraping down the sides of the bowl. Fold in the remaining whites.

Line the bottom and sides of a 3-quart trifle bowl or soufflé dish with ladyfingers, the flat sides toward the center. Spoon in one-third of the filling and top with a layer of ladyfingers. Repeat with two more layers of filling and ladyfingers, arranging the final layer of ladyfingers decoratively over the top, trimming to fit, if necessary. Sprinkle with chocolate shavings. Cover and chill for at least 8 hours or overnight. Dust with confectioners' sugar and serve.

Serves 12.

150 CALORIES PER SERVING: 2 G PROTEIN, 6 G FAT, 19 G CARBOHYDRATE; 68 MG SODIUM; 16 MG CHOLESTEROL.

**4 ounces reduced-fat cream cheese (½ cup), softened
Chocolate shavings and confectioners' sugar for garnish**

Pear-Cranberry Steamed Pudding

English cooks stir their Christmas puddings clockwise for good luck. While our pudding recipe is hardly traditional, it certainly could do no harm to stir in one direction only.

¼ pound dried pears

1 cup buttermilk

3 large egg whites

1 tablespoon grated lemon zest

1 teaspoon pure vanilla extract

1½ cups fresh cranberries, coarsely chopped, plus 9 whole cranberries for garnish

1 cup golden raisins

1 cup all-purpose white flour

1 cup fresh breadcrumbs made from day-old firm white sandwich bread (3 slices)

½ cup sugar

¼ cup chopped crystallized ginger

1 teaspoon baking soda

½ teaspoon ground allspice

½ teaspoon salt

9 whole blanched almonds

Lightly oil a 2-quart pudding mold and lid or coat them with nonstick cooking spray. (*Alternatively, use a deep 2-quart bowl and a sheet of aluminum foil for the lid.*)

Place dried pears in a small saucepan and add water to cover. Bring to a simmer, cover the pan and remove from the heat. Let stand until softened, about 20 minutes. With a slotted spoon, transfer the pears to a food processor. Add ½ cup of the soaking liquid and puree until smooth.

In a large bowl, whisk together pear puree, buttermilk, egg whites, lemon zest and vanilla until smooth. In a small bowl, stir together chopped cranberries, raisins, flour, breadcrumbs, sugar, ginger, baking soda, allspice and salt. Add the dry ingredients to the wet ingredients and stir just until combined.

Arrange almonds and whole cranberries in a decorative fashion in the bottom of the prepared mold or bowl. Gently spoon a little batter into the bottom of the mold to cover the garnish, then add the remaining batter. Cover tightly with the lid or foil, securing the foil with string or masking tape. Set on a trivet or rack in a pot tall enough to hold the mold comfortably. Add hot water to come halfway up the sides of the mold. Bring to a simmer, reduce the heat to low, cover the pot and steam for 1½ hours. (Add more water to maintain the level, if necessary.)

Remove the mold from the pot and let sit on a towel for 10 minutes. Unmold. (*The pudding can be made up to 3 days in advance and stored, well wrapped, in the refrigerator. To reheat, wrap in foil and steam on a rack for 20 minutes.*) Serve warm, with Brandy Custard Sauce.

Serves 8.

309 CALORIES PER SERVING: 7 G PROTEIN, 3 G FAT, 67 G CARBOHYDRATE; 373 MG SODIUM; 1 MG CHOLESTEROL.

Brandy Custard Sauce

Not as hard on one's arteries as a classic hard sauce, which blends butter, sugar and brandy, our version uses evaporated skim milk to lend low-fat richness to brandy's pleasant kick.

In a small, heavy, nonreactive saucepan, whisk together egg and cornstarch until smooth. Whisk in evaporated skim milk, sugar and salt. Whisking constantly over low heat, bring the mixture to a simmer; it will be frothy and thickened. Remove from the heat and stir in brandy. Let cool slightly.

Makes about 1 cup.

56 CALORIES PER TABLESPOON: 1 G PROTEIN, 1 G FAT, 9 G CARBOHYDRATE; 19 MG SODIUM; 27 MG CHOLESTEROL.

1   **large egg**
1   **teaspoon cornstarch**
⅔   **cup evaporated skim milk**
⅓   **cup sugar**
    Pinch of salt
2   **tablespoons brandy**

Lemon Tartlets

Cream-puff pastry baked in muffin cups forms the base for these pretty tartlets.

LEMON CURD

- 1 large egg
- 2 large egg whites
- ¾ cup sugar
- ⅔ cup fresh lemon juice (4 lemons)
- 1 tablespoon grated lemon zest
- 2 tablespoons butter

PASTRY SHELLS

- 2 tablespoons vegetable oil, preferably canola oil
- 2 tablespoons sugar
- ¼ teaspoon salt
- 1 cup all-purpose white flour
- 2 large eggs
- 4 large egg whites
- 1 teaspoon pure vanilla extract
  Confectioners' sugar for dusting

TO MAKE LEMON CURD:

Whisk together egg, egg whites, sugar, lemon juice and zest in a heavy-bottomed saucepan. Add butter and cook over medium-low heat, whisking constantly, until thickened, 5 to 7 minutes. (The curd thickens as it cools.) Transfer to a bowl and let cool. Cover and refrigerate until chilled. (*The curd can be prepared ahead and stored, covered, in the refrigerator for up to 2 days.*)

TO MAKE PASTRY SHELLS:

Place oven rack in the upper third of the oven; preheat to 375 degrees F. Lightly oil 24 three-inch muffin cups or spray them with nonstick cooking spray.

In a saucepan, combine 1 cup water, oil, sugar and salt; bring just to a boil over medium heat. Remove from the heat and add flour all at once. Stir with a wooden spoon until the mixture forms a smooth mass. Let cool for 2 minutes, then transfer to a food processor. In a measuring cup, whisk together eggs, egg whites and vanilla. Gradually add one-quarter of the beaten eggs to the flour paste, processing until the eggs are incorporated. Repeat with 3 more additions of the eggs.

Place about 1 tablespoon of the dough into each prepared muffin cup. Use a spoon dipped in cold water to press the dough to the sides. With wet fingers, press it partway up the sides, forming ⅜-inch-thick shells. Bake for 5 minutes. Remove from the oven and prick the centers with a fork. Return to the oven and bake for 10 to 15 minutes longer, or until puffed and golden. Loosen the shells with a knife and let cool on a wire rack.

TO ASSEMBLE TARTLETS:

Spoon about 1 tablespoon lemon curd into each tartlet shell and dust with confectioners' sugar.

Makes 24 tartlets, serves 12.

159 CALORIES PER SERVING: 5 G PROTEIN, 6 G FAT, 24 G CARBOHYDRATE; 108 MG SODIUM; 58 MG CHOLESTEROL.

Lemon Tartlets

Bananas Foster

Bananas Foster was first served at Brennan's Restaurant in New Orleans in the early 1950s.
This version retains the rich flavor of the original with only one-quarter of the fat.

4   ripe, firm bananas, peeled

2   teaspoons unsalted butter

1   teaspoon vegetable oil, preferably canola oil

1   cup packed brown sugar

¼   cup banana liqueur

¼   teaspoon ground cinnamon

¼   cup dark rum

1   pint nonfat vanilla frozen yogurt

Cut bananas in half crosswise, then cut each piece into quarters lengthwise. Set aside.

In a large skillet over low heat, melt butter with oil. Stir in brown sugar, banana liqueur and cinnamon. Cook for 2 to 3 minutes, stirring, or until the sugar has melted. Add the bananas and toss to coat well. Simmer for 5 minutes, or until the bananas are tender.

In a small saucepan, warm rum over low heat. (Do not boil.) Carefully ignite the rum and pour over the banana mixture. Scoop frozen yogurt into 4 serving dishes and spoon the banana mixture over the top. Serve immediately.

Serves 4.

462 CALORIES PER SERVING: 4 G PROTEIN, 4 G FAT, 109 G CARBOHYDRATE; 105 MG SODIUM; 5 MG CHOLESTEROL.

Cassata Siciliana

In Sicily, cassata is served at Christmas and Easter.

CASSATA

1   cup low-fat ricotta cheese

¼   cup sugar

¼   cup chopped mixed candied fruit (citron, lemon peel, orange peel, pineapple and/or cherries)

1   ounce semisweet chocolate, chopped

1   teaspoon grated lemon zest

TO PREPARE CASSATA:

Line a 9-by-5-inch loaf pan with plastic wrap. In a mixing bowl, whisk together ricotta and sugar. Stir in candied fruit, chocolate and lemon zest. Slice angel food cake with a serrated knife into ½-inch-thick slices. Use the largest slice to line the bottom of the loaf pan, filling in with small pieces if necessary. Brush with one-third of the rum. Spread with half of the ricotta filling. Arrange a second layer of cake slices on top, brush with half of the remaining rum and spread the remaining filling over the top. Arrange the remaining slices over the top and brush with the remaining rum. Cover with plastic wrap and weight down with another loaf pan and a heavy weight or can. Refrigerate overnight.

TO MAKE CHOCOLATE SAUCE:

In a small heavy saucepan, combine cocoa, cornstarch and sugar. Gradually whisk in corn syrup and milk. Stirring constantly, bring to a boil over medium heat and cook for 30 seconds. Remove from the heat and whisk in vanilla and oil. Let cool and serve at room temperature or chilled. (*The sauce can be prepared ahead and stored, covered, in the refrigerator for up to 1 week.*)

TO SERVE CASSATA:

Invert the loaf pan onto a serving dish. Remove the plastic wrap. Slice the cassata and serve with chocolate sauce.

Serves 8.

281 CALORIES PER SERVING: 7 G PROTEIN, 3 G FAT, 56 G CARBOHYDRATE;
121 MG SODIUM; 5 MG CHOLESTEROL.

1 **10-ounce angel food cake (homemade or store-bought)**
¼ **cup dark rum**

CHOCOLATE SAUCE

⅓ **cup unsweetened cocoa powder**
2 **tablespoons cornstarch**
2 **tablespoons sugar**
½ **cup light or dark corn syrup**
⅓ **cup low-fat milk**
2 **teaspoons pure vanilla extract**
1 **teaspoon vegetable oil, preferably canola oil**

Cassata Siciliana

Caramel Pears in Phyllo Nests

Phyllo nests are a delicate, crisp contrast to the tender pears and luxurious caramel sauce.

½   cup plus 1 tablespoon sugar

¼   cup evaporated skim milk

1½ teaspoons frozen orange-juice concentrate

4   ripe pears, preferably Bosc or Anjou, peeled, halved and cored

½   cup fresh orange juice

3   sheets phyllo dough (14x18 inches)

2   teaspoons butter

1   tablespoon vegetable oil, preferably canola oil

3   tablespoons sliced almonds, toasted

For the caramel sauce, combine ½ cup sugar with ¼ cup water in a heavy saucepan. Bring to a boil over medium-high heat, stirring to dissolve the sugar. Cook, without stirring, until it turns a deep amber color, about 5 to 8 minutes. Do not burn. Remove from the heat and carefully swirl in 1 teaspoon water to stop the cooking: be careful, it will spatter. Let cool for 2 minutes, then gradually stir in evaporated milk. Return the pan to low heat and stir to dissolve the caramel; do not boil. Remove from the heat and stir in orange-juice concentrate. (*The sauce can be prepared up to 1 week ahead and stored, covered, in the refrigerator.*)

Preheat oven to 375 degrees F. Set pears in a large round baking dish, with the stem-ends toward the center. Pour fresh orange juice over the pears. Cover with aluminum foil and bake for 30 minutes. Uncover and sprinkle with the remaining 1 tablespoon sugar. Bake for 20 to 30 minutes more, basting from time to time with juice, until the pears are tender. Set aside.

For the nests, cut each sheet of phyllo into 4 squares. Stack the squares and cover with plastic wrap. Set aside. Melt butter in a small saucepan and stir in oil. Brush four 10-ounce custard cups with a little butter-oil mixture. Put one phyllo square in the bottom of a custard cup and brush it lightly with the butter-oil mixture. Set another square on top at an angle to the first, brush as well. Repeat with the third phyllo square. Fill the remaining custard cups in the same manner. Set the cups on a baking sheet and bake at 375 degrees for 7 to 10 minutes, or until crisp and golden.

To serve, gently lift each phyllo nest out onto a dessert plate. Set two pear halves in each nest, top with a generous spoonful of caramel sauce and sprinkle with toasted almonds.

Serves 4.

368 CALORIES PER SERVING: 6 G PROTEIN, 8 G FAT, 73 G CARBOHYDRATE; 135 MG SODIUM; 5 MG CHOLESTEROL.

Caramel Pears in Phyllo Nests

Pumpkin Custards with Hazelnut Caramel

Serve the custards at Thanksgiving or Christmas for a change from pumpkin pie.

1 cup canned pumpkin puree
2 large eggs, lightly beaten
2 cups evaporated skim milk
1 teaspoon pure vanilla extract
¾ cup packed dark brown sugar
1 tablespoon cornstarch
1 teaspoon ground cinnamon
1 teaspoon ground ginger
¼ teaspoon freshly grated nutmeg
¼ teaspoon salt
10 hazelnuts (½ ounce)
½ cup white sugar
4 ounces reduced-fat cream cheese
2 tablespoons confectioners' sugar
½ teaspoon Cognac or pure vanilla extract

Preheat oven to 350 degrees F.

In a mixing bowl, whisk together pumpkin, eggs, evaporated skim milk and vanilla. In a small bowl, combine brown sugar, cornstarch, cinnamon, ginger, nutmeg and salt. Sift into the pumpkin mixture and whisk until incorporated. Divide the batter equally among six 6-ounce custard cups.

Set the cups in a baking dish and pour in boiling water to come halfway up the outsides of the cups. Bake for 50 to 60 minutes, or until a knife inserted in the center comes out clean. Remove the custards from the oven and cool them to room temperature. Chill for at least 2 hours before serving. (*The custards can be prepared 2 days ahead and stored, covered, in the refrigerator.*)

Meanwhile, spread hazelnuts on a pie plate and toast in a 350-degree F oven for 10 minutes to loosen the skins. Rub off the skins and let cool. Chop finely and set aside.

Line a baking sheet with aluminum foil. In a small heavy saucepan, combine white sugar and ¼ cup water. Bring to a simmer and cook, without stirring, until the syrup is a deep amber color, 5 to 10 minutes. Do not let the syrup burn. Pour the hot syrup onto the prepared baking sheet. Quickly tilt it to spread the caramel in a thin layer. Sprinkle on the toasted nuts. Let cool. When the caramel is hard, break it into shards. (*The caramel can be prepared up to 1 week ahead and stored in an airtight container.*)

In a food processor or blender, process cream cheese, confectioners' sugar and Cognac or vanilla until smooth. Garnish the custards with a spoonful of the cream and shards of hazelnut caramel.

Serves 6.

348 CALORIES PER SERVING: 11 G PROTEIN, 7 G FAT, 63 G CARBOHYDRATE; 325 MG SODIUM; 82 MG CHOLESTEROL.

Rhubarb-Peach Shortcake

Juicy rhubarb and fragrant peaches soak deliciously into tender buttermilk biscuits. (Photograph on page 4.)

TO MAKE BISCUITS:

Preheat oven to 425 degrees F. Line a baking sheet with parchment paper or coat it with nonstick cooking spray. In a large bowl, stir together all-purpose flour, cake flour, baking powder, baking soda and salt. Use a pastry blender or 2 knives to cut butter and cream cheese into the dry ingredients until the mixture resembles coarse crumbs. Make a well in the center and add buttermilk; stir with a fork just until a dough forms.

Turn the dough out onto a lightly floured surface and knead briefly. Pat into a ¼-inch thickness and cut 8 biscuits with a 3-inch cutter. Transfer to the prepared baking sheet, brush the tops with egg white and sprinkle with sugar. Bake for about 10 minutes, or until golden brown. Transfer to a rack; let cool slightly.

TO MAKE FILLING:

In a saucepan, stir together rhubarb, sugar and lemon juice. Bring to a simmer over low heat and cook for 1 minute. With a slotted spoon, transfer the rhubarb to a bowl. Increase the heat to medium and boil the liquid until it is syrupy, about 2 minutes. Add the syrup to the reserved rhubarb; set aside.

Blanch peaches in boiling water for 1 minute. Remove with a slotted spoon and refresh under cold water. Slip off the skins. Thinly slice the peaches and add to the rhubarb.

In a chilled bowl, whip cream until firm peaks form. Fold in yogurt.

TO ASSEMBLE SHORTCAKES:

Slice the biscuits in half and place the bottoms on dessert plates. Spoon the fruit filling and a little of the yogurt-cream topping onto them. Cover with the biscuit tops and finish with a dollop of topping.

Serves 8.

266 CALORIES PER SERVING: 7 G PROTEIN, 8 G FAT, 44 G CARBOHYDRATE; 259 MG SODIUM; 22 MG CHOLESTEROL.

BISCUITS

- 1 cup all-purpose white flour
- 1 cup cake flour
- 1 tablespoon baking powder
- ½ teaspoon baking soda
- ½ teaspoon salt
- 2½ tablespoons cold unsalted butter, cut into small pieces
- 2½ tablespoons cold reduced-fat cream cheese, cut into small pieces
- ¾ cup buttermilk
- 1 large egg white, lightly beaten
- 1 teaspoon sugar

FILLING

- ¾ pound rhubarb, trimmed and cut into ½-inch pieces (3 cups)
- ½ cup sugar
- 1 tablespoon fresh lemon juice
- 2 ripe peaches
- ¼ cup whipping cream
- 1 cup nonfat vanilla yogurt

Strawberry-Rum Shortcakes

Colonial Americans knew that a tot of rum now and then was probably good for the soul, and the same holds true in this summer standard. The shortcakes are made with buttermilk, which produces a tender dough that is much lower in fat than a classic recipe. The vanilla cream filling is fat-free.

FILLING

1⅓ cups nonfat vanilla yogurt

⅔ cup nonfat sour cream

3 pints fresh strawberries, rinsed and hulled

⅔ cup sugar

3 tablespoons light rum

SHORTCAKES

3 cups all-purpose white flour, plus extra for forming shortcakes

⅓ cup plus 2 teaspoons sugar

1 tablespoon baking powder

2 teaspoons baking soda

½ teaspoon salt

2 tablespoons unsalted butter, cut into small pieces

1¼ cups buttermilk

1½ tablespoons vegetable oil, preferably canola oil

1 tablespoon skim milk

TO MAKE FILLING:

In a small bowl, stir together yogurt and sour cream. (*The cream can be prepared up to 2 days ahead and stored, covered, in the refrigerator.*)

In a large mixing bowl, combine 1 pint of the strawberries, sugar and rum; mash with a fork. Slice the remaining berries and add to the bowl. Stir to combine well, then let the mixture stand for 30 minutes to 1 hour at room temperature.

TO MAKE SHORTCAKES:

Coat a large baking sheet with nonstick cooking spray or line it with parchment.

In a large bowl, stir together flour, ⅓ cup sugar, baking powder, baking soda and salt. Using your fingertips or 2 knives, cut butter into the flour mixture until crumbly. Make a well in the center and add buttermilk and oil. With a fork, stir until just combined to make a slightly sticky dough. Do not overmix.

Place the dough on a lightly floured surface and sprinkle with a little flour. Knead the dough 10 times, then pat or roll it out to an even ¾-inch thickness. Using a 2½-inch round or star-shaped cutter, cut out shortcakes and transfer them to the prepared baking sheet. Gather together the scraps of dough and cut out more shortcakes to make a total of 8. Brush with skim milk and sprinkle with the remaining 2 teaspoons of the sugar. (*The shortcakes can be formed up to 1 hour before baking and set aside, covered, in the refrigerator.*)

TO BAKE AND ASSEMBLE SHORTCAKES:

Preheat oven to 425 degrees F. Bake the shortcakes for 12 to 16 minutes, or until golden. Transfer them to a rack and let cool slightly.

Using a serrated knife, split the shortcakes. Set the bottoms on dessert plates, spread with some of the vanilla cream, spoon on the strawberries and juices and crown with the shortcake lids. Top with a dollop of vanilla cream and serve immediately.

Serves 8.

434 CALORIES PER SERVING: 10 G PROTEIN, 7 G FAT, 80 G CARBOHYDRATE; 433 MG SODIUM; 11 MG CHOLESTEROL.

Pears Baked in Marsala with Crumbled Amaretti

Crush the cookies between sheets of wax paper using a rolling pin; a food processor will make the crumbs too fine.

Preheat oven to 350 degrees F. Peel pears, leaving the stems intact. Trim the bottoms so they will stand upright. Brush the pears with lemon juice and set in a shallow baking dish. Pour Marsala over and around the pears. Scatter butter over them.

In a small dish, combine brown sugar and cinnamon, then sprinkle the mixture over the pears. Sprinkle the pears with amaretti crumbs. Bake, uncovered, for 50 to 60 minutes, basting with the pan juices 3 or 4 times, or until the pears are tender and the juices are slightly thickened. Serve the pears warm or at room temperature with the pan juices spooned over.

Serves 8.

192 CALORIES PER SERVING: 2 G PROTEIN, 3 G FAT, 35 G CARBOHYDRATE; 65 MG SODIUM; 4 MG CHOLESTEROL.

- 8 small ripe but firm pears, such as Bosc or Anjou (about 3 pounds)
- 2 tablespoons fresh lemon juice
- 1 cup Marsala
- 1 tablespoon butter, cut in small pieces
- 3 tablespoons light brown sugar
- ¼ teaspoon ground cinnamon
- ¾ cup coarsely crushed amaretti cookies (3 ounces)

Peach-Blackberry Ambrosia

Enjoy this fat-free fruit dessert after a day in the sun and a big supper.

In a small saucepan, combine honey and lemon juice. Warm over low heat just until the honey melts. Remove from the heat and stir in lemon zest. Let cool for 5 minutes. Meanwhile, rub the fuzz from peaches with a kitchen towel. Slice the peaches in half, remove the pit and dice the flesh. In a bowl, combine the diced peaches, berries and honey syrup. Stir gently to combine. Spoon into 4 dessert dishes and chill until serving time.

Just before serving, pour ⅓ cup sparkling wine into each dish.

Serves 4.

165 CALORIES PER SERVING: 1 G PROTEIN, 0 G FAT, 28 G CARBOHYDRATE; 6 MG SODIUM; 0 MG CHOLESTEROL.

- 3 tablespoons honey
- 1½ tablespoons fresh lemon juice
- 1 teaspoon grated lemon zest
- 2 ripe peaches
- 1 pint blackberries or raspberries
- 1⅓ cups chilled Asti Spumante or other sparkling wine

Pears Baked in Marsala with Crumbled Amaretti

CHAPTER 16

Frozen Desserts

Chocolate-Raspberry Icebox Torte

Layers of hazelnut-and-chocolate meringue meld with refreshing raspberry sorbet during freezing.
This torte should be made the day before you plan to serve it.

⅓ cup hazelnuts (2 ounces)

⅔ cup confectioners' sugar, plus more for garnish

¼ cup unsweetened cocoa powder, preferably Dutch-process

2 tablespoons cornstarch

5 large egg whites, at room temperature

¼ teaspoon cream of tartar

¾ cup sugar

1 teaspoon pure vanilla extract

3 cups raspberry sorbet

1 pint fresh raspberries

Preheat oven to 350 degrees F. Line two 12-by-18-inch baking sheets with parchment paper. Using an 8-inch cake pan or plate as a guide, draw 3 circles on the paper. Turn the paper over; the lines will show through. (*Alternatively, line baking sheets with aluminum foil, coat with nonstick cooking spray and dust with flour, shaking off excess. Trace the circles with your fingertip.*)

Spread hazelnuts in a pie plate and bake for 8 to 12 minutes, or until lightly toasted and fragrant. If the hazelnuts have skins, place the nuts on a clean kitchen towel, fold the towel over and rub off as much skin as you can. Let cool. Lower the oven temperature to 250 degrees.

Put the toasted hazelnuts, confectioners' sugar, cocoa and cornstarch in a food processor; process until the nuts are ground. Set aside.

In the bowl of an electric mixer, beat egg whites and cream of tartar on low speed until frothy. Gradually increase the mixer speed to high. When the whites begin to form soft peaks, decrease the speed to medium and slowly beat in sugar, 1 tablespoon at a time. Add vanilla; continue beating until the meringue is glossy and stiff peaks form. Sprinkle the reserved hazelnut-cocoa mixture over the meringue and fold in with a large rubber spatula just until mixed.

Spoon the meringue into a piping bag fitted with a ½-inch

Chocolate-Raspberry Icebox Torte

open-star tip. Pipe a layer of meringue in a tight spiral onto each circle on the prepared baking sheet. (*Alternatively, spread the meringue onto the circles with a spatula.*)

Bake the meringue layers until firm to the touch, 50 to 70 minutes. Let cool on the baking sheets placed on racks, then carefully peel off the paper or foil.

Let sorbet soften in the refrigerator for about 30 minutes. Carefully trim the meringue layers to fit snugly into an 8-inch springform pan. Set a meringue layer in the bottom of the pan and spread half of the sorbet evenly over the meringue. Set the second meringue layer on top of the sorbet. Cover with the remaining sorbet and the third meringue layer. Cover the torte with plastic wrap and freeze overnight or for up to 5 days.

Before serving, let the torte soften in the refrigerator for about 30 minutes. Run a sharp knife around the edge of the pan to loosen the cake. Transfer to a cake plate and dust with confectioners' sugar. Garnish with fresh raspberries.

Serves 10.

193 CALORIES PER SERVING: 3 G PROTEIN, 3 G FAT, 43 G CARBOHYDRATE; 34 MG SODIUM; 0 MG CHOLESTEROL.

Baked Alaska, Riversong Style

These individual desserts come from Riversong Lodge in Alaska. They are finished under the broiler, but if you have a propane torch, you can do a masterful job of browning the meringue. If you like, garnish them fancifully with Johnny-jump-ups or nasturtium blossoms.

8   ½-inch-thick slices nonfat or low-fat pound cake

1   pint nonfat vanilla or fruit-flavored frozen yogurt

½   cup plus 1 tablespoon sugar

2   large egg whites

¼   teaspoon cream of tartar

Using a 3-inch round cutter, cut 4 circles from half of the pound cake slices. Using a 2-inch cutter, cut 4 circles from the remaining cake slices. Set the larger rounds on a baking sheet at least 3 inches apart. Top each with a scoop of frozen yogurt. Lightly press a smaller round of cake on top of each scoop; cover loosely with plastic wrap and place in the freezer for at least 15 minutes to firm up.

Bring about 1 inch of water to a simmer in a large saucepan. Put ½ cup sugar, egg whites, 2 tablespoons water and cream of tartar in a metal bowl that will fit over the saucepan. Set the bowl over the simmering water and beat with an electric mixer at low speed, moving the beaters around the bowl constantly, for 3 to 5 minutes, until an instant-read thermometer registers 140 degrees F. Increase the mixer speed to high and continue beating over the heat for a full 3 minutes. Remove the bowl from the heat and beat the meringue until cool, about 4 minutes. Beat in vanilla. Cover with plastic wrap and put in the refrigerator to chill for at least 15 minutes.

When ready to assemble the dessert, preheat the broiler. Gently stir berries, crème de cassis or vodka and the remaining 1 tablespoon sugar together in a small bowl and set aside. Remove the cakes from the freezer and quickly spread with the meringue, swirling it decoratively and making sure it covers the frozen yogurt completely and evenly. Immediately place under the broiler, holding the desserts as close to the broiler flame as possible, until the meringue is lightly browned, about 1 minute. Serve surrounded with the fruit.

Serves 4.

385 CALORIES PER SERVING: 7 G PROTEIN, 0 G FAT, 68 G CARBOHYDRATE; 309 MG SODIUM; 0 MG CHOLESTEROL.

½ teaspoon pure vanilla extract

1 pint raspberries, strawberries or other seasonal berries

1 tablespoon crème de cassis or vodka

Peach Ice Cream

If you plan to serve this ice cream directly from the ice cream maker, add an extra cup of chopped peaches to the mix just before stir-freezing. A crisp almond-flavored cookie served alongside (such as Mocha-Almond Biscotti, page 203) would complement the subtle hint of almond in the ice cream.

3 cups sliced peeled peaches
   (6-8 medium peaches)

2 tablespoons fresh lemon juice

1½ cups Marshmallow Fluff or
   Marshmallow Creme

1 cup low-fat milk

2 teaspoons amaretto or
   ½ teaspoon pure almond extract

In a food processor, puree peaches with lemon juice. Transfer to a bowl. Add Marshmallow Fluff or Creme and mix with a whisk until as smooth as possible. (The mixture will be a little lumpy; the lumps will break down during stir-freezing.) Add milk and amaretto or almond extract and mix well. If necessary, chill until cold.

Pour into the canister of an ice cream maker and freeze according to the manufacturer's directions.

Makes about 1 quart, serves 6.

235 CALORIES PER SERVING: 3 G PROTEIN, 1 G FAT, 57 G CARBOHYDRATE; 47 MG SODIUM; 2 MG CHOLESTEROL.

Strawberry Ice Cream

The best strawberries are those you pick yourself. If the berries are a little sandy, rinse them just before hulling.

1½ pints strawberries, hulled

2 tablespoons fresh orange juice

1½ cups Marshmallow Fluff or
   Marshmallow Creme

1 cup low-fat milk

2 teaspoons orange liqueur
   (optional)

In a food processor, puree strawberries with orange juice. Transfer to a bowl. Add Marshmallow Fluff or Creme and mix with a whisk until as smooth as possible. (The mixture will be a little lumpy; the lumps will break down during stir-freezing.) Add milk and orange liqueur, if using, and mix well. If necessary, chill until cold.

Pour into the canister of an ice cream maker and freeze according to the manufacturer's directions.

Makes about 1 quart, serves 6.

230 CALORIES PER SERVING: 3 G PROTEIN, 1 G FAT, 55 G CARBOHYDRATE; 48 MG SODIUM; 2 MG CHOLESTEROL.

Peach Ice Cream

Chocolate Ice Cream

This fudgy ice cream will satisfy any chocolate craving, but contains only 5 grams of fat in a serving.

3 cups low-fat milk

¼ cup dark corn syrup

2 tablespoons brown sugar

2 large egg yolks

⅔ cup unsweetened cocoa powder, preferably Dutch process

2 tablespoons cornstarch

1 ounce bittersweet chocolate (not unsweetened), chopped

1 tablespoon coffee liqueur or strong brewed coffee

2 teaspoons pure vanilla extract

1½ cups Marshmallow Fluff or Marshmallow Creme

In a large heavy saucepan, combine 2½ cups of the milk, corn syrup and brown sugar. Heat over medium heat, stirring to dissolve the sugar, until steaming.

Meanwhile, in a mixing bowl, whisk together egg yolks, cocoa, cornstarch and the remaining ½ cup cold milk until smooth. Gradually whisk the hot milk into the egg-yolk mixture; then return to the pan. Cook over medium heat, whisking constantly, until the mixture boils and thickens, about 3 minutes. (Because the custard is thickened with cornstarch, it will not curdle when it boils.) Remove from the heat, add chocolate, and stir until melted. Stir in coffee liqueur or brewed coffee and vanilla.

Transfer the custard to a large clean bowl and place a piece of wax paper directly over the surface to prevent a skin from forming. Cool completely. Add Marshmallow Fluff or Creme and mix with a whisk until as smooth as possible. (The mixture will be a little lumpy; the lumps will break down during stir-freezing.) Chill until cold.

Pour into the canister of an ice cream maker and freeze according to the manufacturer's directions.

Makes about 1 quart, serves 6.

320 CALORIES PER SERVING: 7 G PROTEIN, 5 G FAT, 64 G CARBOHYDRATE; 96 MG SODIUM; 76 MG CHOLESTEROL.

Pomegranate Sorbet

When pomegranates are in the supermarkets in the fall, scoop up a dozen to turn into a colorful, refreshing sorbet.

6 pomegranates

1 lemon

1 cup sugar

Cut pomegranates in half crosswise. Gently lift out the seeds, section by section, and place in a saucepan. (You should have about 6 cups of seeds.) Set aside.

Using a vegetable peeler, remove the lemon zest in wide strips (be careful to leave the bitter white pith behind), allowing the strips to fall into the saucepan with the pomegranate seeds. Squeeze the lemon and strain the juice into the saucepan. Add sugar and 2 cups water; bring to a simmer, stirring to dissolve the sugar. Cook over medium-low heat until the pomegranate seeds turn pale, about 10 minutes.

Strain through a fine sieve into a bowl, pressing on the seeds to extract as much juice as possible. (Discard the solids.) Chill until cold.

Pour into the canister of an ice cream maker and freeze according to the manufacturer's directions. (*Alternatively, freeze in a shallow metal cake pan or ice cube trays until solid, about 6 hours. Break into chunks and process in a food processor until smooth.*)

Makes about 3 cups, serves 4.

342 CALORIES PER SERVING: 2 G PROTEIN, 1 G FAT, 89 G CARBOHYDRATE; 8 MG SODIUM; 0 MG CHOLESTEROL.

Blackberry Sorbet

A sorbet is the perfect showcase for this member of the raspberry family; berries start ripening in late summer.

In a bowl, combine sugar, crème de cassis or black currant syrup and ⅔ cup water, stirring to dissolve the sugar.

In a food processor, puree blackberries with lemon juice. To remove the seeds, force the puree through a fine strainer into a bowl. Add the sugar mixture and mix well. If necessary, chill until cold.

Pour into the canister of an ice cream maker and freeze according to the manufacturer's directions. (*Alternatively, freeze in a shallow metal cake pan or ice cube trays until solid, about 6 hours. Break into chunks and process in a food processor until smooth.*)

Makes about 1 quart, serves 6.

184 CALORIES PER SERVING: 1 G PROTEIN, 0 G FAT, 46 G CARBOHYDRATE; 1 MG SODIUM; 0 MG CHOLESTEROL.

1 cup instant-dissolving sugar

2 tablespoons crème de cassis or black currant syrup

1 quart blackberries

2 tablespoons fresh lemon juice

Watermelon Ice

The only thing more refreshing than a slice of watermelon is a scoop of watermelon ice.
Choose seedless watermelon for this ice.

6 cups watermelon chunks
3 tablespoons fresh lemon juice
¾ cup sugar
1 envelope unflavored gelatin

In a food processor, puree watermelon with lemon juice. To remove the seeds and fiber, force the puree through a fine sieve into a bowl. Set aside.

In a mixing bowl, whisk together sugar and gelatin. Pour 1 cup boiling water over the sugar mixture, stirring to dissolve. Add to the reserved watermelon juice and mix well. Chill until cold, about 30 minutes.

Pour into the canister of an ice cream maker and freeze according to the manufacturer's directions. (*Alternatively, freeze in a shallow metal cake pan or ice cube trays until solid, about 6 hours. Break into chunks and process in a food processor until smooth.*)

Makes about 1 quart, serves 6.

147 CALORIES PER SERVING: 2 G PROTEIN, 1 G FAT, 36 G CARBOHYDRATE; 5 MG SODIUM; 0 MG CHOLESTEROL.

Raspberry Frozen Yogurt

Keep raspberries on hand in the freezer year-round so you can make this luxurious, simple dessert anytime.

In a food processor, puree raspberries with lemon juice. To remove seeds, force the puree through a fine strainer into a bowl. Whisk in sugar and yogurt. If necessary, chill until cold.

    Pour into the canister of an ice cream maker and freeze according to the manufacturer's directions. (*Alternatively, freeze in a shallow metal cake pan or ice cube trays until solid, about 6 hours. Break into chunks and process in a food processor until smooth.*)

    Makes about 1 quart, serves 6.

- 3 pints raspberries
- 2 tablespoons fresh lemon juice
- 1⅓ cups instant-dissolving sugar
- 1 cup nonfat plain yogurt

242 CALORIES PER SERVING: 3 G PROTEIN, 1 G FAT, 60 G CARBOHYDRATE; 30 MG SODIUM; 1 MG CHOLESTEROL.

Sangria Sundaes

The sauce can be served while it is still warm from the pan or made ahead and served cold.

In a small saucepan, bring wine to a boil over medium-high heat. Cook until reduced to 2 tablespoons, 6 to 8 minutes. Add marmalade and cook until thickened, 1 to 2 minutes. Remove from the heat and stir in clementines or tangerines and lime juice. Let cool slightly. At serving time, scoop frozen yogurt into 4 dessert dishes and spoon the reserved sauce over the top.

    Serves 4.

- ½ cup dry red wine
- 3 tablespoons orange marmalade
- 2 clementines or tangerines, peeled, segmented and cut in half
- ½ teaspoon fresh lime juice
- 3 cups nonfat vanilla frozen yogurt

231 CALORIES PER SERVING: 3 G PROTEIN, 0 G FAT, 49 G CARBOHYDRATE; 56 MG SODIUM; 0 MG CHOLESTEROL.

Cranberry-Vanilla Bombe

The fun of this festive bombe is discovering the brilliant cranberry sorbet interior.

2 cups cranberries

1½ cups plus 1 teaspoon sugar

6 tablespoons fresh lemon juice

3 tablespoons fresh orange juice

1 quart nonfat vanilla frozen yogurt

Fresh mint leaves for garnish

In a saucepan, combine cranberries, 1½ cups sugar and 2½ cups water; bring to a simmer. Remove about 12 whole berries to a paper towel, sprinkle them with 1 teaspoon sugar and reserve for garnish. Continue to cook the cranberry mixture, stirring often, until the berries are tender, about 5 minutes. Remove about ⅓ cup of the cooked berries and chop them coarsely. Set aside.

Strain the remaining cranberries through a sieve into a bowl, discarding the skins. Let cool. Stir in lemon and orange juice along with the reserved chopped berries. Pour into the canister of an ice cream maker and freeze according to the manufacturer's directions. (*Alternatively, freeze in a shallow metal cake pan or ice cube trays until almost solid, about 6 hours. Break into chunks and process in a food processor until smooth.*)

While the cranberry sorbet is freezing, put a 6-cup bombe mold or deep bowl in the freezer. Soften a container of frozen yogurt in the refrigerator for about 30 minutes. Evenly coat the inside of the chilled mold or bowl with the softened yogurt. Return to the freezer to firm up, about 30 minutes. Fill the center with the cranberry sorbet. Cover and freeze for 5 hours. (*The bombe can be prepared up to 1 week ahead and stored in the freezer.*)

About an hour before serving, dip the mold into very hot water, wipe it dry and quickly invert it onto a serving plate. Cover the bombe with plastic wrap and return to the freezer. About 15 minutes before serving, transfer the bombe to the refrigerator to soften slightly. Just before serving, garnish the top of the bombe with the reserved sugared cranberries and mint leaves.

Serves 12.

166 CALORIES PER SERVING: 2 G PROTEIN, 0 G FAT, 42 G CARBOHYDRATE; 45 MG SODIUM; 0 MG CHOLESTEROL.

THE WELL-STOCKED KITCHEN

A few of the ingredients used in the recipes in The Eating Well New Favorites Cookbook *may be unfamiliar to some readers, or not available at local supermarkets, depending on the region. Ask your grocer for help, or try a nearby health-food or ethnic specialty shop.*

ARBORIO RICE. This Italian-grown grain is a must for risotto, because the high-starch kernels add creamy texture. Arborio is now found in most supermarkets, Italian markets and health-food stores.

ARMAGNAC. A member of the brandy family, noted for its distinct, unpolished flavor with hints of prune. Look for Armagnac at liquor stores.

ARUGULA. Also called rocket, this aromatic green lends a pepper-and-mustard flavor to salads. It is sold in small bunches in the supermarket or farmers' markets. Watercress is a good substitute.

BOUQUET GARNI. A bundle of fresh or dried herbs used in French cooking to flavor slowly cooked sauces, soups, stews and braised meats. A bouquet garni contains thyme sprigs, parsley stems and a bay leaf, tied together with a string or wrapped in cheesecloth. Remove the bouquet garni before serving.

CALVADOS. An apple brandy from France made in Normandy from cider that has been aged for up to two years and distilled.

CAPON. A fine roasting bird, the capon is a castrated rooster. Ranging in size from four to 10 pounds, capons have plenty of breast and thigh meat, making them perfect to serve eight to 12 people. To get one, you may have to place an order with a butcher.

CARAMBOLA. (Also called star fruit.) A glossy golden blimp with ribs, this tropical fruit forms star shapes when cross-cut. The edible skin encloses a juicy, slightly crisp flesh that suggests a milky blend of plums, apples and grapes.

CELERIAC. Beneath the gnarly skin of this root vegetable (otherwise known as celery root) is a white-fleshed interior. Look for celeriac in the produce section from fall through early spring.

CHINESE CHILE PASTE. Ask for this spicy ingredient at Asian markets where you will find some of the most flavorful brands.

CHIPOTLE PEPPERS. Smoked and dried jalapeño peppers. The distinctive smoky heat of chipotles is used to flavor Mexican and Southwestern dishes. They are sold dried and in cans, usually with a vinegar-based sauce called adobo. Found in Latin-American markets.

COUSCOUS. The tiny beads of ground semolina resemble rice, but technically couscous is a kind of pasta. Most of the couscous available in North America is precooked; it requires only a five-minute plumping in hot broth or water. Whole-wheat couscous is available at health-food stores.

CREME DE CASSIS. A sweet cordial flavored with black currants. Buy it at a liquor store.

DAIKON RADISH. This long, white, sweet-tasting radish figures prominently in Japanese cuisine. Look for it in the supermarket produce section.

EAU-DE-VIE DE FRAMBOISE. Eau-de-vie is an 80- to 90-proof clear fruit alcohol. Framboise is raspberry-flavored.

FISH SAUCE. Essential in Thai cooking, fish sauce is a pungent, salty liquid made from fresh anchovies. It's sold at Asian groceries and some supermarkets.

HIJIKI. A dried, squiggly black seaweed high in calcium, hijiki is usually reconstituted before using. Look for it at markets that specialize in Japanese foods.

JICAMA. The bulbous brown root with a crunchy white interior has been making its way from Mexican markets to most supermarkets November to May in recent years. Sweet and nutty-flavored, jícama is a great addition to any crudité platter.

LEMONGRASS. An aromatic, dry-looking tropical grass used to add a pungent, lemony flavor to Asian dishes. It is available fresh at large supermarkets and Asian groceries.

MACHE. Also known as lamb's lettuce and corn salad, this deep green herald of spring has a delicate flavor. If you can't find mâche, substitute very young spinach leaves.

MIRIN. Japanese recipes get added sweetness from mirin, a rice wine related to sake.

PANCETTA. An Italian cured meat made from the *pancia* (belly) of the pig—the same cut used for bacon. Pancetta is salted and lightly spiced, not smoked. Buy it at delicatessens or Italian markets.

PECORINO ROMANO. The pecorino cheeses are made from sheep's milk in Italy. The best known of these is romano. Although Parmesan can be substituted, pecorino romano is preferred when a sharp flavor is desirable.

PORTOBELLO MUSHROOM. This large, meaty mushroom is showing up more and more in produce sections. It is thick enough to slice and grill.

QUINOA. An ancient grain from the Andes, rich in protein, lysine, calcium and iron, quinoa has recently been "rediscovered" by cooks. Look for it in large supermarkets or health food stores.

SCOTCH BONNET CHILES. Among the world's hottest peppers, the Scotch bonnet is 30 to 50 times hotter than a jalapeño. The size and shape of a walnut, the Scotch bonnet has a dimpled crown that, with a little imagination, looks like a Highlander's headgear. The chile can be green, yellow-orange or orange. Wear gloves and don't touch your face when handling Scotch bonnets.

SHIITAKE. This strongly flavored mushroom is used in cooking in dried form or fresh. You can find fresh shiitake at quality produce markets; look for firm, rich-brown mushrooms that are dry but not leathery or pallid. A white bloom is normal. Dried shiitake—also called Chinese, black or Oriental mushrooms—are widely available, especially at health-food stores. Before using, dried shiitake must be reconstituted in hot water or broth.

SOBA. A dark brownish-gray buckwheat noodle popular in northern Japan. Some supermarket specialty-foods or noodle sections carry these, or check an Asian food store.

WALNUT OIL. This expensive oil is best purchased in small quantities—it goes rancid more quickly than other oils. However, its wonderful nutty flavor and aroma ensures that it won't remain in the pantry for long. It can be used in baking or sprinkled on greens, pasta or vegetables. Look for it in gourmet shops.

YOGURT CHEESE. Begin with nonfat plain yogurt that does not contain starch, gums or gelatin. Line a colander with a double thickness of cheesecloth. Set the colander over a large bowl. Spoon in the yogurt, cover with plastic wrap and refrigerate overnight. Transfer the cheese to a separate container. Discard the liquid. (*The yogurt cheese can be stored, covered, in the refrigerator for up to 1 week.*) Six cups of yogurt makes about 2 cups of yogurt cheese.

INDEX

Page numbers in italics indicate photographs